Neurodevelopmental Disorders in Children and Adolescents

Neurodevelopmental Disorders in Children and Adolescents provides an innovative perspective on developmental disorders in youth, one focused on embracing and working with the "messiness" and many variables at play in child and adolescent development. The volume's approach is aligned with the NIMH Research Domain Criteria project, which hopes to move away from categorical diagnosis toward multidimensional analysis. Each chapter focuses on a particular aspect of development, cluster of diagnoses, or clinical concern. The book also emphasizes humility, an awareness of diversity and difference without stigma, and support for collaborative and integrative healthcare. This is an essential volume for practitioners hoping to improve how they evaluate and treat developmental disorders in children.

Christopher J. Nicholls, PhD, ABPP, ABPdN, is a clinical neuropsychologist with more than 35 years of experience working in medical centers, teaching hospitals, and private practice, specializing in neurodevelopmental disorders. He is a Fellow of the National Academy of Neuropsychology, the American Academy of Pediatric Neuropsychology, and the American Academy of Clinical Psychology.

Clinical Topics in Psychology and Psychiatry
Bret A. Moore, PsyD, Series Editor

For a complete list of all books in this series, please visit the series page at:
www.routledge.com/Clinical-Topics-in-Psychology-and-Psychiatry/book-series/
TFSE00310

Neurodevelopmental Disorders in Children and Adolescents
A Guide to Evaluation and Treatment
by Christopher J. Nicholls

Integrating Psychological and Pharmacological Treatments for Addictive Disorders
An Evidence-Based Guide
edited by James Mackillop, George A. Kenna, Lorenzo Leggio, and Lara Ray

Practical Psychopharmacology
Basic to Advanced Principles
by Thomas L. Schwartz

Women's Mental Health Across the Lifespan
Challenges, Vulnerabilities, and Strengths
edited by Kathleen A. Kendall-Tackett and Lesia M. Ruglass

Treating Disruptive Disorders
A Guide to Psychological, Pharmacological, and Combined Therapies
edited by George M. Kapalka

Cognitive Behavioral Therapy for Preventing Suicide Attempts
A Guide to Brief Treatments Across Clinical Settings
edited by Craig J. Bryan

Trial-Based Cognitive Therapy
A Handbook for Clinicians
by Irismar Reis de Oliveira

Neurodevelopmental Disorders in Children and Adolescents

A Guide to Evaluation and Treatment

Christopher J. Nicholls

Routledge
Taylor & Francis Group

NEW YORK AND LONDON

First published 2018
by Routledge
711 Third Avenue, New York, NY 10017

and by Routledge
2 Park Square, Milton Park, Abingdon, Oxon, OX14 4RN

Routledge is an imprint of the Taylor & Francis Group, an informa business

© 2018 Christopher J. Nicholls

Library of Congress Cataloging-in-Publication Data
Names: Nicholls, Christopher J., author.
Title: Neurodevelopmental disorders in children and adolescents :
 a guide to evaluation and treatment / Christopher J. Nicholls.
Description: New York, NY : Routledge, 2018. | Includes
 bibliographical references.
Identifiers: LCCN 2017051782 (print) | LCCN 2017052300 (ebook) |
 ISBN 9781315408668 (eBook) | ISBN 9781138215894 (hardback) |
 ISBN 9781138215900 (pbk.) | ISBN 9781315408668 (ebk)
Subjects: | MESH: Neurodevelopmental Disorders | Child |
 Adolescent
Classification: LCC RJ486.5 (ebook) | LCC RJ486.5 (print) | NLM
 WS 350.6 | DDC 618.92/8—dc23
LC record available at https://lccn.loc.gov/2017051782

ISBN: 978-1-138-21589-4 (hbk)
ISBN: 978-1-138-21590-0 (pbk)
ISBN: 978-1-315-40866-8 (ebk)

Typeset in Goudy
by Apex CoVantage, LLC

To Linda, Spencer and Alex

Brief Table of Contents

SECTION III
The Role of the Clinician 155

Expanded Table of Contents

Series Editor's Foreword

Neurodevelopmental Disorders in Children and Adolescents: A Guide to Evaluation and Treatment is the latest volume in one of Routledge's most popular series, Clinical Topics in Psychology and Psychiatry (CTPP). The overarching goal of CTPP is to provide mental health practitioners with practical information on important topics in psychology and psychiatry. Each volume is comprehensive but relatively easy to digest and integrate into day-to-day clinical practice. It is multidisciplinary in that it covers topics that relate to various specialties within psychology and addresses current issues in clinical psychiatry and psychopharmacology. The Series appeals to the student and the early career and senior clinician. Books chosen for the series are authored or edited by national and international experts in their respective areas, and contributors are highly respected clinicians, educators, and researchers. The current volume exemplifies the intent, scope, and aims of the CTPP series.

Christopher J. Nicholls, board-certified clinical neuropsychologist with over 30 years of experiencing working with children and adolescents, has produced a masterful and comprehensive review of a complex topic. In fact, the function and dysfunction of the developing brain is arguably one of the least understood processes relevant to the fields of psychology, psychiatry, and pediatrics. He reviews the latest thinking on how biology influences neurodevelopment but pays equal attention to the intricacies of family, environmental, and broad social factors. Dr. Nicholls discusses how the clinician impacts the child's development, particularly the diagnoses and interventions he or she assigns. This is rarely done in clinical texts outside of psychotherapy topics. Importantly, he reviews the limitations associated with a categorical approach to understanding a child's development and argues for the consideration of a dimensional framework. And like other texts on the topic, but in a more accessible and nuanced manner, Dr. Nicholls reviews the major neurodevelopmental disorders encountered by practitioners.

The reader will find each and every chapter in this volume of considerable benefit. Unlike edited books, this authored volume flows seamlessly. Dr. Nicholls speaks to you as a colleague and not as a "know-it-all" specialist who demands you accept what he says because he's the expert. He is thoughtful and well reasoned in his presentation of the material, and the information he provides is based on the latest science, not ideology or conformity to a particular approach. Moreover, he is a gifted writer. Contrary to other popular books on the topic, the present volume leaves the reader feeling like he or she just had an informal consultation with an experienced colleague as opposed to having just attended a long and boring conference where presenters reviewed a series of research articles.

I am convinced that *Neurodevelopmental Disorders in Children and Adolescents: A Guide to Evaluation and Treatment* will become one of the lead textbooks in training future neuropsychologists, pediatric and developmental psychologists, and counseling and clinical psychologists. It will also be a valuable resource for child psychiatrists and pediatricians. And, consistent with the main intent of the Series, it will function as an excellent review for early career and experienced practitioners looking for an easily digestible presentation of the latest science on neurodevelopmental disorders.

Bret A. Moore, PsyD, ABPP

Series Editor

Clinical Topics in Psychology and Psychiatry

Introduction

How many people do you know? In fact, how many people have you ever met? Humans are social animals that rely upon connections with others and the development of relationships. Each connection with another person impacts us on some level, some more so than others. Now consider, how many people have you ever seen? We are all born into some form or variety of family, and our attachment to initial caregivers gradually expands as we explore the world, leave the relative safety of our home, and develop ever more relationships with others. We have contact with a growing number of people as we develop, with the numbers of chance interactions increasing at an astounding rate.

What if we had the opportunity to interact with every individual in our hometown or city? Depending upon whether you live in a rural community or a large city, the number of individuals with whom we would need to communicate on some level starts getting unwieldy. What about interacting with everyone in your country? Your continent? The entire world? Wikipedia estimates the number of individuals in the world, in April 2017, to be some 7.5 billion people! ("World population," n.d.). How on earth would you be able to connect with all of these people within your lifetime?

It is within this context that our understanding of the developing brain must be grounded. Although the absolute number is a source of debate, the adult human brain is considered to have between 86 and 100 billion neurons (Azevedo et al., 2009) with many more supportive glial cells that provide structure for the brain. Each neuron furthermore reaches out to communicate with perhaps 1,000 other neurons, resulting in a network of interacting circuits the complexity of which is beyond comprehension, just as the idea is that we could connect with each individual on some 13,000 planets that each have as many people as Earth! And yet, this is in some ways the task of understanding how our brains operate, and the reasons underlying how children and adolescents can develop or acquire impairments in functioning that lead them to come to us for evaluation and treatment. By comparison, the proverbial "finding a needle in a haystack" seems simple!

My goal in this book is to share a perspective that professionals who deal with neurodevelopmental disorders in children and adolescents must develop a systematic approach to thinking about the important variables that might influence the specific child who comes to your attention. Children are a moving target. Just about the time you think you have figured out why a child is being brought to see you, you also realize that the story you are being told is about how the child was over the past months to years, not today. You are handed a stack of minimally organized prior evaluation reports, brochures about this or that tutoring program, several product inserts for medications that have been prescribed, and an apparently misplaced dry cleaning receipt. Your job is to figure out why someone feels there is a problem, what that problem might be, why you are being consulted today (as opposed to previously), and what can be done to make things at least slightly better. You are confident that your years of education about child development, normal and abnormal developmental sequences, and the latest diagnostic manual will help you to get the right diagnosis, and yet you struggle with the whole concept of categorical diagnoses, especially when the person you are to evaluate has gathered a list of multiple diagnoses from multiple providers already. What can you possibly add to the findings of all who have preceded you, and why is this family continuing to seek yet another opinion?

Evaluating and treating children and adolescents with neurodevelopmental disorders is a challenging proposition. Working with adults seems comparatively easier because we (perhaps erroneously) presume they had a history of intact function which was changed as a result of a defined event, such as an accident, a stroke, or a decline in cognition that fits a well-articulated pattern such as prodromal dementia. Adults are "clean" because there is typically a defined change from premorbid functioning, and the insult upon the adult's brain can be relatively clearly measured, imaged, and compared with an extensive research literature. Children, on the other hand, are messy. It is often difficult to sort out the "noise" in the data from the true nature of an emerging and potentially remediable developmental disorder. It is easy to become distracted by a specific symptom, a suggestion that everything can be explained by one variable, or the need to explain why science has disproven commonly held assumptions. Depending upon a host of moderator variables, the same "diagnosis" looks very differently at one age than it does at another. It isn't such a big deal if a 4-year-old runs around noisily until he drops suddenly into an exhaustion driven sleep. If an 8-year-old were to run around a classroom, whooping and wiping the desktops of other students clean in the process, however, there would be a much more vehement demand that "something has to be done."

As of the writing of this book, we don't have a neat algorithm into which we can plug the reams of data available to us and come out with "the truth." Many things are unknown, such as why twins reared together in the same household can be so different from one another. Why is Twin A diagnosed with a debilitating condition while Twin B has almost no symptoms? The goal of this book is to help you, the clinician, develop a comprehensive model of the many variables involved and how they interact with growth and development, environmental change, and progress in healthcare. It is my hope that by the end of this book you will have discarded the categorical thinking characteristic of the early stages of a scientific discipline and instead have an appreciation of the ever-broadening dimensions of consideration which we must consider, in our attempts to understand human behavior. It is also my hope that you will gain an appreciation of your own role in the process of evaluating and treating children and adolescents and that you will recognize the potential you have, to do both good and harm in your work. As the saying goes, the more I think I understand the answers, the less likely it is that I understood the question. This book is therefore about formulating good questions. It is about suspending knowledge in favor of constantly challenging what you have been taught.

Section I of the book addresses the concept of what it means to be different. Although a sense of what is "normal" helps with the recognition of "abnormal," difference is not necessarily undesirable. Many individuals who have struggled with congenital and acquired ways of being different have made great contributions to mankind. The World Health Organization (2017) discusses the concept of disability as being an umbrella term that includes subconcepts of impairment, activity limitations, and restrictions to participation faced by the individual. There is a constant interplay between the person and society, and extremes between ostracism and admiration depending upon context. A presenting concern may range from a mild symptom that has captured someone's attention, to questions of management of multisystem dysfunction that cannot be ignored. While the average person wants to fit in and not stand out, ugly ducklings regularly turn into swans, and the "crippled" become presidents or paradigm-shifting theoretical physicist/cosmologists.

Chapter 1 discusses some of the biological dimensions of difference and covers issues of genetics, prenatal influences upon the developing fetus, perinatal events and variables, and medical illnesses or acquired insults during childhood. Next, we discuss the role of prevention and early identification, and the consequences of failing to consider these important factors. Chapter 2 addresses the influence of the family, diversity, and peer relationships upon the developing child and how protective and deleterious factors can play a strong influence upon a child's outcome. We touch on the concept of special education and the role of the school in shaping the outcome of a child. Chapter 3 provides conceptual "handles" for placing difference in perspective, including the timelines of an individual's efforts to cope with being different, a psychosocial typology of different types of conditions, and the stages of child and family development as they interact with the timing of professionals entering the child's world/system. The first section ends with Chapter 4, in which a discussion is offered regarding the use and misuse of categorical diagnosis and thinking in the evaluation of the developing organism. Rather than fitting an individual into someone's predetermined "boxes" of conceptualization, a call is made for taking a dimensional perspective on what makes for a competent person and for the assessment of strengths and weaknesses in equal proportions.

Section II of this book shifts to the most common presenting concerns for developmental neuropsychology and other child development professionals, from the above perspective. We will discuss what I refer to as "the usual suspects," starting with Chapter 5 in which we review concepts relevant to intellectual and developmental disorders. Chapter 6 addresses attention and executive function impairments. Chapter 7 reviews the concepts of developmental social neuroscience and the autism spectrum disorders, while Chapter 8 reviews academic and specific language disorders. Rather than recitation of the diagnostic criteria and symptoms classic for each condition, each chapter will introduce some of the current thinking about causation, early versus later expression of the problems, conceptualization of the true nature of impairment, and our best guesses as to what works as far as intervention and remediation. Section II emphasizes that an individual's "condition" must be viewed from the context within which that individual lives. What may be more important than the nature of a "difference" is the degree to which it impacts participation within the individual's world.

Consistent with systems theory perspectives that our entrance into a relationship of any kind with a child and his/her family changes the nature of that family system, Section III of the book turns the mirror on ourselves. After providing a possible framework for performing an evaluation in Chapter 9, Chapter 10 covers how we should put all of the information we have gathered together into a written report, and in Chapter 11, I will offer considerations in how one should formulate interventions for neurodevelopmental disorders. In Chapter 12, I will pose questions as to what the role of a clinician might be and how we play a small but potentially impactful role in the totality of the child's experience.

Without presuming to be correct or wise in my own conceptualization of the issues presented in this book, I applaud you for the intellectual curiosity to consider *how* you do what you do, with the goal of being the one who makes a difference in the lives of those with whom we work. I am always surprised when someone tells me that a single remark I had made, or a line in a report that I had written many years previously, had made such a big difference in someone's life. I am humbled by the enormity of that which I do not know or understand. My primary goal is to learn to ask good questions. I hope this book helps you join me.

Bibliography

Azevedo, F. A., Caravalho, L. R., Grinberg, L. T., Farfel, J. M., Ferretti, R. E., Leite, R. E., . . . & Herculano-Houzel, S. (2009). Equal numbers of neuronal and non-neuronal cells make the human brain an isometrically scaled-up primate brain. *The Journal of Comparative Neurology, 513*, 532–541.

World Health Organization (WHO). (2017). *Disabilities*. Retrieved September 17, 2017, from www.who.int/topics/disabilities/en/

World Population (n.d.). *Wikipedia*. Retrieved September 17, 2017, from https://en.wikipedia.org/wiki/World_population

Section I

Dimensions of Being Different

Clinicians in training are often provided with an outline of how to perform an intake interview. Commonly, one asks for demographic information, presenting complaints, the history of the present concerns, etc., etc. I recommend that all clinicians have a "cookbook" manual of "what to do" handy for reference and guidance in gathering this information, as it takes practice in performing intake interviews to become comfortable with the process. We will return to ideas about this in Section III of this book; however, I would first like to invite the reader to think about the process of evaluating and treating children and adolescents in a manner similar to reading a complicated mystery novel.

Invariably, novels involve multiple themes and subplots, often occurring simultaneously and with seeming little connection until one reaches the conclusion of the story. Suddenly, all the threads come together, and the confusion lifts and is replaced by a higher level of understanding, frequently with our smiling in recognition that the clues to the mystery were all there from the beginning. They just needed to be fitted together in previously unseen ways.

Section I discusses several of the subplots involved in evaluating and treating children with neurodevelopmental disorders. Certain themes are purposely repeated, for emphasis; however, there are clearly other considerations that are not covered. It is hoped that the reader will come to realize the importance of asking multiple questions about numerous potential avenues of interest, while recognizing that many turns will involve dead ends while occasionally the path becomes clear and convincing. Section I is therefore about the dimensions within which people differ and the background to their seeking our consultation.

1   Biological Dimensions of Difference

You Don't Pick Your Parents

In the mid-1800s, a farm boy from Austria, who had spent the first part of his life in a rural setting, was recognized by his local schoolmaster to have an advanced aptitude for learning. The schoolmaster arranged for the boy to be sent to a secondary school to cultivate his talents. Although this young man was poor, experienced times of significant depression, and failed some of his school certification tests, he persevered in his studies and ultimately graduated from the Philosophical Institute of the University of Olomouc. He joined the Augustinian order at the St. Thomas Monastery in Brno (currently the second largest city in the Czech Republic), where he was exposed to the research and intellect of the Monastery's friars. He decided to begin his own experiments and planted a garden of pea plants with differing characteristics, systematically cross-fertilizing the pea plants that seemed to have opposite characteristics (Mendelian Inheritance, n.d.)

Gregor, as he was named by the friars, went on to develop two important conclusions from his work. The first conclusion, which he called the Law of Segregation, was that there are some traits that seem to be more powerful and would dominate other traits in the cross-breeding. This was contrary to conventional wisdom at the time, which was that traits would dilute each other through their combination. The other conclusion, which he termed the Law of Independent Assortment, established that some traits were passed on independently of other traits. Although he did little to publicize his work, and much of his work was initially misunderstood, Gregor Mendel's research became the foundation for the understanding of genetics and much of the foundation of biology (Mendelian Inheritance. n.d.).

The laws of Mendelian inheritance suggest that, as the two parts of a gene pair, called "alleles," separate from each other and fuse with another gene pair during sexual reproduction, the new cell has one allele that is dominant to the other. Since Mendel's original work, it is now clear that there are extensions to his principles, including the idea that some alleles are incompletely dominant, that some pairs of genes do not assort independently because they are physically linked on a chromosome, and that some genes are sex-linked. Still, it is widely known and accepted that traits are passed on from one generation to another, and parents will readily tell you that one of their children is more like mother while the other is just like their dad.

Genetics is most commonly thought of in terms of the physical manifestations of reproduction. A sheep that mates with a sheep produces a, well you get the idea. What is less appreciated, however, is the idea that there are non-Mendelian forms of genetic transmission, that single genes can have a huge impact upon behavior, and that there are genetic influences upon such abstract issues as cycles of violence among adults who were maltreated as children. The National Institute of Mental Health's Research Domain Criteria (RDoC) project (National Institute of Mental Health, 2017), for example, has identified over twenty probable genetic influences on the single construct of "fear," as distinct from other forms of anxiety or what they refer to as "negative valence systems." Clearly, the early theories of psychology that postulated that certain behaviors were the product of social learning or mother-child attachment or psychosexual development, while not wrong, represent only the tip of the iceberg and reflect our wishful desire for a nice, simple explanation for just how complicated life is.

Understanding the developing child and things that go wrong must therefore start with an appreciation that humans are the product of genetic, independent assortment. The combination of traits in a child do not always match the combination of similar traits in the parents. The process of "meiosis," where cell division reduces the number of chromosomes in a parental cell by half to produce four reproductive cells called "gametes," is considered to be random. This in turn means that the new cells will not contain all of the mother's or the father's chromosomes and that the new "haploid" cells will contain a mixture of genes from both mother and father. In many ways, having a child is like rolling genetic dice. We know what the dice look like and can point to the different sides of the die, but the result produced by rolling combinations of dice can only be described in terms of probabilities, and our confidence in predicting outcome is demonstrated in the likelihood of your walking away from a craps table in a casino with money in your pocket.

What is important for our purposes is the recognition that some genetic conditions have profound effects upon brain growth and development and may be behind the presentation of a specific child who comes to see you. Common single-gene disorders in children include cystic fibrosis, neurofibromatosis 1, phenylketonuria, and fragile X syndrome. Professionals working with children and adolescents should develop at least an awareness of these conditions, as early identification and intervention is often the key to long-term outcome. Overall, however, it is important to understand that the human life cycle begins with genetically driven patterns of brain development.

Are You Sure They Are Your Parents?

Without going down rabbit holes and distracting you from the central purpose of this chapter, I invite you to at least consider the question of whether the child who presents to the office is actually the offspring of the caregivers who bring them. Society is increasingly flexible in accepting alternative family models, and it is worth asking (privately) whether the child is the biological offspring of the presenting caretakers. Aside from the more obvious variations of foreign adoption and the assumed guardianship of grandparents, aunts, etc., medical science makes available a wide variety of other means of having children. Children may have been the product of a surrogate pregnancy, an in vitro fertilization, donor egg/sperm, etc. Sometimes accidents occur as a result of a one-night stand, or mothers who wish to remain single arrange for impregnation by a man who, by the time they arrive in your office, is described as "never having been involved." The point is that things aren't always what they appear, and asking only about mother's family history may overlook other genetic and familial factors. If you don't ask, you won't know. Perhaps the most sensitive way to approach this is to ask the caregivers to help you develop a "family tree" diagram. This process quickly allows the clinician to learn about the structure of the biological family of the child.

Neurulation and the Growth of the Nervous System

Fertilization involves the fusion of gametes into a new organism, the "zygote." Cell division initially involves no growth, but rather cleavage of the cells into 2, 4, 16, and so on until 128 cells are reached, at which time the embryo becomes called a "blastula." At about 7 days after fertilization, the blastula attaches itself to the uterus and becomes implanted. By day 9, two "germ" layers have become differentiated (an outer or "dorsal" ectoderm and an inner or "ventral" endoderm), and later as a result of the blastula folding inward, a third level (mesoderm) develops between the ectoderm and the endoderm. On day 18 of life, the nervous system begins to form on the dorsal surface (think of the dorsal fin on a shark) of the embryo, and in the third week of gestation, the ectodermal germ layer differentiates into a pear-shaped disk with an upper (cranial) and lower (caudal) end. This disk is called the "neural plate." The more central cells on this plate become narrower on their inner surface, while the cells around them become narrower on their outer surface, which produces a "neural groove" which gradually deepens and eventually folds over onto itself, to become the "neural tube." This tube closes from the middle toward each end, and gradually extends as a fluid filled tube with two open ends that eventually close by about 25 days of life. The cranial end of this tube ultimately becomes the brain, while the caudal end becomes the spinal cord. The reader is encouraged to review any of the multitude of YouTube videos showing the sequences of the above steps which are collectively termed "neurulation."

Neurodevelopmental disorders can have their causation even at this very earliest of developmental stages. If there is a problem with neurulation (the forming of the neural tube) in the third and fourth weeks of life, severe disorders such as anencephaly can occur. Anencephaly refers to the failure of the brain and protective skull to develop and, in most cases, is incompatible with life. Infants born with anencephaly have recognizable faces; however, their heads slope backwards and down from their forehead, and the brain doesn't develop much above the brainstem and spinal cord. The Centers for Disease Control has ongoing research into the causes of anencephaly and is considering genetic as well as environmental factors (Centers for Disease Control and Prevention [CDC], 2017, August 2).

Disorders of closure at the lower/caudal end of the neural tube can cause various forms of spina bifida, in which the neural tube doesn't close all the way and the backbone protecting that section of the spinal cord doesn't develop, often resulting in damage to the spinal cord and nerves. Three subtypes of spina bifida include myelomeningocele, meningocele, and spina bifida occulta. Most people think of spina bifida involving myelomeningocele, the most serious form in which a sac containing fluid and parts of the nervous system protrude out from the baby's back and are damaged. The result is often a quite severe disability affecting such skills as the ability to walk or move one's legs, loss of sensation/feeling in the legs, and problems with how the individual goes to the bathroom. If there is a fluid sac but no nerves are involved, the condition is termed meningocele and has much milder disability-related consequences. The mildest form of spina bifida is called "occulta" and involves a failure of bone growth in a part of the spine but doesn't involve nerve damage and has essentially no developmental impact. Many individuals with spina bifida occulta aren't identified until later in life.

Spina bifida is a good example of why understanding the developmental processes affecting the nervous system is important to the work of professionals who evaluate children and adolescents; however, several other variations in brain growth and development can also have later consequences. Once the neural tube is formed, the cranial end of the tube begins to grow and differentiate into the various sections of the brain, including the forebrain, midbrain, and hindbrain. The brain begins to fold or bend forward (ventrally), and by the fifth week of life, the brain has divided into four sections, which are further specialized by the seventh week of life, at which time we can recognize the major landmarks of the brain—the two hemispheres, the thalamus, cerebellum, pons, and medulla oblongata can all be identified. We now begin to speak of the "fetal period" or "fetus," which begins at about the eighth or ninth week and is associated with the embryo taking on the recognizable features of the human form. Even at this very early stage of life, however, our brains are beginning to have nerve cells "migrate" or move from the germinal layer to different locations based upon their genetic coding. The brain begins to develop layers of nerves and their connecting axons, which emerge at a rapid rate—so fast that, by about the fifth month of gestation, the smooth surface of the developing brain must "wrinkle" in order to provide enough cortical space for all of the nerves to develop. This wrinkling occurs in a regular sequence, and the different areas of the brain become divided into "lobes" defined by the peaks and valleys across the surface of the brain. If you were to spread out the surface of the brain, unfolding all the wrinkles and smoothing the product out, it would be about the size of four sheets of letter-sized paper (Freudenrich & Boyd, 2001).

Here too, things can go wrong. Sometimes the brain doesn't develop its wrinkles, causing a smooth appearance ("lissencephaly") that limits the area in which neurons can differentiate (National Institute of Neurological Disorders and Stroke, 2017b). There can also be a failure to develop large enough wrinkles (microgyria), which also causes restrictions. What is interesting is the fact that the layer of neurons in the cortex of the brain is very thin—between 2 and 4 millimeters, or about the thickness of three credit cards stacked on top of each other. How can three times the thickness of a paperclip be responsible for cognition that ranges from simple recognition of a baby's mother all the way to quantum physics or the composition of a symphony? The answer seems to lie in the fact that neurons grow rapidly or "proliferate" at an astounding rate during fetal development. By approximately 12 to 14 weeks of life, nerve cells are proliferating at a rate of something like 15 million per hour (Ackerman, 1992, p. 6). These cells are genetically programmed to move ("migrate") to set places in the brain, where they become specialized ("cell differentiation") in their functions appropriate to that place. Similar cells group together in the emerging regions of the brains and start to make connections both within that region as well as with other areas of the brain.

The complexity of this process is almost unimaginable. Researchers at the Computational Radiology Laboratory at Boston Children's Hospital are developing electron microscopy techniques that can image individual neurons within the brain, helping us to understand the structure and connectivity of brain circuitry at amazing levels of image resolution (Computational Radiology Laboratory Research, 2015). Their work is confirming estimates that a cubic millimeter of the cerebral cortex—about the size of a grain of sand—can contain some 50,000 neurons that each make some 6,000 connections with the cells around them. These 300 million connections are highly specific and allow communication with some but not other cells, again all according to a genetic plan.

How do the cells start to connect? The neuron cell body has extensions that both send (axons) and receive (dendrites) messages to/from other neurons. At each point of connection, called a "synapse," electricity that has traveled down the axon causes bubbles of chemicals (neurotransmitters) to be released into the small gap between the axon and the dendrite of the receiving cell. By filling receptor gates (think catcher mitts), the chemicals cause excitation of the receiving cell, with aggregation of that excitation in turn triggering communication with the next nerve(s). The axons of the neurons within a certain area of the brain start to group together, to form circuits or "tracts" that allow communication to occur, not only within a specific brain region, but between the various regions of the brain and down into the spinal cord. An image of this process might look something like the members of a household leaving each morning, to climb into their cars and leave their home street to join a main street, connecting with a divided highway that connects with interstates.

As the regions of the brain become more specialized, the connecting tracts specialize into those that are within the specific regions (*association pathways*), those that communicate across the connections between the left and right hemispheres of the brain (*commissural pathways*), and those that send messages to and receive input from the spinal cord (*projection pathways*). Usually, these connections all develop and work efficiently, although as we will learn, some developmental problems can occur because this doesn't happen correctly. One example is something called "agenesis of the corpus callosum," where the thick band of tracts connecting the left and right hemispheres of the brain don't completely develop. The result is a developmental variation upon the concept of the "split brain," research that has looked at how various cognitive functions are affected when the connecting pathways in adults were surgically cut to stop the spread of epilepsy. The Nobel Prize-winning work of Roger Sperry and his colleagues in the 1960s helped us to understand that the left and right hemispheres of the brain perform different kinds of cognitive activities and that severing the communication between the hemispheres results in a "disconnection" between these abilities (Nobelprize.org, 2003), much as might happen if the major bridges across the Mississippi River were all washed away.

One doesn't need to always disconnect regions of the brain in order to have developmental problems, however. There are several types of malformation in the brain that affect cortical development, beginning at these earliest stages of prenatal life. Some problems are associated with insufficient neuronal or glial (structural cells in the brain) proliferation. The result is that not enough brain cells are developed. This can cause brains that are too small (microcephaly) and a child who ultimately has limitations in their intellectual and developmental potential. Some problems are associated with abnormal neuronal migration, either with too little or too much migration in certain areas, as has been found among individuals with dyslexia. Yet other problems can also occur, involving abnormal cell organization or malformations that result from inborn errors of metabolism. While we could have extensive further discussion of these possibilities, patients with these disorders are most typically seen in specialized neurology and developmental clinics and less often seen in the practice of most developmental specialists. For most of us, it is important to become aware of these possibilities, and if necessary to refer to or consult with specialists in the various brain development conditions that can occur. There are also textbooks that describe the many birth defects and genetic anomalies that can occur during this, the earliest stage of brain development.

The Prenatal Environment

Returning to our story about the development of the more typical child, if we assume that the more serious troubles discussed above are avoided, we now have a fetus that is approaching the point where it can survive outside of the mother's protective internal environment. Before we get there, however, we need to consider what non-genetic or neural growth influences may have contributed to the ultimate development of the child who shows up in our office. Here we must consider the health of the mother and the influences upon her maintenance of an optimal uterine environment for the developing fetus. It is becoming increasingly clear that maternal health habits and exposure to noxious events and substances can potentially have a devastating effect upon the unborn child. We have become familiar with the warning stickers on packs of cigarettes or containers of alcohol that warn against their use during pregnancy, and the concepts of fetal alcohol syndrome or fetal alcohol effect are well known in society.

Substances that can produce physical or functional defects in the human embryo or fetus are called "teratogens" and affect the fetus in multiple ways. Important variables include the type of substance exposure, the timing of when during fetal development the exposure occurs, the amount of exposure, and the duration of continuous exposure. According to Chanapa Tantibanchachai of The Embryo Project Encyclopedia (2014), the scientific study of teratogens began in the 1800s, at which time systematic experiments involving subjecting chicken eggs to various manipulations (turning, jarring, subjecting them to temperature extremes) began to document the effects of such manipulations upon the developing chick, with deformities that were observed associated with the trauma exerted on the egg. This progressed to more extensive research in the twentieth century in which teratogens became categorized into physical, chemical, infectious, and maternal conditions. For example, exposure to radiation or extreme temperatures, such as those experienced by the fetus of a pregnant woman who enters a hot tub or suffers a high fever experiences, have been shown to have negative impact upon the developing fetus, causing malformations, microcephaly, and other birth defects. President Franklin Roosevelt's struggles with polio resulted in his formation of the National Foundation for Infantile Paralysis, in 1938, to combat the rise of polio through vaccine development. This program became later/better known as the March of Dimes, whose mission is to prevent birth defects and infant mortality through supporting research, promoting newborn screening and the education of healthcare professionals about the best practices for healthy pregnancies (March of Dimes, 2010). March of Dimes information is routinely provided to families of newborn children, even today.

Although we have a long way to go, these studies have helped reduce the incidence and severity of preventable conditions through educating mothers about what substances and practices to avoid, as well as through recognizing that attention to diet and vitamins can promote healthy pregnancies. For example, anencephaly as discussed above may be prevented by women of childbearing age consuming folic acid on a daily basis (CDC, 2017, August 2). Folate may also prevent spina bifida and other birth defects. Iron deficiency is another and perhaps the most common form of nutritional problem during pregnancy. Iron deficiency increases the risk of premature delivery and delivering a low birthweight baby and, in children, is associated with developmental delays and behavioral problems. Efforts to improve maternal and child health among women at risk for poor nutrition resulted in the Women, Infants and Children (WIC) program, which provides nutritional supplements, nutritional education, and healthcare referrals for low-income women who are pregnant, postpartum, or breastfeeding and for children up to 5 years of age (United States Department of Agriculture, 2017).

Aside from interventions for women who are at risk nutritionally, it is also critical to consider the environment within which the pregnant woman nurtures her unborn child. Problems in fetal and child development are more frequent among those living in poverty and other disadvantaged circumstances. Women who are subjected to domestic violence and partner abuse, second-hand smoke (even if they don't smoke themselves), and high levels of maternal stress and depression are more likely to have children who show developmental and behavioral challenges. And despite their best efforts, pregnant women can become ill, experience ongoing chronic illness, and are encouraged to take certain medications despite an awareness that there could be a negative impact upon their growing child. As an example, fluctuations in a pregnant, diabetic mother's blood sugar can have an impact upon their child's ultimate learning and memory skills that might not be reversible. Tracy DeBoer (Riggins) has found that infants of mothers with poorly controlled blood sugar during pregnancy had subtle memory deficiencies such as not recognizing their mother's voice and not remembering how to do things they had learned the week before (DeBoer, Wewerka, Bauer, Georgieff, & Nelson, 2005). Managing diabetes is hard enough without the worry mothers with diabetes must feel when they become pregnant.

Many other medical conditions during pregnancy, and their treatments, are also sources of worry. Thyroid disorders in which levels of thyroid hormones are abnormal can cause teratogenic effects, miscarriage, and separation of the placenta from the uterine wall. Women with low thyroid levels need to take medications such as Synthroid throughout their pregnancy, and while levothyroxine is not expected to harm an unborn baby, mothers often worry about the impact.

What about depression? Meta-analyses of common perinatal mental disorders finds that, in high-income countries, 10% of pregnant women and 13% of those who have given birth experience some form of mental disorder, usually depression and anxiety. These incidence figures climb to almost 20%—one in five mothers—in low- and lower-middle income countries (Fisher et al., 2012). Depression experienced by mothers prior to their child's birth increases the risk of neurodevelopmental disorders in children and adds to the risk of future maternal illness (Kinsella & Monk, 2009). Yet, while gestational diabetes is far less common than depression in pregnancy, it is routinely screened for while maternal depression during pregnancy is often overlooked. This seems counterintuitive when depression could be effectively treated with psychotherapy and some kinds of antidepressants, which have been found to be relatively safe for use during pregnancy. The primary point to be made here is that we should not overlook the thousands of possible factors that can influence pregnancy and the culture within which our developing fetus grows. While it isn't possible to go back and change things that have already happened, our study of outcomes is important in fueling prevention and healthcare policies.

Prematurity

The work of growing a child typically lasts 40 weeks from conception to delivery. As we have already seen, this is a period of tremendous growth and rapid development of the central nervous system. As the fetus reaches just past the halfway point during this period, it begins to be possible for the child to survive outside of the mother's uterus. Being born too early is termed "prematurity," and the survival rate of extremely low birthweight, and extremely premature infants has improved over the last several decades to the point where it is now possible for a child who has reached 22 weeks gestation to survive (although babies this premature are rarely resuscitated because survival without major disability is rare). The decision to resuscitate a 22- or 23-week gestation infant is the subject of great debate. Some neonatologists and newborn intensive care units offer treatment to babies born at the very limits of viability, while others are withholding treatments that were regularly used a decade ago. The American Congress of Obstetricians and Gynecologists, in a joint statement with the Society for Maternal-Fetal Medicine (American College of Obstetrics and Gynecologists, 2016), suggests that decisions about treating extremely premature infants should be made on the basis of parental preference and the most recent data on outcome. Worldwide consensus seems to suggest that comfort care should be provided at 22 weeks' gestation, increasing to active care at 25 weeks' gestation. But at what cost are these decisions being made?

There have been dramatic advances in the care of these most fragile of newborn children. If the child has a relatively uncomplicated intensive care nursery stay until they are close to their presumed expected date of delivery, the outcomes are quite positive. Nevertheless, so many things can go wrong and a high percentage of premature children will end up with some form of developmental morbidity. Even late-term premature infants, defined as those born between 33 and 36 weeks' gestation (i.e. 7- to 8-month-long pregnancy), have been found to have more neurodevelopmental problems than full-term infants (Romeo et al., 2010), and calls have been made to investigate and identify the predictors of outcome other than gestational age, including factors such as maternal risks and reasons for early delivery, biomarkers such as indications of inflammation and intrauterine growth retardation, and postnatal medical problems and environmental influences. These concepts are important because parents often volunteer that their baby was born prematurely; however, when clinicians hear that the baby was only a few days or weeks premature, they often dismiss the history as unimportant or unremarkable.

The outcome of prematurity also depends upon when in time the baby was born. Neonatology continues to evolve and progress, and the technologies and treatments used to care for these smallest of babies are very different today than they were 5 or 10 years ago. Morbidity has also been reduced by an improved awareness of the impact of care variables on outcome, and while it was previously not uncommon to find large rooms with 30, 40, or even more isolettes in rows next to each other, today's newborn intensive care units are often designed to have smaller rooms in which the baby is either alone or shares the room with just one or two other babies. Attention to infection prevention has also helped, although well-meaning parents who have colds still visit the Newborn Intensive Care Unit ("It's just allergies") and can cause havoc if their colds involve highly infectious conditions such as respiratory syncytial virus (RSV). Premature babies just can't fight infection very well, and contracting RSV when you are also fighting to breathe and regulate your temperature can be a disaster for ultimate developmental potential.

Common problems found among the premature include chronic lung diseases such as bronchopulmonary dysplasia and the need for supplemental oxygen over long periods of time, retinopathy of prematurity in which the infant's eyes develop structural problems that affect vision, and intraventricular hemorrhage where bleeding into the brain's ventricles can cause varying degrees of brain damage. Infants can experience prenatal strokes, have challenges secondary to chronically poor oxygenation, and can develop cerebral palsy due to many possible reasons. Treatment of these conditions is also not benign, and the process of keeping babies alive can have unintended consequences that may not become evident until much later in the child's life, at which time the areas of the brain that were affected reach the time in development where those brain functions become needed (Taylor & Clark, 2016).

The implication is, if a child was born prematurely, the conscientious clinician may wish to obtain and review discharge summaries from the child's newborn intensive care unit hospitalization. The brain is very adaptable; however, one cannot make assumptions based upon normal development if the child's start to life involved early neurological adaptation to potentially traumatic events. The concept of neurological "plasticity" is valuable and suggests that our brains can adapt to early insult and compensate for damage to brain structures. However, if one area of the brain takes over for another potentially damaged area, the skills that the compensating area would have managed may themselves be impacted, possibly not becoming evident until later in life when those areas come "online." This is particularly true for later developing brain regions and functions, such as the executive functions dependent upon frontal lobe development.

Delivery and the Perinatal Period

Society has become familiar with the tragedy of sudden infant death syndrome, where despite a thorough investigation, review of clinical history, and a complete autopsy, an infant less than 1 year of age dies suddenly and for no apparent reason. What is less known is that ten times as many babies die before or during delivery, again with many cases involving no apparent cause. Sometimes there are problems with the baby in terms of birth defects or genetic anomalies, sometimes there are problems in the mother's placenta or the umbilical cord that feeds the baby, and sometimes stillbirth is tied to maternal health issues such as high blood pressure or obesity. Still, many things happen during pregnancy that we don't understand or can't predict with routine pregnancy screenings. Some infants are born with an immediately noticeable medical problem that results in their failure to develop as expected. The hopes and dreams of parents become shattered when the delivery room becomes suddenly quiet and urgent calls for resuscitation teams and neonatologists are made. Parents wait frantically for news that their baby is ok, many times when the mother is herself in a state of medical emergency and shock.

Sometimes babies are born and don't start to breathe for an extended period of time, or are pale in appearance and have a slow or absent pulse. Virginia Apgar, an anesthesiologist in 1952, developed the well-known Apgar Score where a newborn is evaluated at birth across the variables of appearance (skin color), pulse (heart rate), grimace response (reflexes), activity (muscle tone), and respirations (breathing rate and effort). According to the American College of Obstetricians and Gynecologists (2015), an infant is given scores of 0, 1, or 2 on each of these variables, resulting in a score that can range from 0 to 10. An Apgar score is given at 1 minute and 5 minutes for all infants, and at 5-minute intervals up to 20 minutes for an infant with an initial score of less than 7. What is not always appreciated, however, is that Apgar scores do not predict infant mortality or adverse neurologic outcome and that, while the incidence of cerebral palsy increases if the Apgar score is less than 5 at 5 and 10 minutes, most infants with low Apgar scores do not develop cerebral palsy. Also, if an Apgar score at 5 minutes is 7 or more, it is unlikely that neonatal encephalopathy will result from perinatal hypoxia-ischemia. What Apgar scores are fundamentally important for is the initial management and resuscitation of an infant who isn't doing well at birth. Apgar scores can guide resuscitation efforts; however, these efforts are typically begun before the initial 1-minute Apgar rating (American College of Obstetrics and Gynecologists, 2016).

Should an infant suffer significant troubles breathing during the birth process, a condition might arise in which both reduced blood oxygenation of the brain or reduced perfusion of blood to the brain (or both) can occur, secondary to conditions that affect the cardiac and/or respiratory systems. If disruption of sufficient levels of oxygen circulating in the brain occurs in the presence of reduced blood flow, the term "hypoxic-ischemic encephalopathy" is sometimes used. This condition can be secondary to a wide range of medical conditions, including cardiac arrest, carbon monoxide poisoning, prolonged seizures, and even recurrent obstructive sleep apnea; however, in the newborn child, the use of this term may be reflective of a myriad of problems and is not straightforward (Fatemi, Wilson, & Johnston, 2009). What is important is to recognize that developmental disorders, such as cerebral palsy, may result from medical events surrounding the birth process and that it is important to have asked/considered such factors when taking one's initial history.

Another common condition that can negatively impact the newborn child is when an infection experienced by the mother is transmitted to the infant, such as when the mother herself is experiencing an illness related to Group B Streptococcus (GBS). GBS is a type of bacteria that can cause illness in people of all ages; however, newborns can develop especially severe complications from exposure to GBS, including infection of their own blood (sepsis), pneumonia, and sometimes an infection of the fluid and lining around the brain and spinal cord, also known as meningitis (American Pregnancy Association, 2017). The CDC differentiates between early-onset GBS disease, which occurs in the first week of life, versus late-onset disease which occurs between the first week and third month of life (CDC, 2016, May 23). Pregnant mothers are routinely tested for GBS between 35 to 37 weeks of pregnancy, and those who test positive are given antibiotics during labor to prevent the transmission of the bacteria to their baby. Mothers often don't know that they have the infection, however, and may not always be treated. The child's development of meningitis and the potential for subsequent deafness and other developmental problems (even death) is more often associated with late-onset disease—after the delivery period and mother having taken her baby home from the hospital. Clinicians who work with infants should therefore be sensitive to whether children who have not had routine medical follow-up in early infancy may be experiencing an infectious process.

Other infections can also have devastating impact upon the growing child. In 2016, the world experienced a public health emergency when a virus carried by *Aedes* mosquitoes, the "Zika virus," spread rapidly in various areas of the world. Although the virus was first identified in 1947, large outbreaks of human infection caused by this virus occurred in Micronesia (2007), Brazil (2015), and other places and was strongly suspected of causing microcephaly and other neurological problems such as Guillain-Barré syndrome in the infants of infected pregnant women (World Health Organization, 2016). Another condition, human immunodeficiency virus (HIV) can also be transmitted to the infant by the mother. HIV attacks the infection-fighting cells of the immune system and is most typically acquired in childhood through mother to child transmission during pregnancy, labor and delivery, and breastfeeding. Although early treatment may prevent or prolong the progression of HIV to acquired immunodeficiency syndrome (AIDS), dosing of appropriate medicines is challenging, and adherence with medication use can be particularly difficult for children and adolescents (World Health Organization, 2017). As with all chronic illnesses, living with HIV causes stress upon the child, which can often impact their success in school, social relationships, and self-esteem. A complication for the clinician regarding the many infections and illnesses that children and adolescents can acquire is that many individuals will not disclose their status unless the clinician specifically asks.

Prevention and Early Identification

Fortunately, most children are born and negotiate the newborn period without experiencing any of the horrible things we have covered so far. Parents and guardians will often tell you, "Everything was fine, fine" when discussing the child's start to life, although some conditions are not immediately apparent and must be picked up by systematic screening and early intervention. Children who are born into families that have health insurance and access to routine pediatric or family practice care are lucky in that routine laboratory tests and screening of development is a regular part of early childhood healthcare. But what about the uninsured or those who live rurally and far from available healthcare?

Healthcare availability is a political topic about which there are many strongly held beliefs and differing practices worldwide. In 1967, however, the United States Congress introduced the Medicaid benefit for children and adolescents, known as Early and Periodic Screening, Diagnostic and Treatment (EPSDT) program (Medicaid.gov., n.d.). Similar programs are in place in most countries around the world. The purpose of such screenings is to identify factors that can adversely impact child development, as early as possible.

Identification can lead to early intervention, which can minimize the potentially negative impact of both well-defined and as-yet unexplained variables that impact the child. Some conditions will be obvious, such as hearing and visual impairments, and interventions at the earliest stages can maximize positive outcomes, such as the use of eye patching in amblyopia. According to the American Association for Pediatric Ophthalmology and Strabismus, amblyopia refers to decreased vision in one or both eyes due to something that interferes with normal development of vision in infants and children (American Association for Pediatric Ophthalmology and Strabismus., 2017). Often, this is not due to an obvious problem in the eye but, rather, because the nerves that send the visual data from the eye to the brain's visual cortex aren't working correctly. The brain accepts the blurry image from the amblyopic eye, even when glasses are used, and accepts the image from the "good" eye as the one to rely upon. Also called "lazy eye," amblyopia causes reduced visual acuity in the affected eye and is a leading cause of vision impairment. More significant problems can occur when the optic nerve from the eye to other brain-based vision processing systems doesn't grow properly. A condition known as "optic nerve hypoplasia" can result in complete blindness in one or both eyes and/ or significantly impaired vision (American Association for Pediatric Ophthalmology and Strabismus, 2016). While therapies won't help this kind of vision loss, it is important for the child to wear glasses to protect the "good eye" from trauma or injury. Vision screening is an important component of a developmental evaluation, and one can download vision screening software onto a cell phone or tablet for easy use in your office.

Other variables are less apparent at birth and only found through targeted genetic and other forms of screening. The impact of these variables may not be

immediate but, rather, accumulate over time and development, possibly causing devastating consequences if not treated. One example of this process is
the outcome of a rare inherited disorder called phenylketonuria (PKU). PKU
increases the level of a certain substance in the blood called phenylalanine,
a protein building block obtained through our diets. The condition is inherited in what is called an autosomal recessive pattern, which means that both
parents have to carry one copy of the mutated gene but typically don't have
symptoms themselves. Children with PKU can't break down one of the amino
acids found in proteins and, if not identified, can develop significant intellectual disabilities over time. Fortunately, PKU and many other conditions are
identified through newborn screening tests, which are required in the United
States but vary from state to state as far as which tests are required. Typically,
babies are screened before they leave the hospital at birth, with checks of
variables involving the blood, hearing, and heart. The blood tests check for
common genetic conditions, such as PKU, and allow for early identification
and intervention.

Child development specialists, again, are not typically involved in the
screening process but need to become aware of the impact of various conditions as they impact or contribute to the developmental difficulties that present to our offices. Continuing with the example of PKU, the Developmental
Cognitive Neuroscience Laboratory of Adele Diamond, at the University of
British Columbia, has long studied factors that influence how children's minds
change as the grow up. Diamond has had a particular interest in what are
termed "executive functions," reflecting the self-regulatory and self-control
mechanisms of the brain (Diamond, 2013). She hypothesized that poorly controlled diets among children with PKU, which would result in increases in
the ratio of phenylalanine to tyrosine in the blood, would affect the cognitive
functions in a certain area of the frontal lobes of the brain—the dorsolateral
prefrontal cortex. Her findings confirmed her theories that children with PKU
who had higher levels of plasma phenylalanine over a 4-year period performed
more poorly on tasks involving working memory and inhibitory control, as
compared with those children who maintained relatively better dietary control (Diamond, Prevor, Callender, & Druin, 1997). Diamond's work serves as
a mandate for those of us who work with neurodevelopmental disorders to
grasp the broader implications of the disorder a child may present and not be
content to simply perform our evaluation of where the child is functioning on
a developmental continuum.

Developmental Delays

In considering all of the foregoing ways in which early development can go
awry, it is not surprising that some children lag behind others in the achievement of developmental milestones. Just as there are reference charts for height
and weight across the childhood years, against which physicians compare a
child's growth trajectory, there are norms for when children should acquire

various developmental stages. The scientific field of developmental psychology is a rich source of knowledge about how children move from one stage to another. There are many factors involved such as attachment, separation and individuation, and ultimately identity development and self-concept. Normative data helps us to identify children who may be lagging behind expectations in various areas, so that we can involve those children in early intervention activities to help them catch up.

So what are the areas in which a child could demonstrate developmental delay? Some children may exhibit global delays across all areas of development, while others may have specific delays in only one or two areas. Very premature infants often show global delays relative to their chronological age, which makes sense because they had less time to develop and integrate the various neurological systems that are necessary for normal development. If a child was born at 30 weeks' gestation, they were 10 weeks or 2.5 months early. If we recognize that the average child sits up at about 3 months of age, the fact that the premature child would be neurologically only 3 1/2 months old at that point, if they had been carried to term, impacts whether they will have matured enough for this specific developmental phase. The premature child's development may further be compromised by the fact that they spent much of their early life experience lying flat in an isolette or nursery bed, sometimes even with their arms loosely tied down to prevent their dislodging various tubes and lines. They don't get the "normal" experience of movement that occurs both prenatally and in the first months of life. If the premature infant is restrained, they do not get to build the proprioception and strength that full-term, healthy babies experience. The question arises as to whether they are delayed or disadvantaged.

Because they are at times under bright lights, premature infants are also often given eye protective masks, which may restrict the usual processes of the brain learning to create vision secondary to processing movement and varying levels of light. Babies who are intubated so that a respirator can breathe for them are deprived of the experience of normal breathing and often develop feeding problems because they are fed by a tube or intravenously. Our brain's development requires movement and experience to establish and refine sensory and motor pathways within the brain. Once such infants are discharged home, they have to "start over" in developing their strength and coordination— no wonder they can show delays as compared with full-term infants!

To account for these experiences, developmentalists often "correct" for prematurity by comparing infants to their gestational rather than their chronological age. Conventional practice is to gradually stop this process by about age 2, because although 2 1/2 months is a significant part of 6 months, it is less significant as compared with 24 months. Despite statistical corrections, however, the fact is that very small preemies are delayed relative to full-term children and are at a greater risk of having long-term consequences of such delays. The answer is therefore that we must provide early intervention in all areas of need, including gross motor development, fine motor development, feeding and oral-motor/speech development, cognitive stimulation, social interaction, and language development.

Acquired Medical Illness and Injury

If, seemingly miraculously, we make it through early childhood without any of the above predisposing factors causing problems, a careful review of a child's history may reveal other factors that need to be put into the equation of variables we need to consider in understanding developmental problems. Perhaps the most common condition about which we should ask is whether the child experienced frequent ear infections during their early years. Due to the anatomical structure of the young child's head and neck, the Eustachian tube that connects the upper part of the throat with the middle ear can become blocked or plugged. You have probably experienced this when flying or driving through the mountains, where your ears may feel plugged or full or you hear a popping or clicking sound. Adults can easily clear this sensation by yawning or opening their mouths wide; however, young children's Eustachian tubes are shorter and straighter than adults', which makes it easier for germs to travel to the middle ear or fluid to become trapped there. The term "otitis media" refers to an inflammatory process that results from fluid becoming trapped, and children's reduced capacity to fight infection can result in complications that can lead to permanent hearing loss at certain frequencies, which in turn can affect how well the child can subsequently learn (National Institute on Deafness and Other Communication Disorders, 2017). Ear infections are therefore an example of an acquired illness during childhood that we should ask about, particularly if the child presents with language concerns. Many other infections and acquired illnesses are also relevant to our study of the development of the child, and a thorough history can help to pick up on conditions that otherwise might have been forgotten about by the parents.

Acquired problems don't have to be only about an illness, however. Sometimes a child may spontaneously develop seizures for which there is not a clear causative factor. While most seizures can be controlled and do not cause brain damage, uncontrolled and ongoing seizures may cause more permanent damage. It is also common for children with epilepsy to develop associated behavioral and emotional problems, and for many, the risk of seizures can restrict their independence and involvement in various recreational conditions (National Institute of Neurological Disorders and Stroke, 2017a). Even absence seizures, which are typically brief and involve staring, blinking, and interrupted consciousness, can lead to learning troubles that are much more significant than just brief lapses in attention. Children with absence seizures have a much higher incidence of other psychiatric conditions, especially attention-deficit/hyperactivity disorder (ADHD), and treatment needs to be conscientiously implemented in order to prevent further progression. The watchful clinician should be sensitive to even brief lapses in a child's engagement with a task or activity, particularly if such lapses appear to occur more than once.

Sleep disorders are also commonly overlooked in childhood and can have substantial impact upon a child's performance in school. There are many contributors to disorders of initiating and maintaining sleep in childhood, both biological as well as psychological. Many children resist going to bed or "train" their parents to lie in bed with them to help them get to sleep. The "midnight intruder" is also a common phenomenon where children prefer to come into parents' rooms and try to get into the warm bed of their parents, rather than remaining in their own, less appealing bed. The disruption of parental sleep can lead to exhaustion that prompts giving in "just this once" and develops a learned cycle of behavior. Physiological causes can include such things as sleep-related breathing disorders, most commonly caused by enlarged adenoids and tonsils, and restless leg syndrome which involves repetitive, stereotypic leg movements that occur in non-rapid eye movement (REM) sleep (Dodzik, 2011). Sleep disorders are found to be associated with several developmental disorders including ADHD, autism spectrum disorders, and others.

Any number of accidents and traumas can affect the developing brain, including head injuries, near-drowning events, and other medical events that might have an impact upon the brain. For the most part, children recover completely from a single, mild, uncomplicated traumatic brain injury (TBI) such as a sports-related concussion (Anderson, Godfrey, Rosenfeld, & Catroppa, 2012). Mild TBI is thought of as being primarily a "software" problem of chemical regulation at the synaptic level. If a child who has had such an injury is protected and allowed to recover with a gradual return to both cognitive and physical activities, the brain proves remarkably resilient and capable of returning to its premorbid state without measurable deficits. When a child is subjected to repeated concussions, or not given time to fully recover, however, the picture becomes more complicated. Particularly if the insult to the brain is rated as moderate to severe, and/or if there are associated complications such as bleeding into the brain tissues or tearing away of brain connections, the outcome can become much worse and result in longer-term disability (Babikian & Asarnow, 2009). Loss of oxygen to the brain, whether from near-drowning or electrocution, tends to produce deficits along a time grid, with more prolonged reductions in brain oxygenation associated with more significant acquired brain injury. Likewise, spinal cord injuries can result in associated cognitive impairments above and beyond the sensory and motor loss that produces varying stages of weakness and paralysis.

Finally, children can acquire brain injuries as a result of accidental poisoning or exposure to toxins within the environment. The identification of high levels of lead in the blood of children younger than 6 years of age, in Flint, MI, during the period from 2013–2016, became a public health crisis secondary to our knowledge that increased blood levels of lead are associated with lower intelligence, more frequent learning problems and even death. More broadly, the Centers for Disease Control and Prevention estimates that there are at least 4 million households in the United States in which children are being exposed to unsafe/high levels of lead (CDC, 2017, February 9). There are many other conditions that can impact the developing brain, including brain tumors and the treatment of other forms of cancer. Medical science has come a long way in identifying and treating medical disorders in children, with improved survival rates across many conditions. While most would agree that the benefits associated with such treatments outweigh the risks, the long-term consequences can nevertheless at times be substantial.

Conclusions

Professionals who work with neurodevelopmental disorders have a responsibility to be aware of what seems to be an overwhelming body of scientific knowledge. New clinicians find it hard enough to learn to give a standardized test of some ability in accordance with administration requirements, to score it correctly, and to understand the implications of the results. But we are not simply technicians, and we must have a broad view of how the child in front of us came to present with their concerns. We have reviewed a few of the biological influences that may have contributed to the challenges a child or adolescent who visits your office may experience. Most of our patients will likely not have a significant history of the topics we have touched upon; however, it is important to have asked the questions and gathered the background history.

This book is not designed to provide a comprehensive review of all of the possible genetic, prenatal, perinatal, and postnatal events that can contribute to the developmental difficulties children can acquire. There are multiple reference books on the topic, and specialists in major cities with whom a conscientious clinician can consult. Your job, therefore, is to learn to ask good questions and not overlook background information that may be highly relevant to your understanding of the child. Life is a movie, and if you miss the opening scenes, the causation of later events may be less clear.

Bibliography

Ackerman, S. (1992). *Discovering the brain*. Washington, DC: National Academies Press.

American Association for Pediatric Ophthalmology and Strabismus (AAPOS). (2016, April). *Optic nerve hypoplasia*. Retrieved August 7, 2017, from www.aapos.org/terms/conditions/83

American Association for Pediatric Ophthalmology and Strabismus (AAPOS). (2017, March). *Amblyopia*. Retrieved August 7, 2017, from www.aapos.org/terms/conditions/21

American College of Obstetrics and Gynecologists (ACOG). (2016). Periviable birth. *American Journal of Obstetrics and Gynecology, 127*, 157–169.

American Congress of Obstetricians and Gynecologists (ACOG). (2015, October). The Apgar score [Committee Opinion No. 644]. *Obstetrics & Gynecology, 126*, e52–55.

American Pregnancy Association (APA). (2017). *Group B strep infection: GBS*. Retrieved August 7, 2017, from http://americanpregnancy.org/pregnancy-complications/group-b-strep-infection/

Anderson, V., Godfrey, C., Rosenfeld, J. V., & Catroppa, C. (2012). 10 years outcome from childhood traumatic brain injury. *International Journal of Developmental Neuroscience, 30*, 217–224.

Babikian, T., & Asarnow, R. (2009). Neurocognitive outcomes and recovery after pediatric TBI: Meta-analytic review of the literature. *Neuropsychology, 3*, 283–296.

Centers for Disease Control and Prevention (CDCP). (2016, May 23). *Types of infection.* Retrieved August 7, 2017, from www.cdc.gov/groupbstrep/about/infection.html

Centers for Disease Control and Prevention (CDCP). (2017, February 9). *Lead.* Retrieved August 7, 2017, from www.cdc.gov/nceh/lead/

Centers for Disease Control and Prevention (CDCP). (2017, August 2). *Facts about anencephaly.* Retrieved August 7, 2017, from www.cdc.gov/ncbddd/birthdefects/anencephaly.html

Computational Radiology Laboratory Research (CRLR). (2015). *Petascale analysis of electron microscopy images of the nervous system.* Retrieved August 7, 2017, from http://crl.med.harvard.edu/research/neural_ultrastructure/index.php

DeBoer, T., Wewerka, S., Bauer, P., Georgieff, M. K., & Nelson, C. A. (2005). Explicit memory performance in infants of diabetic mothers at 1 year of age. *Developmental Medicine & Child Neurology, 47*, 525–531.

Diamond, A. (2013). Executive functions. *Annual Review of Psychology, 64*, 135–168.

Diamond, A., Prevor, M. B., Callender, G., & Druin, D. P. (1997). Prefrontal cortex cognitive deficits in children treated early and continuously for PKU. *Monographs of the Society for Research in Child Development, 626*, 1–206.

Dodzik, P. A. (2011). *The handbook of pediatric neuropsychology: Pediatric neuropsychology and sleep disorders* (pp. 901–920). New York: Springer Publishing Company.

The Embryo Project Encyclopedia. (2014, January 22). *Teratogens.* Retrieved August 7, 2017, from http://embryo.asu.edu/handle/10776/7510

Fatemi, A., Wilson, M. A., & Johnston, M. V. (2009). Hypoxic ischemic encephalopathy in the term infant. *Clinical Perinatology, 36*, 835–858.

Fisher, J., Cabral de Mello, M., Patel, V., Rahman, A., Tran, T., Holton, S., & Homes, W. (2012). Prevalence and determinants of common perinatal mental disorders in women in low- and lower-middle-income countries: A systematic review. *Bulletin of the World Health Organization, 90*, 139–149.

Freudenrich, C., & Boyd, R. (2001, June 6). How your brain works: higher brains. *HowStuffWorks.* Retrieved August 7, 2017, from http://science.howstuffworks.com/life/inside-the-mind/human-brain/brain7.htm

Kinsella, M. T., & Monk, C. T. (2009). Impact of maternal stress, depression & anxiety on fetal neurobehavioral development. *Clinical Obstetrics and Gynecology, 52*, 425–440.

March of Dimes. (2010, August 26). *A history of the March of Dimes.* Retrieved August 7, 2017, from www.marchofdimes.org/mission/a-history-of-the-march-of-dimes.aspx?utm_campaign=semevergreen2017&gclid=EAIaIQobChMIuLgtNnF1QIVlJd-Ch3kEAoOEAAYASACEgIjWPD_BwE

Medicaid.gov. (n.d.). *Early and periodic screening, diagnostic, and treatment.* Retrieved August 7, 2017, from www.medicaid.gov/medicaid/benefits/epsdt/index.html

Mendelian Inheritance. (n.d.). In *Wikipedia.* Retrieved August 7, 2017, from https://en.wikipedia.org/wiki/Mendelian_inheritance#Law_of_Segregation

National Human Genome Research Institute (NHGRI). (2015, October 1). *All about the human genome project.* Retrieved August 7, 2017, from www.genome.gov/10001772/all-about-the—human-genome-project-hgp/

National Institute on Deafness and Other Communication Disorders (NIDCD). (2017, May 12). *Ear infections in children.* Retrieved August 7, 2017, from www.nidcd.nih.gov/health/ear-infections-children

National Institute of Mental Health (NIMH). (2017). *RDoC snapshot: Version 3.* Retrieved August 7, 2017, from www.nimh.nih.gov/research-priorities/rdoc/constructs/rdoc-snapshot-version-3-saved-5-18-2017.shtml

National Institute of Neurological Disorders and Stroke (NINDS). (2017a). *Epilepsy information page.* Retrieved August 7, 2017, from www.ninds.nih.gov/Disorders/All-Disorders/Epilepsy-Information-Page

National Institute of Neurological Disorders and Stroke (NINDS). (2017b). *Lissencephaly information page.* Retrieved August 7, 2017, from www.ninds.nih.gov/disorders/all-disorders/lissencephaly-information-page

Nobelprize.org. (2003, October 30). *The split-brain experiments.* Retrieved August 7, 2017, from www.nobelprize.org/educational/medicine/split-brain/background.html

Romeo, D. M., DiStefano, A., Conversano, M., Ricci, D., Mazzone, D., Romeo, M. G., & Mercuri, E. (2010). Neurodevelopmental outcome at 12 and 18 months in late preterm infants. *European Journal of Paediatric Neurology, 14*, 503–507.

Taylor, H. G., & Clark, C. A. C. (2016). Executive function in children born premature: Risk factors and implications for outcome. In *Seminars in perinatology* (Vol. 40, No. 8, pp. 520–529).

United States Department of Agriculture (USDA). (2017). *Women, infants and children (WIC).* Retrieved August 7, 2017, from www.fns.usda.gov/wic/women-infants-and-children-wic

World Health Organization (WHO). (2016). *Zika Virus.* Retrieved October 18, 2017, from www.who.int/mediacentre/factsheets/zika/en/

World Health Organization (WHO). (2017). *HIV/AIDS.* Retrieved October 18, 2017, from www.who.int/mediacentre/factsheets/fs360/en/

2   Familial and Social Dimensions

Children are not born into a vacuum. Just as a seedling depends upon the nutrients of its soil, the amount of sunlight and water it receives, and the degree to which a gardener attends to or neglects its care, the outcome of a child's development is in many ways impacted by the environment into which the child is born. Plants grown in a controlled temperature and humidity greenhouse inevitably thrive more so than the seed that sprouts in a crack in a sidewalk. Plants that are pruned and shaped often grow stronger than plants that are subjected to harsh treatment by other organisms within the environment. This chapter therefore addresses some of the variables that are in the child's world, within which development must occur.

Family Environment and Characteristics

The stereotypical family in the United States has been portrayed in television and movies as involving two married parents and their biological offspring, plus or minus extended family members such as a grandparent. Indeed, among many cultures of the world, this form of family structure was historically ensured by arranged marriages, carefully planned by parents for the purposes of maintenance of social class or business relationships. Social scientists, moreover, have long suggested that a child being raised in a two-biological married parent household would be better off than a child reared in an alternative arrangement.

The reality of this family structure as typical of the world into which children are born is, however, changing. According to the 2016 U.S. Census Bureau (United States Census Bureau. 2016, November 17), although the majority of children lived with two parents, the percentage of children living in families with two parents had decreased from 88% to 69%, during the period between 1960 and 2016. In the same period, the percentage of children living with their mother only nearly tripled, from 8% to 23%, and the percentage of children living with their father only increased from 1% to 4%. It is also the case that 4% of children don't live with either biological parent, and variations on the theme of family structure are becoming increasingly diverse. Some children live with same-sexed parents, some live with grandparents, and about 38% of opposite-sex unmarried couples have a child under the age of 18 in their household.

The nature of child rearing is also changing. Many families have two parents who work, with children receiving many different forms of childcare and before- and after-school programming. The busy parent who picks their child up after work, rushes home to prepare dinner and do laundry, often doesn't have the energy and time to spend with their developing child in the kinds of activities that we presume have a positive impact upon development—such as playing with or reading to the child.

This chapter focuses upon the questions you might ask about the environment into which a child wakes up every morning and spends their day. While some clinicians find it "easier" to think only about a specific child's information processing strengths and weaknesses, this is similar to watching only one character in a movie. You may be accurate in your observations, but you may also miss the context.

The Hangover of Old Models

Many of the tools we use for evaluating or assessing a child's abilities are developed and standardized on fairly narrow populations of individuals. One of the best examples of this is the Denver Developmental Screening Test (DDST) (Frankenburg & Dodds, 1967), which for decades was perhaps the most commonly used method of determining if an infant or young child was reaching developmental milestones at appropriate ages. Quick and relatively easy to score, the clinician would observe whether an infant was able to support their weight on both arms, roll over, etc., and could estimate the developmental age level demonstrated by the infant. Expectations for what was "normal" based on this measure became common knowledge among clinicians, and the determination that an infant was delayed often led to a referral for early intervention services.

An interesting finding regarding the use of the DDST, however, was the recognition that infants who were not representative of the cultural composition of Denver at the time of the test's development didn't always fit the norms. Children growing up in China, for example, were considered to lag behind in gross motor development during the first year of their life, as measured by the DDST but then found to subsequently "catch up" to their international peers after infancy. Observation of infants within the occidental culture and under the influence of a cosmopolitan city (Hong Kong), however, found them to be different from infants raised in more rural North Chinese regions (Fung & Lau, 1985). These differences were thought to be attributable to the parenting practices of heavily wrapping infants and placing them in a supine position by parents in more rural settings (with obvious impact upon motor skill development) as compared with less protective parenting of infants growing up in a city. Analogies can be drawn to the performance of other children whose cultural background differs from that of a test's normative background, for example, when a Canadian college student attending school in the United States is asked questions on the Wechsler Adult Intelligence Scale, Fourth Edition (WAIS-IV), which requires knowledge of American history and government. Such individuals would likely obtain a lower score than if they were administered a Canadian version of the WAIS-IV (Wechsler, 2008).

It is also important to think about the economic diversity of the families of children who present for evaluation. A child from an advantaged family within a wealthy suburb of a major metropolitan area likely has a different body of experience from a similarly aged child who grew up without electricity and running water, miles from the nearest town. Note that these differences in experience do not necessarily imply a better or worse outcome, as demonstrated in the story of Sandra Day O'Connor, the first woman appointed to the U.S. Supreme Court. Justice O'Connor grew up on a farm on the high desert plateau of the New Mexico-Arizona border, where her only adult contact was with her parents and the cowboys who worked the ranch (O'Connor & Day, 2002). It was 35 miles from her home to the closest town, a trip that was made only once per week to get groceries. Ultimately, O'Connor was sent to El Paso to live with her grandparents, where she attended a private girls' school and ended up attending Stanford University, becoming a role model for many. Differences in backgrounds are therefore important to recognize but may or may not have an impact.

As a general rule, it is always important to learn about the environment from which the child you evaluate has traveled to meet with you. According to the U.S. Census Bureau, the median estimated poverty rate for school-aged children was 16.5% of children enrolled in one of the 13,245 U.S. school districts in 2016 (United States Census Bureau, 2016, December 14). Many children go to bed and wake up hungry, and their performance in school (and in your office) can be greatly influenced by whether they have had breakfast on a given day. The author has found that having inexpensive but nutritious snacks available for the children who come for evaluations not only is a great way to establish rapport, but possibly helps children to put forth better effort and more accurately show their abilities.

Limited financial resources also impact the learning environment of the child. Children from areas of lower socioeconomic status often attend schools with fewer resources taught by teachers who may themselves not be able to provide the materials necessary for effective teaching. Well-meaning but resource-strapped parents may place their young children in front of a television rather than having books to read to the child or the energy to do so. Contrast this with the affluent family with a stay at home parent who volunteers in the child's well-equipped and increasingly electronics-based classroom. Children who grow up attending expensive preschools and aftercare programs understandably have an advantage over those who aren't provided this privilege.

Thankfully, governments often provide a bridge for the gap between the haves and the have-nots. The United States Office of Head Start, for example, promotes the school-readiness of low-income children from birth to age 5, through programs and agencies in the child's local community. Head Start began as a part of Lyndon B. Johnson's 1965 War on Poverty and has served well over 30 million children across all the United States as well as the District of Columbia, Puerto Rico, and the U.S. territories (U.S. Department of Health & Human Services, 2017, June 15). Professionals can refer children from 6 weeks to 3 years of age to a local Early Head Start program, or children 3 years and older to a Head Start program. The key is that early intervention for children who are at risk for developmental disorders can often help to minimize the impact of causative variables that, left unaddressed, can result in a lifetime of difficulty. Such interventions must continue, however, to prevent "back sliding" once they end.

Variations on Family Systems

Interaction with a non-traditional family can raise multiple issues for the professional, ranging from legal considerations involving who has the authority to consent to your involvement with a child, to personal reactions on the part of the clinician or belief systems that may influence your activity. We are increasingly a multicultural world that presents challenges for some in being able to understand and feel comfortable with the diversity of beliefs, religions, sexual orientations, skin color, and political persuasions of our clientele. None of us is immune to our own personal reactions to such variables, and we need to take responsibility for avoiding assumptions based upon prejudice. While the concept of "microaggression" is currently a matter of debate (Lilienfeld, 2017), we must remain vigilant to the possibility of our presumptions influencing our work. Despite our protestations otherwise, we are not immune to the teachings and influence of those with whom we have grown up, and subtle, possibly subconscious attitudes may influence our thinking processes as we perform our evaluations.

Take, for example, a pink-haired caregiver who is unemployed but lives with her professional partner of several years, who brings the partner's 9-year-old biological son to your office for an assessment of social challenges at school. The boy is of small stature, has hair that reaches the middle of his back, and is wearing a sequined jean jacket. He hangs behind the caregiver in a shy manner, declining to speak with you and unwilling to separate from his protective caregiver. Alternatively, consider the oppositional teenage daughter of a heavily tattooed, 300-pound man who has brought his daughter to your office on the back of his motorcycle, telling you that his daughter has been mandated to get counseling because of her "attitude." Finally, consider the plight of an undocumented woman from Mexico who, in a mixture of English and Spanish, tells you that her 6-year-old son is struggling to learn to read. Particularly when clinicians work in public health settings or with individuals who have significant differences from ourselves, it becomes essential for us to perform a "civility check" to make sure that our own biases and filters don't lead us to draw unjustified conclusions.

It is natural to make implicit assumptions about possible contributors to a child's presenting problems, even though these assumptions may have nothing to do with the child's difficulties. For example, in your intake interview, you learn that a Hispanic boy who can't read was born in the United States, lives in a middle-class neighborhood, has only ever spoken English, and excels in mathematics and science. You nevertheless find out that his school has placed him in an English Language Learner classroom, where there has been no specific instruction in phonological awareness or early reading skills. You also learn that the boy's father is a highly skilled welder who, himself, never became a fluent reader but is being considered for foreman at his company.

Clinicians must also consider issues of guardianship and consent when performing evaluations and treatment with children and adolescents. In most Western cultures, some 90% of people become married by the age of 50; however, about half of these marriages end in divorce, with the rate of subsequent divorce being even higher (American Psychological Association, 2017). When a minor presents to your office with a request for services, from whom do you need consent and with whom do you communicate? Depending upon the laws governing your jurisdiction, the legal guardian of a child may be any of several individuals, or a combination of individuals. It is generally important to obtain the informed consent of the legal guardian(s) before you provide any services, but challenges can arise when individuals with joint legal guardianship disagree over whether to provide such consent to you, or not. What about when the grandparent or aunt/uncle of a child brings them to your office and tells you that the child's mother "knows" about the appointment but has to work today. We must also try to obtain the assent of the children to be evaluated or treated themselves. What do you do if the child/adolescent pointedly says to you, "I don't want to be here and there is nothing wrong with me."

We must also stop to consider if the presenting problem resides within the child. For the most part, children referred to your office are likely to have some form of cognitive, social, learning, or medical problem that you are asked to figure out and treat. Sometimes, however, the "identified patient's" troubles reflect a broader family system issue, a characteristic of the parent, or events that change parental perceptions of the child and influence their upbringing. This possibility was identified in the mid-1960s by Morris Green and Albert Solnit of the Departments of Pediatrics at Indiana University and the Yale School of Medicine (Green & Solnit, 1964). In an article entitled "Reactions to the Threatened Loss of a Child: A Vulnerable Child Syndrome," twenty-five children with a history of an illness or accident that was expected to result in their death, actually recovered. Follow-up study of these children revealed that the children often had difficulties with separation, infantile behaviors, bodily over-concerns, and school underachievement, none of which were related to the medical condition they experienced. This concept was further refined to include recognition that the central concept of the vulnerable child syndrome, an increased parental perception of child vulnerability to illness or injury, led to strong influences upon the child, parent, parent-child relationship, parent-clinician relationship, and family functioning (Thomasgard & Metz, 1995). Indeed, the work of Richard Q. Bell clarified that the traditional views holding that parents influence children's socialization were too limited to accommodate data from the studies of human and animal development (Bell, 1968). Alternatively, congenital factors in children were shown to also influence parents, such that research documenting a correlation between parent and child behavior must be considered bidirectional—i.e. children are just as likely to influence parental behavior as vice versa. As all parents quickly discover, children can "train" their parents to act in certain ways, and the relationship between a parent and one child is often different than the relationship between that same parent and another of their children.

Professionals can also influence how parents feel and act, with consequent impact upon the developing child. One example of this phenomenon is found in the growing attention being paid to the impact of sports-related concussions upon children's learning and behavior. The popular press accounts of acquired, devastating cognitive impairment, depression, and even suicide among high-profile football players has led many parents to restrict their children's access to sports that have a potential for head injuries. Many parents seem to take the position that it is "just not worth the risk" to allow children to play contact sports. What the press doesn't report, however, is that the preponderance of evidence in the study of uncomplicated, mild traumatic brain injuries in children indicates that full recovery without persisting symptoms occurs in the vast majority of children (McCrea, 2008). Likewise, concerns about the unlikely negative consequences of immunizations in young children has led an alarming number of parents to decline to protect their children against the devastating effects of what are otherwise preventable illnesses. Living in fear of unlikely possible events does not promote confidence and resilience in children.

The term "helicopter parent" has emerged to describe caregivers who attempt to control and prevent potential dangers in their child's life. The term has been used by many individuals but may have first been reported by Haim Ginott in his book *Between Parent & Teenager* in which a teen complained that his mother "hovers over me like a helicopter" (Ginott, 1969). Teachers and school administrators use this term to describe caregivers who advocate for their children in a manner that they find becomes intrusive and annoying. I have found many such anxious parents to nevertheless become amused when I reassure them that, in order to protect their child from danger, it may be possible for them to eventually move into their child's college dorm room with them. Part of a clinician's job is to sensitively tease apart actual versus perceived impairment in children, whose worried parents bring them for a "comprehensive evaluation." It can be reassuring to such parents if we find that aside from normal strengths and weaknesses, the child does not have a significant problem, and children often smile at such news and tell their parents, "I told you so!" I remember one intelligent youngster who entered my office at the beginning of an evaluation, looked me in the eye as he shook my hand and stated with a smile, "You know, I may *not* have autism!"

Caregivers are, for the most part, appropriately focused upon the protection and nurturance of their child. Most of us devote untold hours of our lives in caring for our children, encouraging their growth and independence, and denying our own selfish wants to grow a child who can turn out better than we did. For some parents, however, this is not an easy task. The tasks of parenting are much more difficult if the parent has their own cognitive or developmental impairment. Nature has programmed parent-infant bonding and attachment to the extent that even intellectually and developmentally disabled parents can meet the needs of newborns and infants, fairly well. Indeed, The Arc for people with intellectual and developmental disabilities asserts that, contrary to what many people think, individuals with intellectual disabilities can be good parents (The Arc, 2011). Multiple factors deserve consideration in determining whether individuals with intellectual disabilities can successfully parent, including their ability levels, support systems, motivation, and response to training and education. It is also the case that, at all levels of cognitive abilities, sometimes children are "smarter" than their parents, particularly if the child is of advanced intellectual competence. It is common to hear parents bemoan the fact that they can't help their child with their homework because they don't understand it themselves. Advances in education have resulted in some high school students taking classes that their parents may have never taken, or only when they were in graduate school (e.g. matrix algebra). It is always important to inquire about how far in school each parent went and whether they, themselves, also had some form of neurodevelopmental difficulties. This can lead to good-natured teasing of one parent by the other that "See, it's all your fault!" to which the clinician can remind the parents that we genetically pass on both our strengths as well as our limitations and that almost everybody has some area in which they struggle.

Some parents have more significant challenges, however, which often need to be addressed as a part of our contact with the child or adolescent. Keeping in mind that the family is the patient, clinicians need to be sensitive to indications that the caregiver of a referred child may themselves have either an acute or more chronic psychiatric disorder. Depressed parents have a significantly negative impact upon their children. The Center on the Developing Child at Harvard University has extensively documented that maternal depression can interfere with the development of young children and that children who must cope with maternal depression in early life may demonstrate lasting effects on their brain architecture and function that persist into adolescence and can disrupt the normal stress response system (Center on the Developing Child at Harvard University, 2009). Other parents may have different psychiatric illnesses that make them unavailable to their children and create uneasy home environments, which lead children into adult roles far too early in their lives. The child who worries about a parent's substance abuse has less cognitive energy to devote to school and peer relationships, and some children must care for younger siblings after school, taking away from their own opportunities to play and remain innocent in their view of the world. It doesn't seem right, but some caretakers place their own needs ahead of those of their children, at all levels of socioeconomic status. Some advantaged children are "sent away" in the guise of a "tremendous opportunity" to attend a school or program far from home but suffer the loneliness and homesickness that results.

Family Stages and Cycles

Even among children who live at home with both biological parents, family systems theory has identified multiple cycles or patterns of family interaction that can result from or exacerbate neurodevelopmental disorders. To consider these variables, we must first recognize that, just as children go through developmental stages, there are also stages in the life of a family. The developmental tasks of each stage are different, and a comprehensive model of family life cycle phases includes the concepts that emerging young adults differentiate themselves from their family of origin and emancipate into self-sufficiency and independence. Forming a couple relationship with another requires a commitment to a new and expanded family system. The birth of the first child causes the family to accept new members into the system and initiates the "families with young children" stage, which gradually moves into the families with adolescents phase, during which increasing flexibility of family boundaries permits the independence of young adults. The launching pad phase requires the acceptance of possibly multiple exits from and entries into the family system, followed by the necessity of accepting shifting generational roles as families reach the late middle ages. Finally, as families have members that near the end of life, demands are made to accept the realities of family members' limitations and death. The most recent edition of Carter, Garcia-Preto, and McGoldrick's classic textbook, *The Expanding Family Life Cycle* (2016), also addresses the societal changes that influence the life cycle, associated with shifting patterns of household composition, work demands, non-traditional relationships, etc. Becoming cognizant of all the potential influences upon the family system in which the child you are evaluating resides can indeed become quite complex!

So how does a family cope with the identification of one of their children having a need for more intensive attention and services than expected, or more so than the needs of the child's siblings? While it is often asserted that parents love their children equally, differences in the relationships of parents and children and children with their siblings naturally occur in all families. The child born with a chronic illness or emerging disability requires more attention, and subtle shifting in the nature of the family's relationships can gradually occur. Take, for example, the premature child who requires frequent respiratory treatments and medications and must be repeatedly be driven to various doctors and therapies. In some families, the burden of such care is shared between the adult caregivers, who provide ongoing support to each other to lighten the load. In other families, however, one caregiver becomes primary and attends to all of the child's needs, while the other caregiver spends more hours at work so as to generate the money to pay for everything. One parent's career or continuing education must be put on hold, while the other parent may become emotionally distant and disengaged. A "psychological divorce" may develop even though it is not discussed or possibly even recognized. In turn, the at-home caregiver's relationship with the affected child can become symbiotic—each providing for the other's emotional needs during times of distress and loneliness. If a child's developmental difficulties or weak immune system causes that child to become socially isolated, who does the child turn to for friendship?

There have been many models of family functioning, one of the most studied of which is David Olson's Circumplex Model of Marital and Family Systems (Olson, Sprenkle, & Russell, 1979). This model proposes three key concepts to consider when trying to understand family functioning: cohesion, flexibility, and communication. A self-report assessment scale, the Family Adaptability and Cohesion Evaluation Scale (FACES), has been used in conjunction with this model in over 1,200 published articles and dissertations and has resulted in an agreement that healthy families tend to be more balanced, while unhealthy families tend to be more unbalanced across these three primary concepts. Healthy families are neither enmeshed nor disengaged in their interactions, rigid nor chaotic in their problem solving, and tend to have positive communication skills that allow the family system to flexibly alter their levels of cohesion and flexibility in response to life's stressors (Olson, 2011). Clearly, the identification of a neurodevelopmental disorder in a child represents a source of potentially significant distress, and how the family adjusts their system to meet the demands of raising that child can often influence/determine the quality of the child's ultimate outcome. A flexible, connected family that has open and constructive communication will fare better than a more chaotic and disengaged, or rigid and enmeshed, system or one that operates under the principle of "We don't talk about it."

Siblings also are impacted by a child's developmental difficulties. If one's brother or sister struggles with a medical, learning, or social disorder, there can often be a combination of guilt and relief on the part of the unaffected sibling that they don't have the same problem. Many healthcare professionals will privately tell you that one of the reasons they went into their field is because of a desire to help others, born of their childhood observations of their sibling's struggles. There is a concept of being an "insider" versus an "outsider" that those who have never themselves been ill or hurt or embarrassed by academic failure have a harder time placing themselves in the shoes of their patients, despite the best of intentions. I also worry about the siblings of some of the children who come to see you, who are perfectly behaved, straight A students but worry excessively about their parents' and siblings' wellbeing, often putting their own needs aside. Other siblings resent what they perceive as excessive levels of attention heaped upon their siblings and can become challenging, secondary to oppositional and defiant behavior as an expression of their understandable distress. Asking siblings to describe the interactions within their family's non-public lives can be illuminating.

Extended family members can also have a powerful effect on whether or how a child might be evaluated and/or treated for developmental difficulties. Some members of older generations may minimize the impact of the child's difficulties and chasten anxious parents as they discuss spending their limited resources to help their children. Claims that "he's all boy" and "you grew out of that" may cause parents to put off an evaluation or decide that "it's not really that bad." Infrequently, some grandparents give the message that it is the parent's fault that the child has their troubles, or the fault of the other parent, noting, "We never had anything like that in our family." It can be heartbreaking to learn that your own parents don't support you, or minimize your worries about your child, and some parents go to great lengths to keep news that their child has been given a diagnosis or is entering treatment private from not only grandparents but aunts and uncles, too, as if it is a badge of shame that one's child has a developmental disorder. Naturally, this can extend to the social circle of the parents and the siblings. Brothers and sisters may be embarrassed by the affected child's challenges, especially if they are visible or apparent to others. Casual strangers may offer unsolicited advice or ask intrusive questions, as if they have the right to violate one's privacy—even in the grocery store.

Of course, the above scenarios aren't the only reactions of family members, and many times, extended family members serve as a source of great compassion, support, and help to both parent and child. Grandparents often help with the financial burden of getting services for a child, transport children to appointments and therapies, provide respite for exhausted parents by having the child spend the night or weekend, and even become the primary caregiver when things go too wrong for the biological parent. It is an expression of love when a grandparent, who has already raised their own children, volunteers to once again take on the stress of parenting another generation. Aunts and uncles also get involved, provide support, and help to ease the burden of the parent and child. Weekend trips to see the cousins represent a safe haven where parents can feel assured that their child will be well cared for and loved.

Multiple factors are bantered about as causative of the current divorce rates, including marriages at a young age, lower income and education, extramarital affairs, etc. It is also the case that raising children is hard under the best of circumstances and that having a child with some form of developmental disorder adds to that difficulty. Some parents react to the news that their child is "different" by blaming their partner, blaming themselves, or leaving the marriage for a multitude of other reasons. Divorce is a parent issue, not a child's doing; however, the children in divorce are often negatively affected by their confusion, emotional reactions, and sometimes a sense of guilt that their parents split because of something they did or their developmental problems. The education of children as to what divorce is all about and their role in the family change is hard enough without the additional complication that the child may have difficulties with emotional regulation, understanding abstract concepts, or being able to use sufficient "theory of mind" to put themselves in their parents' shoes. Siblings may blame the identified child as the cause of the separation and harbor resentment toward the parent who remains behind.

Having two homes to live in causes additional challenges. There are the usual hassles of what clothes are kept in which home, who is going to take children to school or practice, and how well the parents are able to resolve their differences so as to maintain a parenting partnership free from putting the children in the middle of ongoing conflict. If a child has ongoing medical or developmental needs, however, how well can the estranged parents agree on what services are provided, who is going to pay, and who will take the child to the doctors or therapists they need? Issues around the management of the child's needs can become the focus of continuing conflict between the parents, demonstrated through such behaviors as one parent refusing to give the child medication when at their home, another parent refusing to allow the child to receive special education services, or refusal to provide the financial support necessary for the child to receive optimal care. Caregivers of younger children worry that the other caregiver may not pay close enough attention, will supervise appropriately, will help the child finish their homework, or will be sure to get the child to bed on time.

Unfortunately, it is a sobering fact that many children experience adverse events in their early lives. Felitti and colleagues (1998) sent a questionnaire to 13,495 adults who had undergone a standardized medical evaluation, 9,508 of whom responded. The questionnaire asked if, as a child, the adults had experienced psychological, physical, or sexual abuse; violence against their mother; or lived with household members who were substance abusers, mentally ill or suicidal, or had ever been imprisoned. More than half of respondents reported at least one of these adverse events, and one-fourth reported more than two adverse events. Persons who had experienced four or more of the categories of childhood exposure had a four- to twelve-fold increase in multiple health risk factors later in life. It is easy to extrapolate to a conclusion that such adverse experiences would also have a negative impact upon a child's development, learning, and socialization.

Peer Influences

Nature provides several models of the degrees of social group engagement that are possible. Solitary vertebrates include many of the wild cats (tigers, leopards, etc.), bears, moose, and rhinoceroses, while group animals include penguins, lions, schools of fish, etc. In part, this distinction is based upon survival needs, such as the availability of food within a solitary animal's territory; however, social needs are important for others who depend upon safety in numbers, shared caregiving, and the social learning of such activities as parenting and group hunting techniques. Humans seem to cross these categories in that some people are fiercely independent and isolative, while many are group oriented and actively seek out affiliation and group membership. Children depend upon their caregivers for protection and survival during the early years, but some children grow up with only one or even no friends, while others "run with the pack" and define their identity based upon their group membership. Having a neurodevelopmental difference seems in many ways to be independent of this choice, possibly with the exception of developmental social disorders such as autism, but for most children with disabilities, social relationships are a critical contributor to how well one copes. Self-esteem is developed, at least in part, by one's acceptance by others and our focus upon what is right about us rather than what make us different. Even children with fairly severe disabilities make the most of life when they have someone their age with whom to compare notes, share secrets, and learn about life.

Children with chronic illnesses are often the most isolated secondary to illness-related factors. Youth with cystic fibrosis, for example, are typically advised to avoid group meetings with others who have CF out of a concern for the possibility of spreading certain potentially dangerous infectious illnesses. Children with complex medical needs may miss out on sleep-overs and camping trips because of parental concerns that their blood sugar may need to be checked to determine insulin dosing or that a child with epilepsy may have a seizure in the middle of the night. While efforts are made to have supervised group experiences for some of these children, such as having a diabetes camp that is staffed by volunteer physicians and nurses, the importance of providing an opportunity to be "normal" cannot be overstated, and parents need occasional respite and reassurance that their child will be ok if they are not there to look after them. Medications can be pre-packaged, and coaches and counselors can be given advanced knowledge and training of what to do in various circumstances. The alternative scenarios are not always ideal, as exemplified in *The Glass Menagerie* by Tennessee Williams, a five-act play about a fragile girl, Laura, who has developed disabling anxiety and shyness secondary to her having a polio-related limp and an overprotective mother (Williams, 1945).

Developmental disorders, at least on some level, impact the child's skills and facility in developing close friendships and peer relationships. Children with visible or noticeable conditions, such as a stutter, are often teased and even bullied, and those who lack emotional self-regulation react to sometimes innocent fun by becoming explosively angry or upset. It is not uncommon for parents to sadly tell you that their child has never been invited to a birthday party or that, although she is welcome in group events, no other girl responds to her invitation for a play date or sleep-over. Children with developmental difficulties need to be taught assertiveness skills and educated about the social dance of relationships. Peer activities need to focus around the child's strengths rather than increasing their sense of isolation secondary to tapping into their weaknesses. Not all children are athletic, and it is painful for a boy who cannot run fast to be engaged in a race to the other side of the soccer field.

Youth sports are inclusive and provide participation trophies at the youngest ages; however, competition soon leads to the in-group and the out-group and a need for the identification of another type of activity in which to succeed and build self-esteem. Clinicians should always champion what is right about our patients and encourage involvement in some activity that results in success and praise from others.

School Influences

Once a child leaves the toddler years, it is common to leave the protective "nest" of the family and enter a world in which there are many other children and unfamiliar adults who are called teachers. This transition is often the first venture into the big new world and, depending upon one's prior experiences with individuation and independence, can be either exhilarating or frightening. Suddenly the child is not the center of the universe, and his/her needs must fit into an environment in which others' needs may be placed above one's own. A premium is therefore placed upon the developing executive functions of emotional regulation, activity control, attention and persistence, problem solving, and the theory of mind-dependent initiation of social reciprocity and communication. Initial requirements of bowel and bladder control are combined with reduced needs for naps during the day and the expectation that the child will learn rule-governed behavior.

The development of these "executive functions" may well be tied to the development of motor skills. As mentioned earlier, Adele Diamond, currently at the University of British Columbia, has studied the development of the prefrontal cortex of the brain and its relationship to the development of self-control for several decades (Developmental Cognitive Neuroscience Lab of Adele Diamond, n.d.). Her laboratory has shown that the play of young children is intimately tied to the development of cognition and the regulatory processes that help guide development. Diamond has shown that organized motor activities, such as involving young children in Tae Kwon Do or the "intentional make-believe play" strategies of the Tools of the Mind curriculum (Tools of the Mind, 2017) help preschool children develop the self-regulatory, cognitive, and social-emotional skills that are needed in life and can help set the course for future learning. Pre-school experiences are therefore much more than simply playtime: they help young children to emerge from the relative isolation of the home and stick their toes into the pool of life before them!

Entering school for the first time is usually accompanied by some degree of anxiety secondary to the lack of familiarity with the new environment, separation from parents and the comforting routine of the home, and the requirement of growing levels of some kind of "performance." Inborn temperament interacts with cognitive and other developmental competencies to result in a child who is either confident and excited to learn, or apprehensive and fearful of failure. For some children, going to school represents the very first time of being on their own and comparing oneself to other children. Conflict between approach and avoidance can stimulate some children while paralyzing others. Those who have some form of developmental disorder soon "stick out" and begin to be referred to what for some is their initial evaluation process.

Differing school environments quickly reveal themselves to be either more focused upon the emotional comfort and nurturance of the child versus a focus upon the development of academic competence. Some teachers emphasize the growth of confidence and security while others are more task-oriented and want to achieve class-wide goals of achievement. This is often a conflict for parents, as well, who may surprise the clinician by talking about their goal for their child to attend a prestigious university, even in the early elementary school years. There are many pressures upon the child, the teacher, and the parents.

In large part, these pressures derive from the evolution of the Elementary and Secondary Education Act (ESSA), which was signed into law by President Lyndon B. Johnson in 1965. President Johnson emphasized that full educational opportunities were a basic civil right, and the Act provided grants emphasizing opportunities for low-income students as well as those with disabilities (U.S. Department of Education, 2017). In 2002, the No Child Left Behind Act (NCLB) replaced ESSA and emphasized regular assessment of schools and the children who were not making adequate progress, resulting in "high-stakes testing" that proved untenable for many. Suddenly parents began to report that their schools and teachers seemed more concerned about achieving high marks as a school, rather than emphasizing the development of individual children. Schools seemed to become more focused upon teaching children how to pass the high-stakes testing and began eliminating the "fun" activities of extracurricular activities, elective coursework in art and music, and even the time period of the day most prized by students themselves— recess. NCLB next morphed into a new definition of ESSA—the Every Student Succeeds Act (U.S. Department of Education, n.d.), which was signed by President Obama on December 10, 2015. How this version of guidance for public education will work out remains to be seen; however, many parents have begun a shift to alternative methods of educating their children, including alternative school choices such as public charter and private schools, as well as online educational programming.

For the child with a developmental disorder or disability, another federal law comes into play—the 1975 Education for All Handicapped Children Act, which was subsequently named the Individuals with Disabilities Education Act (IDEA) (U.S. Department of Education, 2017). The provisions of this law ensure services to children with disabilities throughout the nation and governs how states and public agencies must provide early intervention, special education, and related services to children from ages 3 to 21. The clinician who performs evaluations and treatment of children with developmental disorders needs to develop more than a passing familiarity with this law, as it will govern important decisions made about the recommendations we write in our reports. Clinicians should also become familiar with Section 504 of the Rehabilitation Act of 1973, which in part states:

> No otherwise qualified individual with a disability in the United States, as defined in section 705 (20) of this title, shall, solely by reason of his or her disability, be excluded from the participation in, be denied the benefits of, or be subjected to discrimination under any program or activity receiving Federal financial assistance.
>
> (United States Department of Labor, n.d.)

According to this law, almost any child who has been diagnosed with an eligible disability may be afforded reasonable accommodations for their disability, regardless of the student's grades or academic achievement. Indeed, in July of 2016, the U.S. Department of Education released guidance that clarifies that schools must not rely upon the generalization that a student who is getting good grades cannot also have a substantial limitation in learning and may have a disability (Lhamon, 2016). This guidance explains that school districts must perform evaluations of students who may have special needs, including those who appear to have behavioral challenges or troubles with distractibility, which may reflect an underlying disability.

Many parents may feel, nevertheless, that the public school setting is not the best for their child. Some children who are identified early on as having medical or developmental needs are viewed by parents as best served through homeschooling, where the parent can maintain close supervision and provide needed treatments or services, themselves. Concerns that such children are "overprotected" or may suffer from a lack of exposure to other children and the school environment are likely unfounded, and there are multiple outlets for homeschooling support and resources. Such programs are not just for children with special needs, however, and many homeschooling curricula are centered around religious philosophies and beliefs.

Other parents may emphasize their beliefs that most school programs are not sufficiently advanced or rigorous and opt for more academically demanding and results-oriented teaching. The Charter School movement is based upon a parent's right to seek an excellent education for their children regardless of where they live or their socioeconomic status. Such schools are subsidized by government funding and are present in countries across the globe, including Canada, Colombia, Europe, and Australia. Private schools and online schooling round out the options available, and each may have its unique advantage for one student versus another.

Unfortunately, however, the emphasis upon academic achievement has, in some settings, resulted in an increased sense of pressure being placed on students and parents. Private programs often market their schools by publishing the percentage of their students who were admitted to prestigious colleges or cite their national rank among private schools. This level of competition can, at times, result in the students feeling substantial pressure to perform and anxiety when they feel that they can't keep up with their peers or expectations. The clinician who works with children and adolescents is aware that such pressure can lead to clinical levels of anxiety, depression, somatic distress, and family conflict. Far from needing external motivation to complete homework and study, some children need to be encouraged to accept "good enough" and to put time into their social life and recreation, rather than studying all night.

Another alarming development over the past couple of decades is the growing awareness of the potential for horrific things to happen in life. In our world of instant media, parents and children are confronted with breaking news of school shootings, child abduction, sexual abuse, and maltreatment of children by traditionally trusted authority figures. Of course, it is prudent to educate and protect students from excessive risk; however, schools have become high-fence, gated facilities with safety officers and a subtle paranoia that has shattered the carefree assumption that childhood is a time of free play, riding bikes, and innocent fun. Many children with developmental difficulties require more, not fewer, rest breaks and the opportunity to get up and run around, so as to burn off energy and refocus their attention. Many children cannot sit still for extended periods of time and long for the freedom of running out on the playground, playing tag, and making friendships. Indeed, the playground is the social laboratory of many elementary school-aged children, who learn about dominance and submission, social hierarchies, and teamwork through their interactions. Naturally, such efforts occasionally result in conflict; however, a "zero-tolerance" policy of managing such conflict often results in children being punished for behavior that traditionally has been seen as relatively benign. Children need to learn to be assertive, to stand up for themselves, and to refuse to be bullied but may not learn such vital life lessons if they are overprotected by well-meaning school personnel and don't get the opportunity to participate in "teachable moments."

Conclusions

Life does not exist in a vacuum, and it is essential to consider the context/setting from which the child or adolescent comes to see us. Many children do not live in a household with two, married, biological parents. Increasingly, we must appreciate and celebrate variations in family structure. As our world becomes multicultural, we must learn about those who are different from us and clarify that our assumptions about the background of the children we see are accurate. Learning in a two-room schoolhouse is very different from the experiences had within the inner-city mega-school. In the process of our evaluations, we must ask questions to understand the home setting, school setting, peer relationships, and social life of the children we evaluate and treat. We must think about the stage of development of not just the child, but of the family within which the child is developing. Assumptions must be discarded and replaced with respectful questions and an honest desire to learn about the day-to-day experience of our patients.

Bibliography

American Psychological Association (APA). (2017). *Marriage & divorce*. Retrieved August 7, 2017, from www.apa.org/topics/divorce/

The Arc. (2011). *Parents with intellectual disabilities*. Retrieved August 7, 2017, from www.thearc.org/what-we-do/resources/fact-sheets/parents-with-idd

Bell, R. Q. (1968). A reinterpretation of the direction of effects in studies of socialization. *Psychological Review, 75*, 81–95.

Center on the Developing Child at Harvard University (CDCHU). (2009). *Maternal depression can undermine the development of young children*. Working Paper No. 8. Retrieved August 7, 2017, from https://developingchild.harvard.edu/resources/maternal-depression-can-undermine-the-development-of-young-children/

Developmental Cognitive Neuroscience Lab of Adele Diamond (DCNLAD). (n.d.). Retrieved August 7, 2017, from www.devcogneuro.com/AdeleDiamond.html#Pubs

Felitti, V. J., Anda, R. F., Nordenberg, D., Williamson, D. F., Spitz, A. M., Edwards, V., . . . Marks, J. S. (1998). Relationship of childhood abuse and household dysfunction to many of the leading causes of death in adults. *American Journal of Preventive Medicine, 14*, 245–258.

Frankenburg, W. K., & Dodds, J. B. (1967). The Denver developmental screening test. *The Journal of Pediatrics, 71*(2), 181–191.

Fung, K. P., & Lau, S. P. (1985). Denver developmental screening test: Cultural variables. *The Journal of Pediatrics, 106*(2), 343.

Ginott, H. (1969). *Between parent & teenager* (p. 18). New York: Scribner.

Green, M., & Solnit, A. J. (1964). Reactions to the threatened loss of a child: A vulnerable child syndrome. *Pediatrics, 34*(1), 58–66.

Lhamon, C. E. (2016). *U.S. Department of Education: Dear colleague letter and resource guide on students with ADHD*. Retrieved August 7, 2017, from https://www2.ed.gov/about/offices/list/ocr/letters/colleague-201607-504-adhd.pdf

Lilienfeld, S. O. (2017). Microaggressions: Strong claims, inadequate evidence. *Perspectives on Psychological Science, 12*(1), 138–169.

McCrea, M. A. (2008). *Mild traumatic brain injury and postconcussion syndrome: The new evidence base for diagnosis and treatment*. New York: Oxford University Press.

McGoldrick, M., Garcia-Preto, N. A., & Carter, B. A. (2016). *The expanding family life cycle: Individual, family and social perspectives* (5th ed.). New York: Pearson Allyn & Bacon.

O'Connor, S. D., & Day, H. A. (2002). *Growing up on a Cattle Ranch in the American Southwest*. New York: Random House.

Olson, D. (2011). FACES IV and the circumplex model: Validation study. *Journal of Marital and Family Therapy, 37*, 64–80.

Olson, D. H., Sprenkle, D. H., & Russell, C. S. (1979). Circumplex model of marital and family systems: I. Cohesion and adaptability dimensions, family types, and clinical applications. *Family Process, 18*, 3–28.

Thomasgard, M., & Metz, W. P. (1995). The vulnerable child syndrome revisited. *Journal of Developmental & Behavioral Pediatrics, 16*(1), 47–53.

Tools of the Mind. (2017). *What is tools?* Retrieved August 7, 2017, from https://toolsofthemind.org/learn/what-is-tools/

U.S. Department of Education. (2017, June 6). *Individuals with disabilities education act.* Retrieved August 7, 2017, from https://www2.ed.gov/about/offices/list/osers/osep/osep-idea.html

U.S. Department of Education. (n.d.). *Every student succeeds act (ESSA).* Retrieved August 7, 2017, from www.ed.gov/essa?src=ft

U.S. Department of Health & Human Services. (2017, June 15). *About the office of head start.* Retrieved August 7, 2017, from www.acf.hhs.gov/ohs/about

United States Census Bureau (USCB). (2016, November 17). *The majority of children live with two parents, census bureau reports.* Retrieved August 8, 2017, from https://census.gov/newsroom/press-releases/2016/cb16-192.html?cid=cb16192

United States Census Bureau (USCB). (2016, December 14). *Census bureau releases 2015 income and poverty estimates for all counties.* Retrieved August 8, 2017, from www.census.gov/newsroom/press-releases/2016/cb16-tps153.html

United States Department of Labor. (n.d.). *Section 504, Rehabilitation Act of 1973.* Retrieved August 7, 2017, from www.dol.gov/oasam/regs/statutes/sec504.htm

Wechsler, D. (2008). *Clinical assessment Canada.* Retrieved August 7, 2017, from www.pearsonclinical.ca/en/products/product-master.html/item-89

Williams, T. (1945). *The glass menagerie.* Oxford: Heinemann Educational Publishers.

3 Conceptual Dimensions

Dealt a Different Hand

Individuals come for evaluations at different points during their lives. One of the first questions that needs to be asked is "why now?" Specifically, why is the child or adolescent being brought to your office at this point in their development, rather than previously, or not until later? Some conditions are apparent at birth, whereas others emerge more slowly, over time. Sometimes we are the first professional to see a patient; sometimes we are simply one in a long line of excellent clinicians who have all performed competent assessments. Taking a longer-term perspective is often useful in formulating the nature of the challenges presented, even if it is at the beginning of the process.

John Rolland of the Chicago Center for Family Health discussed this concept within the perspective of chronic illness, when he was medical director of the Center for Illness in Families, New Haven, CT, in 1987. Rolland proposed a psychosocial typology for understanding the interface between a chronic illness and the family life cycle (Rolland, 1987). The unfolding of a chronic illness was conceptualized in terms of the interaction of three factors: the illness itself, the individual, and the family life cycle. This model applies equally well to developmental difficulties and allows us to develop a language to describe the developmental relationship between conditions and the individual's phase of life and setting. Rolland also suggested that one could categorize a timeline of illness, impairment, and disability into the broad phases of prediagnostic, the diagnostic crisis, the process of grief and adaptation to the newly identified condition, the long haul, and for some conditions a decline in function and possibly even death (Rolland, 1987). Such a model can also be applied to neurodevelopmental conditions.

The prediagnostic phase exists before there is recognition that there are symptoms or impairment. If your condition is present and immediately apparent at birth, the prediagnostic period is limited to the innocence of expectation associated with hopes that most parents have during pregnancy. Even if your child is born prematurely, parents hope that everything will be okay and that there will be no long-term consequences to the child. Nevertheless, there are often early symptoms that appear and raise worry in the parent's mind that something may not be right. Often it is the mother who is the most aware of their infant's struggles, their lack of a skill development, or an abnormality/difference in the process by which skills emerge. In alternate form families, there may be another primary caregiver who is the first to have concern.

There is naturally an interaction between the child's age and the nature of symptoms which emerge. The infant who fails to roll over, sit up, or crawl at the approximate times that most children do suddenly seems "different," especially as compared to other children of the same age. Parents take their children to their pediatrician or family practice physician and ask whether they should have concerns, and there often emerges a watchful waiting period during which it is hoped that the child will catch up. Sometimes the individual who is most concerned receives a message from other caregivers that they shouldn't worry so much. Comments such as "don't worry" or "she'll be ok" are offered in a dismissive fashion and do little to comfort the concern of the worried parent. Resources needed for evaluation and early intervention may be too expensive, or not readily available, sometimes leading to a decision to put off a formal evaluation or treatment. Nagging concerns can often lead to tense interactions between primary caregivers, with one parent accusing the other of making "too big a deal" of the problem while the other parent may feel unsupported and abandoned during this time.

Ultimately, as the symptoms either worsen or the developmental skill that is absent continues to lag behind expectations, a decision is finally made to seek out a professional evaluation. But where? How does one find a competent professional to evaluate the development of one's child? Specialists are often too far away, too expensive, or have waiting lists that last months prior to being able to get in. Some physicians and primary caregivers are very sensitive to questions of development, whereas others may be less aware and offer platitudes. Many caregivers ask their friends if they know where they should go or where services can be received, often resulting in a referral to an agency or service provider who may or may not take the broad perspective necessary for competently deciding what is wrong. It is common, for example, for parents to have someone suggest that their child is demonstrating a developmental delay because of a problem that can be cured by a promising, new, pop-culture intervention that has received recent publicity within the community. Unfortunately, many providers with little formal training in child development, evaluation, and therapy open franchise clinics where a certain form or brand of such therapy is offered. These take on a one-size-fits-all approach, where regardless of the nature of the child's difficulties, the favored therapy is deemed as the best intervention for the child, without any form of evidence of effectiveness. On some level, the program might make sense, and such programs often offer testimonials to support their claims. "Well it can't hurt, and it might help" becomes a rallying cry for parents to spend time and money on such services, without guarantees and sometimes even prior to an evaluation that indicates a need for the program. The obvious concern for this strategy is that the child keeps getting older. The developmental issues are not appropriately addressed and may in fact become worse as time moves on.

Another source of concern is the expense associated with getting a competent evaluation. It is a paradox that insurance companies often will not pay for services unless they are associated with a diagnosis, and yet before you have an evaluation, you aren't sure what the diagnosis is. Insurance companies may also deny claims for developmental services based on a policy provision that such services should be provided by the educational system, even though many schools do not have professionals who are well trained to perform evaluations and provide services in the specific area of need. In the United States, if the patient and/or family is on Medicaid, in some states, you are not allowed to see professionals who have the best qualifications necessary to perform a comprehensive evaluation, and alternatively, you are referred to a center where mental health technicians are caring as they listen to your concerns but do not have the knowledge necessary to identify the early signs of what could be a more serious disability.

And how do you explain this to your child, or their siblings, or your other relatives? Some parents are reluctant to state that they are seeking an evaluation for their child, out of concern for the stigma that might ensue if there were a problem. Sometimes the child's difficulties become the "family secret" that is talked about in hushed tones and not shared with other members of the extended family.

Most children associate going to the doctor with getting a shot, and the very process of being packed up and driven to a clinician's office can, in and of itself, be a nerve-racking experience. No child wants to be told that there is something wrong with them, and many become anxious or oppositional about the concept that they will be identified as somehow being different from their peers. Going through a diagnostic assessment is stressful. The child might ask, "Why am I being asked these questions? What do you think is wrong with me?" The sensitive clinician must recognize this fact and ask about the child's understanding of why they are visiting the office and what they understand will happen. It is important to reassure through the provision of concrete and yet comforting explanations of what will happen during the evaluation, when they might get a break, where the bathroom is, and the clinician's honest interest in what the child or adolescent thinks about the situation or process.

The Diagnostic Crisis

No one likes to hear that there is anything wrong, especially as it relates to one's children. The provision of diagnostic news is often a painful experience for parents or caregivers, who naturally wish to protect their vulnerable family members from any harm. Diagnostic terminology changes from year to year and is often complicated by the fact that caregivers have preconceived notions about what a diagnosis means. Regardless of how sensitive we are in providing news, some parents will receive the information we provide to them as a crushing blow and a personal affront. In their minds, we must be wrong, we have made a mistake, or we don't know what we're talking about.

It is therefore important to try to achieve buy-in from the child and family at each stage of the evaluation process, and it is often useful to wait until the very end of the feedback session before providing a diagnostic "label" or terminology that may apply. This is because once a parent hears the diagnosis, they may hear nothing else afterwards. The diagnostic crisis involves a sense of shock and often numbing of one's senses and awareness. Many parents remember very little of what is said after they hear the diagnosis, while others remember every word that is used. I have had patients tell me that they remember the exact phrasing of my feedback, 15 years later, and that the way I presented the bad news was critical to their ability to move on in a positive fashion. Clinicians should never underestimate the damage that could be done by callous or insensitive presentation of evaluation findings in a hurried fashion. It is essential to provide news with enough time that the recipients can absorb the information, react emotionally, and have time to ask initial questions. Clinicians should guard against a "hit and run" approach to feedback sessions. Of course, we are all busy and have other appointments and responsibilities; however, the impact we have when we give diagnostic feedback can last for extended time periods, even years. The mantra of "first do no harm" is therefore central to our job. It is also important to provide an opportunity for follow-up contact, either with you in person, by telephone, or via email, so that important questions can be clarified.

I also must emphasize how unhelpful it is for an individual or family to receive overly technical feedback and lengthy written reports that are full of jargon, statistics, and descriptions of the tests that we use to perform our evaluations. This will be reviewed in more detail in a later chapter; however, long, jargon-filled reports and feedback sessions that focus upon our demonstrating our brilliance in understanding the statistical nuances of some test's profile of scores is simply not useful to the patient or their family. In most cases, this approach represents a professional shield behind which we hide, so that we don't have to accept responsibility for the emotional impact of our news. Wise clinicians learn this early in their careers, and there is no gentle way to give certain forms of bad news. What is important is to provide information plainly, in language that can be understood, and in a compassionate manner. I encourage the use of vocabulary terminology which may be below the educational level of the recipient, because we can always add more information in response to questions asked, but it is hard to take away the negative impact of coming off as superior or more educated than our patients. Sometimes it is even appropriate to formulate your diagnostic impression in a short sentence that is repeated multiple times during the feedback session. It is also therefore important to ask the patient and/or caregivers what they heard you say, and what that means to them, prior to ending the feedback session. Clarification can be provided for misconceptions at this point, and asking the patient and/or caregiver to restate your findings in their own words helps the clinician to clearly understand whether the news has been received accurately. Finally, clinicians should always be humble about how well we do our job. We are evaluating a specific individual at one point in their life—there may be multiple factors influencing our evaluations, about many of which we are unaware at the time. Sometimes the conclusions we reach are simply wrong.

Initial Reactions and Grief

Assuming that you have done a thorough job of performing your evaluation, conveyed the information plainly, achieved buy-in from the patient and/or family, and gained initial acceptance of your findings, one can expect that the next step in the process of adapting to the news by the patient/caregiver may be one of initial disbelief. "It" now has a name, and individuals go through a myriad of reactions to the news and the process of naming what has previously been a vague sense of knowing that something wasn't quite right. Some individuals will tell you that they knew this is what would be found and that your evaluation confirms their suspicions. Others will argue with you, the clinician, because of their being unable to accept what they did not want to hear. This can sometimes cause defensiveness on the part of the clinician, who may think, "Well, I am a brilliant and educated professional; how dare you question my conclusions?"

Such a reaction by the caregiver does not reflect upon the clinician, however, who should react not defensively but rather with compassion and understanding that no one wants to hear bad news, especially about someone they love. Supportive silence and asking the individual to share their reactions to the news with you can often bring out strong feelings of grief, guilt, sorrow, and even anger. Many caregivers will shake their head and criticize themselves for not having sought an evaluation previously. There is a feeling of guilt that if they had only done X or Y, things might be better. Others will grieve the fact that they did not trust their suspicions and arrange for early intervention services, which might have prevented the condition from worsening. Sometimes family members will blame each other for waiting so long. Sometimes family members will criticize themselves for some imagined action that they may have taken, that might have caused the condition. The sensitive clinician will hear many questions about whether some action that the parent had taken was the reason why the child has developed the condition. Anger toward the healthcare field is another common reaction, such as the multiple individuals who wish to attribute the rise in autism spectrum disorders to the immunizations that children received to prevent even more horrific conditions.

The conclusions we reach are typically not just shared with caregivers, however. The child or adolescent about whom the diagnosis is given will have their own reactions. Depending upon the child's level of cognitive development, they will have a differing capacity to understand what the diagnosis means and how it will impact them. Many youngsters want to be reassured that they are "okay" and need help to understand that any diagnosis represents only a part of who they are, not the entirety of their identity. It is helpful to assist youngsters in recognizing that they continue to have their areas of strength and success, despite whatever condition you have identified that may be interfering with their smooth progression through childhood. It can be helpful to provide information to the child/adolescent on a level that they can understand and in a way that assures them that they are not the only individual who has the specific diagnosis. There are many picture books written for younger children about various conditions, which may be read with a parent, and allows some degree of universality of the emotions being felt. I have read some of these books with children directly and have experienced their exclaiming with a sense of relief, "That kid is just like me!" Allowing children to react to a new diagnosis by comparing themselves with such characters will facilitate recognition of the similarities and differences between their own experience and that of others who are going through the same thing.

Following the initial shock of diagnosis, many caregivers experience a period of grief over the loss of the perfect child they thought they had (or had hoped for). All parents hope that their child will become successful and happy, and there is a true sense of loss experienced by many parents when they are told that their child has some degree of developmental disorder. Many a mother has broken into tears with comments like "my poor baby," at this early postdiagnostic time. The clinician should respond by recognizing that the feedback session is a time for reassurance, empathy, and compassionate acceptance of the caregiver's grief.

Perhaps the best potential outcome of this initial postdiagnostic time period is the recognition that at least now we know what we are dealing with and we can formulate a plan of action. Grief can be transformed into motivation to actively do something to help the child, and the family can take steps toward minimization of the impact of whatever condition you have identified. It is therefore essential for the clinician to provide hope and optimism and to help families to keep whatever condition is diagnosed in perspective. Some clinicians utilize models of other individuals' successful coping with their diagnoses, as an example of how one can be successful in spite of the diagnosis, and it can indeed be useful to emulate a sports star, politician, or actor as someone who has struggled with the same condition that we have.

Living With It

Once a diagnosis has been established (or hasn't as the case may be), we enter into what Rolland termed the "long haul" phase of coping with whatever condition has been found (Rolland, 1987). For some, it takes a while for the full impact of a diagnosis to sink in, while for others the diagnosis is confirmation of the thinking that the caregiver has had for quite some time prior to the actual diagnosis. Even within a given family, different family members may be more or less accepting of a diagnosis, and while some caregivers wish to immediately "do something," and jump into intervention strategies quickly, others may want to go slowly and need a longer time in which to fully contemplate what they are willing to do. This may lead to a disconnect between various family members, and it is likely that differing caregivers within a system will cope at differing speeds or rates. To some degree, this places an increased strain upon the relationships between caregivers, who now need to incorporate this new information into their family system. The sensitive clinician can sometimes be helpful by predicting this potential disagreement and emphasize that there is no one "right way" to cope with chronic conditions. It can be helpful to "give permission" to "take it slowly" to those family members who are more reticent to jump into interventions, while reassuring the caregiver who wants to immediately intervene that there are many things they can do individually, until the other family members are ready to move forward.

It can take a while for some caregivers to understand the disorder we identify. Many caregivers will initially embark upon an exhaustive internet search regarding the condition you have diagnosed, and the studious caregiver will likely be able to find evidence to support whatever belief system they bring to bear upon their child's condition. Sometimes a caregiver will reject a diagnosis because their child doesn't show this or that specific symptom. Some individuals post on the internet, spread misinformation or "alternative truths" that can confuse caregivers and children themselves, and may seem to disprove your findings or challenge their validity. This is where the clinician can be of service by directing families to quality, scientifically valid information regarding whatever condition has been found in the child. Standard sources of information would include the Centers for Disease Control and the National Institute of Mental Health, and I recommend InfoAboutKids as a source of carefully reviewed resources (InfoAboutKids, 2017). Many of these organizations have extensive website resources that ask and answer many of the common questions caregivers and children might have during the early period of adjusting to a diagnosis.

It is also essential that caregivers be guided toward scientifically valid intervention programs and receive education about what "evidence based" really means. Families should be steered away from programs that rely upon testimonials or *ipse dixit* (because I said so) justifications for the use of the service. Many private practice offices will say that their form of therapy will be *the* answer, although they offer that form of therapy for all presenting concerns and cannot point to any research justifying the choice of that approach. The National Center for Education Evaluation and Regional Assistance has a website titled "What Works Clearinghouse" (2017). Review of this website allows the clinician and/or caregiver to learn about the evidence/degree of effectiveness that is published regarding various forms of intervention and therapy strategies. Each program is discussed in terms of the goal of the intervention, provides an effectiveness rating, reviews studies meeting the standards for respectability, etc. Clinicians should advise caregivers to be very cautious prior to signing expensive contracts with service providers who are unable to point to research documenting the effectiveness of their approach.

The Course of a Condition

Sometimes after we have performed an evaluation and recommended evidence-based interventions, parents will ask, "How long is this going to take?" While we may not be able to grow out of some conditions, it is possible to speak to the likely areas of improvement and appropriateness of various goals for intervention. As an example, it is unlikely that a child who has an intellectual and developmental disability will eventually function within the Average range of general intelligence; however, it is very appropriate to speak in terms of the goals of improving adaptive behavioral functioning, the development of a supportive peer network, and the transition of an adolescent into independent adulthood vocational and living arrangements. Other conditions are more likely to have a dramatic response to the appropriate forms of intervention, and caregivers need to learn about the level of investment that will be required and the likely timeline for improvement. As an example, training in phonological awareness has been shown to be effective in improving reading decoding skills among children who have phonological dyslexia; however, the degree of improvement appears to be tied to the intensity of intervention. It may therefore help to explain to parents that a bigger investment in services, early on, will have a greater impact than the same quantity of services spread over time. Early interventions for autism seem to be particularly important in achieving "optimal outcome" in the long run.

Still, intervention for developmental difficulties can be expensive. Ideally, caregivers can rely upon governmental agencies and public school systems to provide much of the intervention that is necessary; however, many school districts are financially strapped, do not offer the best forms of intervention for a particular child's needs, or may argue with parents about whether the child qualifies for services. I have known of families who have taken out a second mortgage on their home in order to pay for the kinds of services a child might need, and families must sometimes make painful decisions about forgoing a vacation or buying a new car because there simply is not enough money. Children receiving the services may themselves feel guilty that they are taking money away from their siblings or family, and extended family members may sometimes become involved in terms of financial support for the individual. Thankfully, advances in computer and internet systems allow for many self-help programs to be developed and delivered in a more cost-effective fashion, although once again the evidence supporting their quality needs to be carefully evaluated. There are no easy answers to the question of financing intervention services; however, it is often helpful to bring up the topic and initiate a discussion with caregivers, which demonstrates your sensitivity to the concerns. In many communities, there are individuals who can help with special needs planning and have expertise in the process of accessing government, charity, and not-for-profit sources of funding, all without placing the family's financial security at risk. For more significant disabilities, applications to the Social Security Administration's Disability Determination Service

Administration, in the United States, or other government-funded programming in other countries, can be very helpful.

The burden of providing services to a child with developmental difficulties is not just financial. Taking a child for therapy or tutoring takes time, energy, and other resources such as the necessity of paying for gasoline or parking near the service provider. The time spent waiting for a child in tutoring could have been spent taking a sibling to the park or maintaining the romance within a relationship. Children who are required to attend frequent therapies or tutoring often miss out on other extracurricular activities, such as involvement in sports teams, religious groups, or other fun activities. Siblings may be resentful about having to lose out or, alternatively, may try to become a "superstar" so as to reassure caregivers that they don't need their own nurturance. None of this is necessarily a significant problem, and in general, most members of the family system do the best they can to support each other. Indeed, the siblings of children who have significant difficulties are commonly found among healthcare professionals, many years later. Growing up with a sibling who has some form of developmental challenges creates a great deal of sensitivity to what is valuable in life and a desire to give back to those less fortunate than we.

Tragically, in some circumstances, the condition we're addressing does not get better and in fact may result in a gradual decline into complete dependence and even death. Some children's medical conditions have significant mortality and morbidity, in spite of the best efforts provided by caregivers and healthcare professionals. There are many issues associated with the preparation of the child and their caregivers for death; however, such a discussion is beyond the focus of this book. For those who are interested in the topic, I recommend the book *When Bad Things Happen to Good People*, by Harold S. Kushner (1981). While most neurodevelopmental disorders do not have a terminal phase, some conditions don't seem to improve substantially, and aging parents begin to worry about who will care for their child when they are no longer able to. Sometimes another family member or sibling may step in to help; however, the clinician must consider what other resources are available to the individual who, as an emerging adult, may have needs in the areas of residential placement, financial guidance and conservatorship, healthcare, etc.

The Qualitative Nature of the Disorder

Returning to Rolland's psychosocial typology, additional considerations in our understanding of the impact of various medical and developmental conditions include questions of the condition's onset, course, and outcome (Rolland, 1987). Some conditions have an acute onset, such as when a child experiences a stroke, a head injury, or some other traumatic event which results in the chronic developmental disorder. Such situations cause an immediate requirement that families adapt to unexpected news and changes in their system, and the ability of family members to manage such demands is often tied to the ultimate outcome. More typically in developmental conditions, however, the onset of impairment is gradual, and sometimes there is no real impairment until the child reaches a developmental stage at which the missing competencies become important for continued development. This is quite prevalent, for example, in the bright child who has no learning disabilities and manages well during the high structure years of elementary school but suddenly experiences difficulties as they reach middle school because they had an undiagnosed attention-deficit/hyperactivity disorder. The demands of independent utilization of executive functions were not present previously, and the sudden decline in performance associated with the requirements of juggling different classes, teachers, and longer-term assignments can sometimes catch parents by surprise. In this case, the onset of problems is gradual, not sudden.

The concept of the "course" of chronic conditions refers to the idea some conditions are static and remain at the same level of impairment across the lifespan, while others get better and are more manageable over time, while still others are progressive in their impact, meaning that symptoms tend to become worse over time. Conditions that can improve include speech articulation disorders, reductions in motor hyperactivity as the child with ADHD grows older, or the reading competence of a child with dyslexia who receives early and appropriate interventions. Other conditions have a constant course, meaning that the severity of impairment does not change over time. Individuals who suffer some insult to the nervous system that stabilizes medically may have a persisting level of impairment and functional limitation; however, the changes are semi-permanent and stable and, ultimately, predictable over individual's lifespan. The premature child who is found to have mild to moderate visual impairment, and some level of spastic diplegia represents an example of this type of situation, and these impairments are constantly present even if they are not disabling or don't interfere with the individual's development in other areas. Unfortunately, some conditions tend to get worse with time, such as muscular dystrophy and some forms of cancer. Families coping with these conditions have progressive and intensifying challenges, such as the individual with Down syndrome who develops dementia of the Alzheimer's type, as they grow into adulthood. Periods of relief from the demands of caring for an individual with a progressive disorder are infrequent, and caregivers must continually adapt to changing demands as the individual grows older.

Rolland speaks to a third type of condition course which he describes as relapsing or episodic, such as asthma or epilepsy (Rolland, 1987). These kinds of conditions often provide periods of stability of varying lengths, characterized by a reduced level of intensity of the impact of the condition and periods of time within which relative normalcy can occur. The reappearance of symptoms is sometimes unexpected and causes frequent transitions between times of crisis and stability, with uncertainty as to when the next event might occur. Differing demands are placed upon family members and the child himself, when faced with this type of condition, and indeed sometimes, the treatments are productive of symptoms that are equally bad as the core problem, from the child's perspective. As an example, prophylactic medication used to stave off repeated seizures can often have cognitive, emotional, and social impacts secondary to medication side effects. One certainly would prefer to avoid the child having repeated grand mal seizures; however, the reaction of some children to certain anticonvulsants is to demonstrate slowed thinking, a "zombie like" appearance, and they may be prevented from participating in certain activities that other children enjoy. The psychosocial impact of neurodevelopmental disorders is substantial, and complex.

The Developmental Parameter

It is often difficult to predict the outcome of a developmental disability. Some conditions can respond dramatically to appropriate interventions, to the extent that, several years later, there are no signs that the condition was ever present. In other conditions, our goal is to minimize impact although clear signs of the disorder remain. This is especially apparent within the Autism Spectrum of Disorders, where an individual may be intelligent, graduate from college or even professional school, and have the appearance of being highly successful. I have had patients who had successful medical practices or worked in prestigious law firms, who nevertheless continued to struggle with reciprocal social interaction, theory of mind, and other components of a developmental social disorder. Individuals who are found to have cerebral palsy may struggle with participation in the "typical" activities of childhood and early adolescence, yet transition into adulthood to achieve great things. Clinicians need to recognize that developmental disorders tend to involve changing demands upon coping and adaptation, and while ultimate outcome represents a nagging question in the minds of most caregivers, it is more productive to focus upon immediate needs and short-term goals as a focus of intervention.

Obviously, a neurodevelopmental disorder will have a different presentation and impact at different ages. A straightforward example is the fact that one can carry an infant who has some form of motor impairment, but this becomes increasingly difficult as the baby gets bigger and grows to adult proportions. Similarly, the impact of visual impairment, while significant in early childhood, becomes life-changing as the individual reaches the age at which most individuals obtain a driver's license in their quest to pursue independence. Understanding the interaction between impairment and development is therefore critical, and the clinician working in this field must have at least a passing knowledge of the developmental psychologies of cognition, identity, morality, and the social tasks facing individuals at different ages. We must be careful not to become blinded by narrow conceptions and models, and clinicians must constantly challenge assumptions made about our patients.

Many clinicians approach development from a cognitive perspective, for example, ignoring the central role movement has in brain development. Human beings are, first and foremost, animals who learned to move to negotiate their environment. Cognitive schemas develop as a result of such exploration of the world, and the first few years of life represent a time of experimentation with the environment, as demonstrated by how fast one can run, what the highest step is that one can jump off without hurting oneself, etc. Exploration of the world also occurs verbally and, through language interaction, and socially, through interpersonal relationships. Having some form of impairment in a basic developmental process will necessarily impact how well the individual develops skills, not only in that specific area, but in other areas that are in part dependent upon lifetime experience and development. Infancy, for example, is a relatively protected time, within which the child learns to roll over, sit, crawl, pull to stand, and walk independently. Language development progresses through stages of vowel sounds, consonant sounds, babbling, imitation, and ultimately expressive language; however, equally important is the progression of non-verbal communication as it involves joint visual attention, the perception and production of facial communication, and the perception and production of non-facial communication (body language). It is through the child's development of skills in each of these areas that they develop a sense of agency, that they have an impact upon the world and other people. This in turn helps to develop a sense of independence/difference from others, leading to separation and individuation as the infant enters the second year of life.

Toddlerhood involves "magical thinking" wherein direct logical understanding of the world slowly emerges because of experimentation and observation. This occurs both on a physical and cognitive level, but also socially as any parent of a child who has gone through the "terrible twos" can attest. Suddenly one does not have a baby anymore, and the child has become a real "person." The family system must adapt to this now mobile, opinionated, and demanding child, who requires all the various cognitive and developmental skills necessary for the process to occur smoothly. Take, for example, a child who has delayed expressive language skills. Rather than learning to utilize speech and language to express their needs, this child often reverts to behavioral action to communicate. Typical parental responses to the child to "Use your words!" likely will not work, and yet parents may not realize the source of the frustration for both the child and themselves. Early assessment of these difficulties can lead to intervention that includes such strategies as the use of sign language to bypass the core deficit.

Social and emotional maturity can also impact the separation of a child from family members as they enter school, daycare, or another environment outside of the home. Sometimes this is unavoidable because the parents must work to provide for their families; however, anxiety remains as to whether the surrogate caregivers/babysitters/daycare workers will be sensitive to the needs of the child who has the developmental difficulty and what level of distress the child might experience without the presence of the parent. It is not uncommon to hear parents of a child with a significant attention-deficit/hyperactivity disorder complain that their child was "thrown out of" multiple preschools or daycare settings. Sometimes the message is more subtle and takes the form of the center director suggesting that their program "is not a good fit" for the child's needs; however, the message is clear, and parents often feel a combination of frustration, anger, shame, and helplessness in the face of needing to deal with finding yet another opportunity for childcare.

It is in many ways a blessing that young children are egocentric and don't discriminate against (or perhaps even notice) children who are different from them. Birthday parties in the early years are often open to include all members of a child's class or group; however, the child with developmental difficulties may face gradual exclusion as it becomes clear that they are unable to keep up with, play the games of, or interact appropriately with their peers. A revealing question that can be asked at the beginning of an intake process is "How often is your child invited on play dates or to birthday parties?" Some parents respond by saying that the offers are frequent but that they receive critical feedback about their child's behavior during these times. Other parents will tell you that their child has not been invited to a birthday party in several years. Once again, inquiry into the day-to-day social activities of a child is very helpful in understanding their lives.

The foregoing statements do not mean that all children need to be actively involved in a large group of friendship-based activity. Sometimes having just one friend is sufficient for a child to feel that they are not alone and from whom to derive support. Normal development involves risk taking and experimentation with identities and patterns of behavior, the utility of which is judged based on the reactions of others. Having a friend tell you that they do not like something you just did is powerful feedback, whereas a child who must control all social interactions and dictate what others are to do will soon find themselves without many willing followers.

As a child grows older, most prefer to fit in and not be different, and in this way, the child with a learning disability or "invisible" developmental problem is luckier than a child who has a mobility impairment, some form of physical malformation, or some disturbance in their appearance as might be found in a child with a dermatological disorder. The dynamics of social group power hierarchies often lead to ostracism and even victimization of group members who appear different from others. Clinicians must be sensitive to how assertive a youngster is and how well they are able to manage good-natured teasing, which when mismanaged quickly turns into bullying. Here again, a systems perspective is useful, because the child who is bullied exists within an environment that actively or passively allows the bullying to occur. Sometimes teachers or school administrators minimize the concerns of the student who reports either their own or another student's victimization, which gives the message that there is implicit approval of the bullying. Conversely, some school personnel or parents swing the pendulum too far to the other side and set up artificial layers of protection for a victimized child which prevents that child from learning to stand up for themselves, be assertive, and manage interpersonal conflict. These are critical life skills which we all need to develop, and the process of a developmental assessment gives an opportunity for the clinician to inquire about how successfully the child is managing these developmental tasks.

One of the best means of immunizing a child against the dangers of ostracism is to encourage participation of that child in peer group activities. In the younger years, anyone can join a T-ball team or a soccer team, although it quickly becomes apparent which children are the natural athletes as opposed to those who will need to find an alternative source of identity. Not all children are born athletes, and some can shine in the pursuit of playing an instrument, developing their artistic skills, taking a role within a dramatic production, participating in a faith-based organization, or exploring leadership capabilities within school government. Content-specific participation in a rocket club, 4H, or a chess team all help to give the message to a youngster that they belong, that they have a place in the world, and that they have value. The clinician should become very concerned when they hear that a youngster is not involved in any extracurricular or outside of the home activities.

The transition of the students from elementary into middle school represents another developmental hurdle. The student must change from having a single teacher, in a single classroom with a stable group of classmates, to multiple teachers, classrooms, and different students in each class. Youngsters of this age are also coping with the physiological maturation of their bodies and the wide variation in the age of onset of puberty. The development of secondary sexual characteristics can become a personal crisis for many children if it occurs too prematurely or is delayed relative to others one's age. Precocious physical development exposes the youngster to a world of sexuality for which they may have minimal understanding or capacity for coping. Particularly if one has an information processing disorder that makes understanding the subtleties of social interaction difficult, the sudden appearance of being older and more mature is inconsistent with the child's ability to manage often unwanted attention from older individuals, both male and female. Children vary widely in their understanding of sexuality and the language that is used to discuss the various issues involved in the physiological transition into adulthood. It is difficult to know how to cope with rumors about one's behavior that one doesn't understand, or the subtleties of language that are often used in the communication of early adolescence. Challenges with executive functions can be multiplied by the necessity of dealing with basic bodily functions such as spontaneous erections in young men or menstrual periods in young women. Sexual education clearly needs to become a part of the clinician's focus and should follow the American Academy of Pediatrics' recommendation that sexual education occur throughout the lifespan, at a level of understanding appropriate to the age and understanding of the youngster (Breuner & Mattson, 2016).

Delayed puberty can have equally devastating impact upon a child who has a developmental disorder. Many children with developmental difficulties appear to be more comfortable playing with children who are younger than themselves; however, the experience of being one of the only students in your class who has yet to hit a growth spurt or whose voice has not dropped can add to a sense of difference and inadequacy, experienced by so many youngsters who have learning and other developmental disorders. Rather than allowing such thoughts to go unexplored, clinicians should make an effort to raise questions as to a youngster's understanding of the physical, psychological, and interpersonal aspects of sexual development. There are many useful educational materials available, which can be shared with parents and youngsters to enhance their understanding and which make the "birds and the bees" talk easier for parents to provide. Children with developmental disabilities should be viewed as being at risk for sexual exploitation and manipulation and should receive specific skills training in how to manage unwanted advances by others. Clinicians may be able to help youngsters learn the difference between attention that they are receiving based upon their positive qualities and characteristics versus attention that, while flattering, often seems designed to satisfy less honorable intentions.

The above considerations cumulatively impact the development of one's personal identity. A healthy, differentiated self-concept involves recognition that we all have strengths and limitations. It is important to keep one's limitations in perspective and to not become defined by them. It is equally and perhaps more important to help youngsters focus upon their capabilities and strengths. Help them to pursue activities which provide a positive response from one's world and results in the growth of one's confidence. Identify and nourish interests and talents as early as possible. Even if one is not a strong athlete, participation in a process in which there are winners and losers within the context of sportsmanship (even video games) helps to develop frustration tolerance, resilience, and the realization that effort often trumps capability.

Identity development may in part rest upon how one perceives one's developmental difficulty. The child who has always experienced the world from the perspective of having a disability does not have an alternative perspective, meaning that the child with a hearing impairment has never heard in the way that others do and doesn't necessarily recognize that their auditory experience of the world is different. The child who is farsighted may not be aware of their difficulties with close vision prior to being introduced to the concept of reading. Early-onset difficulties are therefore different from acquired disabilities, or those that emerge when youngsters are confronted with an inability to perform some action or skill with which other children seem to have no difficulty. The manner in which this is framed by the clinician is therefore critically important. If a child doesn't know they have an impairment, it is important that we place that impairment within the context of being a part of who the child is. Children are not dyslexics. Some children have difficulty learning to read. Children are not "retarded"; some children have difficulties with intellectual and other developmental progression. The concept that "God doesn't make junk" speaks to the value of all human beings, and the potential that everyone has to make a positive mark upon the world. Children need to hear the expectation that they will achieve to the best of their abilities and will find their own niche in life. This is a far different message from the child who hears that it is such a shame that they have some form of disability or that they will likely not achieve their goals in life because of something that they "can't" do.

One of the first steps of helping youngsters to feel competent is in helping them with self-care and self-management skills. Some children who have poor fine motor coordination have extreme difficulty learning to tie shoelaces. Well-meaning caregivers often take over and tie their shoes for them, both because it relieves frustration on the part of the child but also because it is more convenient and allows the family to meet deadlines of time and getting out the door in the mornings. The message provided to the child, however, is one that suggests that suggesting they lack competence in an important self-care activity. Providing alternatives such as slip on shoes, shoes with Velcro, etc., presents an alternative message that the child can accomplish an expected activity/responsibilities equally as well as others, just in a different manner. Teaching a child to comb their own hair and complimenting their effort is more productive than having a parent take over to "improve" upon the efforts of the child. The take-home message is; ultimately children become adolescents, who become adults, and that caregivers must foster independence, confidence, and responsibility for the choices that each youngster makes on a day-to-day basis. The choices and/or skills involved may be more difficult for some students with developmental challenges; however, the message that caregivers expect success and competence leads the youngster to also expect success, and many students with disabilities grow up having never read the book that says that they will struggle. Individuals with disabilities don't have a choice in the matter. They face the same challenges every day upon awakening and must learn that managing and overcoming obstacles in life ultimately results in a greater level of personal satisfaction.

Most parents ultimately have the expectation that their children will grow up, leave home, and live a long and productive life. The endpoints of this process may differ; however, the path is often similar. It begins with venturing outside of one's home to explore the big wide world. Exposure and opportunities lead to a sense that one has a purpose in life, and independence can at first be developed through separation from caregivers in gradual portions. The toddler who is encouraged to visit another friend's house is given an opportunity to observe how different families function and how different caregivers treat their children. Confidence in one's ability to manage life's demands can begin with an activity as simple as having a sleep-over at a friend's house, where one has to demonstrate self-control, independence, and the ability to manage basic biological functions and accept one's role in fitting in within a social setting. As the child gets older, they may attend after-school outings, clubs, and activities, again reinforcing the idea that the youngster is capable of managing themselves in a variety of circumstances. Summer camps, field trips, and other activities allow the youngster to explore the world in a protected fashion and to observe how others one's own age manage the stresses involved.

The gradual development of interpersonal skills and confidence inevitably leads to the formation of one or more close relationships, initially involving friendship and companionship but often progressing to a desire to establish a special relationship on a romantic level. Regardless of sexual orientation, the risks and rewards of making overtures to another person for a romantic involvement cause many individuals to initially experience an almost crisis level of stress and insecurity. Having someone accept you for who you are and be willing to reciprocate feelings of affection can soothe many old wounds and help even the most fragile of individuals suddenly feel capable of taking on the world. The impact of a developmental difficulty upon relationships is not insignificant, nevertheless. Many learning disorders can impact the subtleties of romantic relationships, whether on the level of communication, problem solving, social awareness, or acceptance by the family of one's romantic interest. These issues need to be discussed, clarified, and examined. It is a well-known statistic that half of all marriages end in divorce, often for predictable reasons. The involvement of young adults who have developmental difficulties in an appreciation of common stumbling points within relationships can sometimes be preventive of relationship troubles and facilitate a positive outcome. Sensitive education of the individuals romantically involved with our patients, regarding the strengths and limitations our patients possess, can sometimes help to clarify misunderstandings, place a developmental concern in perspective, and even allow the individual to be a dynamic source of support for patients during times of stress.

Getting one's first job is a similar experience. Whether a youngster had chores and responsibilities in their home, or not, the experience of having an unrelated person pay an individual for their efforts places things in a whole new perspective. Whether engaged in cutting lawns, babysitting, or other initial activities, the youngster learns that their efforts can be rewarded in a tangible fashion and begins to develop a sense that it is one's abilities in life that matter, not one's disabilities. A very positive development has been the employment of individuals with developmental disabilities within supermarkets and restaurants, performing tasks at a level commensurate with their abilities. The courtesy clerk who bags one's groceries and collects the carts from the parking lot feels important, valued, and is developing life skills that prepare them for independence. Secondary skills development occurs in terms of money management, the necessity of obtaining a bank account, and the emergence of an understanding of budgeting and saving, all of which helps to stretch one's perception of life as a process with a foreseeable future.

Conclusions

The individuals who come to our attention did not choose to have their developmental disorder. Children are supposed to exceed our own accomplishments, make us proud and happy for their achievements, and all parents strive to give their child the best chance they can, given their own unique circumstances. Whether inherited, acquired, or developed, the identification of a potentially disabling diagnosis triggers a process of coping and adaptation for which individuals and families who do not have a diagnosis are often unaware. Our clients have no choice about having their challenges, and they must live with them every day of their lives. It is helpful for clinicians to take a longer-term view of the processes involved and to appreciate the nature of the disorder, the course of its progression, the qualitative manifestations of the impairments, and the interaction of the disorder both with individual and family development.

Ultimately, it is the goal of most parents to have their children leave home and become independent. This stage of development is often terrifying for the parents of individuals with learning and developmental disorders. Anne Ford, the former chairman of the board of the National Center for Learning Disabilities, has described her own experiences of raising a child who has a learning disability in her memoir *Laughing Allegra* (Ford, 2003) and subsequently in her book *On Their Own* (Ford, 2007), which reviews many of the issues we have discussed from one parent's perspective. Ford tells the story of learning of the diagnosis of her daughter's learning disabilities, her struggles to cope, her relationships with others, her graduation from high school, her transition into adulthood, and issues related to college and employment. Ms. Ford shares her own experiences as well as her interactions with others who have taken the journey. Such courageous individuals offer a positive role model for our patients and their families. The "stigma" of having a disability is quickly shattered when critical issues are openly examined, discussed, and managed. Youngsters, their parents, and we as clinicians must keep in mind that disability does not mean a lack of ability. Impairment does not mean handicap. For most of the individuals with whom we interact, the sky is the limit.

Bibliography

Breuner, C. C., & Mattson, G. (2016). Sexuality education for children and adolescents. *Pediatrics, 138*.

Ford, A. (2003). *Laughing allegra*. New York: New Market Press.

Ford. A. (2007). *On their own*. New York: New Market Press.

InfoAboutKids. (2017). Retrieved August 8, 2017, from http://infoaboutkids.org

Kushner, H. S. (1981). *When bad things happen to good people*. New York: Anchor Books.

Rolland, J. S. (1987). Chronic illness and the life cycle: A conceptual framework. *Family Process, 26*, 203–221.

What Works Clearinghouse. (2017). Retrieved August 8, 2017, from https://ies.ed.gov/ncee/wwc/

4 On Categories and Dimensions

"The evaluation findings indicate that the patient is not capable of logical reasoning; however, the patient offered several good reasons why this conclusion is possibly untrue."

Categories Are Comfortable

Categories are typically the result of consensual agreement reached by many people, regarding similarities between things that have shared characteristics. In science, categories are called taxonomies and are a scheme of classification. The American Psychiatric Association's Diagnostic and Statistical Manual of Mental Disorders (DSM) (American Psychiatric Association, 2013) represents a categorical taxonomy, in that it is "intended to serve as a practical, functional, and flexible guide for organizing information that can aid in the accurate diagnosis and treatment of mental disorders" (American Psychiatric Association, 2013, p. xli). The DSM-5 defines the presence or absence of a diagnosis on the basis of algorithms that stipulate the presence of X symptoms within Y criteria under Z conditions of severity, age of onset, etc. Agreed-upon taxonomies are helpful for professionals early in their careers as well as for more seasoned professionals in that they allow for the description and study of phenomena and promote science and healthcare through the adoption of a common language.

The criteria for the DSM-5 diagnoses were arrived at through expert consensus derived from the review of hundreds of papers, monographs, and journal articles, by thirteen separate work groups, over a period that spanned from 2000 through 2013 (American Psychiatric Association, 2013, p. xliii). The product was the result of a truly massive effort and should not be dismissed or minimized. Indeed, the introduction to the DSM-5 clarifies that the criteria for the various diagnoses were the result of a balance between previously too rigid categorizations and the recognition that emerging theories of mental healthcare are taking on a more dimensional approach. The reader should therefore not conclude from the following discussion that the author categorically rejects categories of thinking as not being useful.

It is also important to recognize that the use of categorical thinking reduces uncertainty and improves communication by assuming a shared understanding of a phenomenon. Defining a smooth, semi-liquid substance as ice cream invokes a different mental percept from describing the same substance as plumbing caulk. Categories represent organizational strategies for understanding new concepts and involve language that cannot be unlearned. Once one has learned the concept of "cat," one cannot look at a member of the feline species and not consider them to represent that category. Similarly, the concept of "dog" is immediately differentiated from "cat," and although young toddlers who are just learning categorical organization will sometimes initially confuse the names of animals, few children ultimately have difficulties in learning an astounding number of concepts and applying them to daily life. Categories therefore allow us to take broad examples of a concept and gather them together under one conceptual "handle."

In many fields of science, this process allows for objectification of our observations and improves communication of findings and the sharing of strategies of evaluation/assessment and treatment. Thus, for example, physicians can perform a laboratory analysis of certain bodily fluids and determine whether they should treat your infection with one antibiotic versus another. Engineers can determine the ability of a structure to support various functions based upon categorical measurements and mechanical principles. Categorical thinking therefore promotes research methodologies. Questions are formed as hypotheses, and methods are developed to determine whether a new event, object, or experience fits or does not fit within our conceptual understanding of the category.

Some forms of categories have led to highly precise measurement tools. In earlier times, we learned that we can measure a certain length and call it a "foot," based upon various bodily features that often differed from one region to the next. The lack of precision in such an approach resulted in the standardization of an inch in the British Parliament's Weights and Measures Act of 1824 (Weights and measures act (UK), 1824), based upon the size of three barleycorns as representing an inch. Obviously that standard would depend upon the health of the barley, and measurement has always included a certain degree of error. Professionals who rely upon exactitude have developed ever-improved theory-based methods of measuring objects in space; however, a quick internet search reveals that one must accept the premise that science is based upon assumptions. The acceptability of a metric for measurement is the product of societal convention, regardless of the precision of how one arrives at such measurement. Think, for example, of the difference in measurements of a kitchen remodeler who determines the dimensions of your kitchen with a laser-driven measurement device, as opposed to a tape measure. Gender identity has also moved beyond a definition based upon observable physiology at birth, to an expanding list of alternative gender identities and terminology. Indeed, the concept of heterosexuality may itself be a product of societal convention, rather than an historical reality, as examined in a BBC article that describes the "invention" of heterosexuality (Ambrosino, 2017).

Categories Can Be Useful

If we can agree upon the assumptions underlying categories, we can agree upon measurement strategies. Thus, an intellectual disability can be consensually agreed-upon to represent cognitive functioning as reflected by a certain score below a certain percentile, on a certain test standardized on a defined population. A learning disability may be defined as a discrepancy between intellectual potential and academic performance, an attention-deficit/hyperactivity disorder may be defined as a certain level of elevation on a behavioral rating scale, and an autism spectrum disorder may be defined as a score that exceeds a cutoff score on a tool such as the Autism Diagnostic Observation Schedule (Lord et al., 2012). Use of these diagnostic "rules" not only promotes a sense of comfort in sorting through the volumes of data about an individual, they are a method of helping individuals who are new to the field of evaluating childhood differences to do so in accordance with a consensual process. Students and early career professionals can learn and follow guidelines for which tests and measurements to use, what diagnostic formula to use, how to plug data into the formula, how to consider confidence intervals, etc., all of which allow for supervisors and professors to grade student clinicians based on their compliance with this consensual, formulaic approach. Such a diagnostic process comforts the clinician that they are following community standards in their work.

Another value of categorical thinking is that we can study and perform research on something that we agree is roughly defined by a certain category. For example, if we define a category as involving large, four-legged mammals that run fast and have a mane and a long tail, we can agree to study and to discover more about creatures that we categorize as "horse-like." We realize horse-like creatures are different from whale-like creatures, and the study of this category can become increasingly nuanced, refined, and published. Science is a discipline, in part, based upon the publication of thoughts, data, and experimental findings, all of which support or refute an argument of whether a given subject case fits within a given category. Discussion within professional circles indeed can become quite heated over whether a category has a certain defining variable or not and what the best method of evaluating that variable might be. Publishing companies expend huge sums of money in developing and promoting their special tools as the very best available to perform a certain form of assessment of a certain form of category. Intelligence testing may be the best example of this idea, and in some people's minds, there have emerged "gold standard" methodologies or tools, which "everyone" should use. Scientific debate then progresses to questions regarding appropriate use of that tool, the data the tool creates, and interpretation of the findings, all with the goal of trying to understand "What does it all mean?" As more knowledge is derived, the tools change, the theoretical models on which they are based evolve, and suddenly we have a new consensus that somehow seems very different from that of 100, 50, or even 5 years previously.

The Major Categorical Systems in Developmental Neuroscience

In the evaluation and treatment of childhood developmental disorders, the two largest categorical systems include the Diagnostic and Statistical Manual (American Psychiatric Association, 2013), and the International Classification of Disease manual of the World Health Organization (World Health Organization, 2017). As we all know, a "diagnosis" from either of these schemas involves the recognition that certain forms of behaviors or "symptoms" cluster together, and an individual is given a diagnosis when they meet the "criteria" for how many symptoms occur together, with or without certain other factors being present. Once again, this way of thinking is comfortable and convenient. Categorical eligibility decision-making is very important at some levels, especially in terms of whether you will be found eligible for certain services, whether insurance will reimburse your professional activities, or whether certain forms of treatment should be applied.

The categorical taxonomies of the Diagnostic and Statistical Manual (DSM) and the International Classification of Diseases (ICD) are fluid, and the criteria for their diagnoses change with each subsequent revision. Consider, as an example, the removal of the term "Asperger's Disorder" from the DSM-5, which returned to an older concept of an Autism Spectrum of Disorders as being a better fit for the knowledge that has been gained over the time between the publication of DSM-5 and its predecessor, DSM-IV. ICD is also evolving, with the change from ICD-9 to ICD-10 resulting in part from an interest in new/additional diagnostic specifiers and diagnostic accuracy (APA Practice Organization, 2016). ICD-11 is currently being prepared for release, with a goal of allowing collaborative, web-based editing and use in electronic health applications and information systems. The developers of ICD-11 reportedly feel that only modest gains can be made in determining the validity of classification of mental disorders but that meaningful progress can be made toward improving ICD-11's clinical utility (Keeley et al., 2016). The proposed ICD-11 system will be a free download for personal use. (World Health Organization, 2017).

Limitations of Categories

Use of a diagnostic taxonomy clearly has many benefits and uses. Categories are nevertheless limiting, and arguments ensue over whether one should apply a diagnosis if one doesn't meet all of the criteria as laid out in a given diagnostic manual, or if your "score" on a given diagnostic tool doesn't exceed the "cutoff" for assigning a diagnosis. At face value, the logic seems to be that, if you don't fit all the criteria, you either don't have a problem or you have a subclinical level of a problem. While this makes sense, the result is that our patients are often denied certain services based upon their failure to check all the boxes. Such reasoning is circular, in that if you are denied services needed to remediate your disorder the problems often don't get better, and if you have a disorder that affects the rate of your development as compared with others your age, the problem often actually gets worse. If the problem does indeed get worse, and the distance between you and others in your peer group widens, then ultimately you are referred for a re-evaluation which often finds that the problems are now sufficiently bad that you actually do meet the criteria for the condition. Congratulations, you now have a diagnosis!

In educational circles, this is sometimes described as a "wait to fail" process, when it is well recognized that early intervention might ideally have corrected a problem or at least helped to prevent further decline. A simple example involves early intervention for phonological dyslexia. We have reached the stage where we can recognize signs of this condition very early in life. Nevertheless, services are often not provided until the child demonstrates a significant learning disability, has fallen behind their peers to the extent that they now need specialized or individualized instruction, and their self-esteem has taken multiple hits, resulting in the child feeling on some level that they must be "damaged goods." Alternatively, if early interventions were provided in the form of specific training in phonological awareness, even before the child reaches school age or starts to learn to read, our remarkable brains can often compensate, rewire, or otherwise bypass the cellular migrational anomaly that is presumed to have caused the problem. Presto! We have prevented later problems by early intervention, in a cost-effective manner that results in the child experiencing success and the development of resilience and an "I can do it!" attitude.

An alternative to the unquestioning utilization of categorical thinking is to gradually train our brain to think in a more dimensional manner. Indeed, the authors of the DSM-5 acknowledge the boundaries between diagnostic categories are more fluid over the lifespan than previous versions of the DSM recognized (American Psychiatric Association, 2013). Categorizing individuals into narrow groupings reduces our ability to detect differences between members of that grouping. We lose track of how different or similar things can be. Categorical thinking also focuses our attention on the boundaries between the categories and distracts us from thinking about the categories in broader terms. Whether one does or does not meet a sufficient number of criteria for a given diagnosis does not mean that the individual may not be somewhere within the general category that the diagnosis covers. Categorical thinking therefore leads us to explain very complex and broad concepts in terms of either one or just a few specific variables. Most individuals do not fit completely within a category, and if you line up ten people with a given diagnosis, you'll see ten different people.

In medicine, the use of diagnosis is designed to lead to specific treatments. The diagnosis of ADHD, for example, typically stimulates a medical decision-making process that often includes the prescription of a stimulant medication. Unfortunately, not all individuals with ADHD respond to stimulants, or if they do, they may respond to one type of stimulant, for example, amphetamines, but not to another, for example, methylphenidate. The field of behavioral health and developmental neuropsychology is still within its infancy, as compared with other medical fields such as infectious diseases, which has many, many more years of research to guide the decisions being made.

Categories also change as we accumulate more knowledge. The work of Leo Kanner in his description of infantile autism was unknown by Hans Asperger, as he described individuals who, for a period of time, were given a diagnosis with his name. It was not until Lorna Wing, a British psychiatrist, translated the original works of both authors from German into English that she realized that they were speaking about the same general spectrum of disorders, and she coined the term "autism spectrum disorders" (Wing, 1993). Still, in America, our focus upon categorical diagnostic schema resulted in separate diagnoses within the fourth edition of the DSM for Autistic Disorder and Asperger's Disorder. Categorical thinkers went to great lengths to discuss the different neurocognitive profiles of each condition, primarily arguing that autism involved a language impairment implicating left brain hemisphere dysfunction, whereas Asperger's Disorder was characterized by more right hemisphere difficulties with visuospatial reasoning and concept integration. Members of the public and professional experts agreed and asserted that autism and Asperger's Disorder were separate conditions, should be treated separately, and had different outcomes. Nevertheless, as additional data was gathered over the ensuing years, it became clear that the primary difference between most individuals with autism and most of individuals with Asperger's Disorder was within the realm of intelligence. The term "High Functioning Autism" began circulating, and the DSM-5 committee ultimately decided that there was insufficient justification for the continued differentiation between autism and Asperger's Disorder, deciding instead upon a unitary category of Autism Spectrum Disorders (American Psychiatric Association, 2013, p. xlii).

The Value of Dimensions

Whereas categorical thinking limits our understanding, dimensional thinking expands our conceptions of the phenomena we study. An example is found in racial profiling, which is based upon an assumption that everyone within a certain group has a certain characteristic, for example, dangerousness. This assumption leads to sociopolitical activities that discriminate against individuals within the group, without evidence that the assumption upon which the conclusion is drawn is valid. On the other hand, diversity profiling is based upon assumption that we are all combinations of multiple factors of ethnicity, culture, opportunity, education, etc. Opportunities for advancement and achievement should be based upon multiple factors, rather than just one. As an example, the use of Graduate Records Examination (GRE) scores to determine which graduate school applicants are even considered for admission to advanced degree programs has been found to be discriminatory toward certain groups of individuals. These individuals are often underrepresented within graduate programming, unfairly. A GRE score more appropriately is considered as only one component of a multifaceted evaluation of an individual's potential for success in graduate school, rather than an exclusionary "rule" which may prevent many who have tremendous potential from even being allowed to participate.

Categorical thinking leads to a reduction in information known about the phenomenon we are investigating. If I state that I have a red car, I am minimizing the information that it is a convertible, two-seat sportster with leather bucket seats, wire wheels, a Bose sound system, etc. as distinct from an old jalopy with faded paint that is missing a hubcap. Categories therefore reflect the process of "nominalization" in which a thing becomes its name. Categories are static and imply an inability to change whereas dimensions are fluid and offer many options for change. The statement "I am depressed" suggests a static condition that explains my mood. The statement "I am depressing myself" suggests that I am making a choice and that there are options for me to explore such that I could stop depressing myself. Stating that a child has severe executive function impairment, as if it is a "thing," may stop us from deciding that we are going to spend the next 2 weeks helping that child to learn how to independently brush their teeth, get dressed, and be ready to attend school.

There is great value in difference. Evolution is a continuous process of natural selection of traits that are designed to ensure preservation of the species. At the animal level, there is a continuous competition in mating, such as the lone mockingbird who loudly advertises his availability by singing his song well into the evening hours, after all other birds have apparently gone to sleep. Television programs such as National Geographic or the Discovery Channel routinely demonstrate the quest for being the biggest, baddest, or most beautiful among one's species, just as within the human race, huge sums of money are spent in the areas of fashion, grooming, the right cologne, and the pursuit of the best school so that our children can become the most intelligent and highest educated among their peers. What is clear, however, is that being different on certain level is in fact attractive. The first person to try a different style of dress may be considered a nerd by some, or innovative and a trendsetter by others. The person who thinks outside the box and comes up with a different perspective is often viewed as creative and a "divergent thinker." The question therefore becomes whether difference equals deficit or if being different makes one interesting.

It is a central thesis of this book that our job as clinicians is to ask better questions, rather than to find "the" answer. We need to train ourselves be broad thinkers who consider variance to reflect interesting considerations, rather than annoying facts that don't fit our diagnostic impression. If someone has some of the symptoms of a given condition, but not others, how is that person different from one who meets all the diagnostic criteria? If one patient is provided intervention opportunities based on their meeting all a set of diagnostic criteria, what happens to the other patient who is denied such opportunities because they did not meet a few of the diagnostic rules? This book is about identifying the dimensions that may be relevant, and thinking about the questions to ask. If in fact we can ask better questions, we may find that the answers promote a new theoretical model and that prior conceptualizations begin to lose their usefulness. Indeed, the progression of theory often results in the development of new models of assessment, and prompts new questions to be asked. An example is the progression from considering intelligence to reflect "g" or a general level of ability, to next considering the difference between "verbal" versus "non-verbal" abilities, to an increasingly complex model of information processing as characterized by the Cattell-Horn-Carroll (CHC) model of information processing (Alfonso, Flanagan, & Radwan, 2005).

Dimensional assessment involves consideration of questions such as what, where, and how the impact of an individual's difficulties might affect their lives. Is the presenting complaint something that interferes only in the home setting, at school or in the workplace, or in the individual's relationships with other people in their lives? This question gets back to the concept of illness course and Rolland's psychosocial typology of illness. Some conditions have broad impact but lower levels of impairment, whereas others are significantly disabling but are confined to a narrow area of functioning. Dimensional assessment therefore requires asking the patient themselves to define the nature of their experience, the realms in which they suffer, and what they would like to know about themselves. Clinicians who record these concerns and begin their feedback sessions by directly assessing the questions that the individual patient has are more likely to have the remainder of their findings listened to and hopefully accepted, as compared to the clinician who says, "Well you fit the diagnostic category called XXX."

Dimensional assessment also points to potential strategies for intervention. Here it is important to conceptualize an individual's difficulties in terms of "can't" versus "doesn't" versus "won't." If an individual has a true deficit in a certain skill set that's being measured, they "can't" use that skill set and will score poorly on measures/tests of that ability. Should such an individual be found to have consistently poor performance on different strategies for measuring that same skill set, one can more reliably conclude that there is a deficit that may need to be remediated or compensated for. Alternatively, if several measures of a similar skill yield differing findings (i.e. the child performs well on one measure of processing speed but not on another), the clinician must ask themself whether there are specific aspects of the task demands that results in this inconsistency or whether it is a question of inconsistent application of the skills involved. This is the concept of "doesn't" as it applies to a child's performance. Parents will often tell you that they observe that their child can pay attention when engaged in something they enjoy but doesn't pay attention when asked to perform activities that are less preferred, such as performing homework. The concept of "doesn't" addresses the inconsistent ability of an individual to utilize skills that they possess, rather than showing that they cannot use those skills regardless of how they are measured.

The final consideration is whether the child does have the skills that we are measuring, and can demonstrate those skills in our evaluations, but "won't" perform the skills in day-to-day life. Some children perform poorly during our evaluations because they don't want to be there in the first place. Perhaps they are relatively oppositional or defiant to any request made of them, possibly because they are too anxious to perform well, possibly because they have a significant depression and don't care about how well they perform, possibly due to a host of other reasons. Does the child miss easy items while getting more difficult ones correct? Does the child have a "Swiss cheese" profile of testing with multiple errors on the way to their successfully completing very difficult items? There are many questions to ask about how some forms of impairment are manifested, and recommendations for intervention will need to consider each of these possibilities.

If the case is that an individual "can't" perform a certain skill, reflecting a deficit in that capability, dimensional thinking next questions whether there are interventions that would focus upon attempting to build the skills needed or, alternatively, whether we should try to accommodate the absence of those skills, through the use of "bypass" techniques. Here again, a young child who has poorly developed phonological awareness may respond to a systematic program of focused instruction in this core basis of language and reading. An older child, however, may be less responsive to such interventions due to the gradually reduced flexibility and adaptability of the brain as we grow older. We may need to focus upon supporting the individual's efforts to compensate for their challenges, for example, through the use of audiobooks with an adolescent who decodes reading poorly/slowly, since the likelihood of "fixing" the core deficit gradually declines as we get older. It is therefore important for us to clearly identify and describe the dimensions on which the student has skill deficits, which can support that student's categorical eligibility for services; however, our understanding the dimensions involved helps to point to mechanisms for delivery of remediation and support activities. Caregivers and other professionals generally appreciate an explanation of *why* an individual has trouble in a certain area, more than they do if only given a simple statement that the deficit exists (which is probably known even prior to our evaluation). Understanding why an individual has their difficulties naturally leads into strategies for remediating or helping that individual.

If the nature of the difficulty we are evaluating fits more within the "doesn't" category, a different pattern of intervention is likely necessary. Often times these types of difficulties reflect underlying biological processes, such that consultation with our colleagues in medicine and other therapeutics becomes part and parcel of our recommendations for intervention. As will be discussed later, the evidence of effectiveness of treatment of attention-deficit/hyperactivity disorders clearly indicates that carefully monitored and appropriately titrated stimulant medication is far and away the best form of intervention and that other intervention strategies are much less effective without the use of medication.

Environmental factors must also be considered for non-biological components of the condition we are evaluating. If a student demonstrates inconsistent alertness and attentiveness in class because they do not obtain sufficient hours of sleep at night, attention to matters of sleep hygiene may be a more effective intervention than anything else. Recent evidence suggests a growing tendency for youngsters to be engaged with electronic devices that emit blue light, just before going to sleep, and to have greater difficulties with falling asleep and maintaining their sleep, due to the impact of blue light upon the brain's production of melatonin, the natural hormone that helps us to regulate our sleep cycles (Bradford, 2016). It is therefore important to ask questions about the individual's environment and its potential contribution to any areas of impairment that the person shows, as modification of those environmental factors often changes "doesn't" into "does."

Dimensional analysis also values the perspective of the functional value of the behavior. Psychology has taught us that all behaviors have antecedents and consequences and that a functional assessment of behavior can determine what factors may be triggering or maintaining the presence of what outwardly seems to be a maladaptive process. Clinicians need to ask what purpose behaviors serve, with common categories including the provision of some sensory stimulation, the seeking of a tangible reward for the behavior, the opportunity to escape from unpleasant experience, efforts to avoid potentially unpleasant situations, and/or the potential biological or medical value of the behavior. The outcome of a functional assessment of behavior often can suggest what type of intervention might be helpful, in what environment/setting, associated with which cues in the sequence of the behavior, and whether it is more helpful to work toward prevention/avoidance of the behavior or the application of positive or negative consequences for the behavior. Should we address specific behavioral concerns (or the alternative missing positive behavior), or should we coach the development of more adaptive processes that will reduce the need for the behaviors of concern? Are we working with the system (either family or school) that may be maintaining the behavior, or do we need to work individually with the child or adolescent through a psychotherapeutic process? These factors become important in deciding the nature and scope of intervention for any disorder that we identify, with many of the answers being derived from a dimensional, process-level assessment rather than a categorical diagnosis.

Conclusions

Science progresses from initial observations of phenomena to their description. Descriptions can be grouped according to similar features, and study of the features can promote a classification system or taxonomy for the identification of categories, such as the diagnostic categories of the DSM or ICD. Such efforts are necessary and foundational for a science to mature, as theories derive from observations and testing of the boundaries of categories and their criteria. Categorical diagnosis will likely benefit from the rapid development of artificial intelligence and machine learning as it analyzes ever-increasing numbers of data points about our patients. At a certain point, however, the nuances of variations on each category's theme become more productive, instructive, and valuable when we wish to apply our acquired knowledge to the case of an individual—such as our patients. It is certainly important to differentiate between a learning disability and an intellectual disability. It is perhaps more important, however, to describe each individual's strengths and weaknesses, goals and aspirations, support systems and needs and to monitor the variability of the manifestation of an individual's disability over the course of time and development. Life is a movie. Categories are photographs.

Bibliography

Alfonso, V. C., Flanagan, D. P., & Radwan, S. (2005). Contemporary intellectual assessment: Theories, tests, and issues. In *The impact of the Cattell-Horn-Carroll theory on test development and interpretation of cognitive and academic abilities* (pp. 185–202). New York: Guilford Press.

Ambrosino, B. (2017, March 15). The invention of heterosexuality. *BBC Future*. Retrieved August 8, 2017, from www.bbc.com/future/story/20170315-the-invention-of-heterosexuality

American Psychiatric Association (APA). (2013). *Diagnostic and statistical manual of mental disorders* (5th ed.). Arlington, VA: American Psychiatric Association.

APA Practice Organization. (2016, September 22). *Fourteen mental health ICD-10-CM codes changing on Oct. 1*. Retrieved August 8, 2017, from www.apapracticecentral.org/update/2016/09-22/changing-codes.aspx

Bradford, A. (2016, February 26). *How blued LEDs affect sleep*. Retrieved September 13, 2017, from www.livescience.com/53874-blue-light-sleep.html

Keeley, J. W., Reed, G. M., Roberts, M. C., Evans, S. C., Medina-Mora, M. E., Robles, R., . . . Saxena, S. (2016). Developing a science of clinical utility in diagnostic classification systems: Field study strategies for ICD-11 mental and behavioral disorders. *American Psychologist, 71*, 3–16.

Lord, C., Rutter, M., DiLavore, P. C., Risi, S., Gotham, K., & Bishop, S. L. (2012). *Autism diagnostic observation schedule (ADOS-2)* (2nd ed.). Torrence: Western Psychological Services.

Weights and Measures Act (UK). (1824). *In Wikipedia*. Retrieved August 8, 2017, from https://en.wikipedia.org/wiki/Weights_and_Measures_Acts_(UK)#Weights_and_Measures_Act_1824.

Wing, L. (1993) The definition and prevalence of autism: A review. *European Child and Adolescent Psychiatry, 2*(1), 61–74.

World Health Organization (WHO). (2016, November 29). *Classifications*. Retrieved August 8, 2017, from www.who.int/classifications/icd/en/

Section II

The "Usual Suspects"

The DSM-5 Disorder Category labeled "Neurodevelopmental Disorders" contains seven subdivisions of focus: Intellectual Disabilities, Communication Disorders, Autism Spectrum Disorders, Attention-Deficit/Hyperactivity Disorder, Specific Learning Disorder, Motor Disorders, and Other Neurodevelopmental Disorders (American Psychiatric Association, 2013). For our purposes, we will be focusing upon four slightly broader categories of difficulty, which can be referred to as the usual suspects underlying referrals to child and adolescent developmental specialists. We will be examining some of the core issues and concepts within each area, taking the perspective that, from a dimensional point of view, similar components of human development cross the categorical groupings and differ primarily in the emphasis, severity, or presentation of impairments in each dimension.

The reader is thus asked to think conceptually about the issues involved in cognitive/intellectual and developmental disabilities, attention and executive function impairments, developmental social neuroscience, and academic and specific learning disorders. Clinicians should be aware of the major components of communication disorders, including core concepts in language function, articulation, fluency, and pragmatics; however, a good relationship with a colleague who is a speech/language pathologist is essential for referral and collaboration. Likewise, movement and motor disorders may be best evaluated and treated by neurologists, occupational therapists, and physical therapists, although child development specialists should acquire sufficient awareness and knowledge to effect referrals to these colleagues, when necessary.

Bibliography

American Psychiatric Association (APA). (2013). *Diagnostic and statistical manual of mental disorders* (5th ed.). Arlington, VA: American Psychiatric Association.

5 Intellectual and Developmental Disabilities

Historical Considerations

The development of a science of measuring mental faculties, often referred to as "psychometrics," resulted in efforts to develop a process for the formal measurement of intelligence. This field traces its origins to the work of Sir Francis Galton, who performed the first systematic measurement of human abilities, primarily involving sensory discrimination and motor functioning (Francis Galton, n.d.). In 1896, Lightner Witmer, who has been termed "the first school psychologist," attempted to link measurement of individual characteristics to specific educational interventions (Lightner Witmer, n.d.). Perhaps the most famous psychometrician, however, is Alfred Binet, who along with his student, Theodore Simon, gathered together and combined performance on a wide range of tasks to give a global estimate of intelligence (Wasserman, 2012). Binet's original assessment scale primarily measured what we now call "crystallized intelligence," referring to one's acquired body of knowledge that has been learned about the world and one's culture. This test was found to accurately predict success in schooling, and even from the beginning, therefore, "intelligence tests" have always been at least partly "achievement tests."

The early 1900s were a time of great political upheaval around the world, and with the large numbers of draftees in World War I, psychologists started to discuss the possible roles they could play in the war efforts. Robert Yerkes, who was the President of the American Psychological Association in 1917, along with Edward Thorndike, who had been President of APA in 1912, created the Army Alpha and Beta intelligence tests, which were combined to determine qualification for enlistment in the United States armed forces (Edward Thorndike, n.d.). These tests were later adapted by David Wechsler and resulted in his development and publication of the Wechsler-Bellevue Intelligence Scale (Wechsler, 1946).

Following World War I, the growing rise to power of Adolf Hitler's regime led many German scientists to decide to leave their native land and emigrate elsewhere. Heinz Werner from the University of Hamburg and Alfred Strauss from the University of Heidelberg were two such scientists. In 1936, Strauss accepted an appointment as a research psychiatrist at the Wayne County

Training School in Michigan, and Werner, who had been working at Harvard, joined Strauss and the research departments of the University of Michigan. It was their observations of the "mentally retarded" residents of the Training School that led to some of the first discussions about variations among children with brain injuries and intellectual disabilities. It was observed that some residents seemed to be relatively high functioning and to be free from comorbid medical conditions, while others had much greater levels/severity of impairment that were often associated with genetic conditions, congenital abnormalities such as hydrocephalus, or acquired brain injuries (Hallahan & Cruickshank, 1973).

With the refinement of intellectual testing and the emergence of other forms of cognitive assessment, in the middle of the twentieth century, levels of severity and categories of cognitive impairment began to be described. Intellectual testing soon identified large numbers of individuals who didn't look impaired but who in fact had statistically lowered levels of cognitive potential. Research into the biological causes of intellectual disabilities also began to identify multiple factors that were not inherited, including metabolic disturbances, infection, trauma, and perinatal causes. Political movements, including the Social Security Act of 1935, also documented the growing societal acceptance of individuals with disabilities, as was the necessity of integrating soldiers returning from the World Wars who had acquired brain injuries and cognitive impairments. The interested reader may wish to explore *The Story of Intellectual Disability* (Wehmeyer, 2013) for detailed historical information regarding societal changes in response to our growing understanding of intellectual disorders.

Categorical Diagnosis

The categorical diagnosis of limited cognitive potential, within both the DSM and ICD diagnostic schemas, has, for the past 50 years or so, identified the necessity of documenting limitations in intellectual functioning, difficulties adapting to environmental demands, and an early age of onset (operationalized to be prior to age 18). These factors continue to represent the defining criteria for the diagnosis that we currently call "intellectual disability." As an awareness increased regarding the negative impact of "labels" and diagnoses upon the individuals to whom they are applied, however, the American Association of Mental Retardation in 2010 released its eleventh diagnostic manual which was titled *Intellectual Disability: Definition, Classification, and Systems of Supports* (American Association of Intellectual and Developmental Disabilities, 2017a). Shortly thereafter, the American Psychiatric Association's DSM-5 (American Psychiatric Association, 2013) followed suit by switching terminology from the previously used "mental retardation" to the current use of the term "Intellectual Disability." Perhaps more accurately, the current DSM-5 uses the term "Intellectual Disability (Intellectual Developmental Disorder)," which it defines as a "disorder with onset during the developmental period that includes both intellectual and adaptive functioning deficits in conceptual, social, and practical domains" (American Psychiatric Association, 2013, p. 33). Interestingly, the addition of "Intellectual Developmental Disorder" in the parentheses following "Intellectual Disability" was, at the time of the DSM-5's publication (2013), designed to align the diagnosis with draft versions of ICD-11 available at the time. In actuality, the World Health Organization has since changed its terminology to "Disorders of Intellectual Development," once again reflecting the ambiguity and continuing change of the labels applied in categorical diagnoses (World Health Organization, 2016).

The DSM-5 diagnosis of Intellectual Disability requires three criteria be met (American Psychiatric Association, 2013, p. 33). The first is that the individual demonstrates deficits and intellectual functions involving such skills as "reasoning, problem solving, planning, abstract thinking, judgment, academic learning and learning from experience, and practical understanding confirmed by both clinical assessment and individualized, standardized intelligence testing." A second requirement is listed as involving "Deficits in adaptive functioning that result in failure to meet developmental and sociocultural standards for personal independence and social responsibility." This criterion identifies the fact that individuals with intellectual disability require ongoing support, the absence of which would limit functioning in one or more activities of daily living such as "communication, social participation, and independent living, across multiple environments, such as home, school, work and community." Finally, the DSM-5 requires that the onset of the individual's measured deficits must be during the developmental period, thereby removing the somewhat arbitrary onset of younger than 18 years.

The World Health Organization offers a similar definition including "disorders of intellectual development" for a group of etiologically diverse conditions originating during the developmental period, characterized by significantly below-average intellectual functioning and adaptive behaviors that fall approximately two or more standard deviations below the mean (i.e. approximately less than the 2.3rd percentile). Determination of such impairment should be based on appropriately normed, individually administered standardized tests. If appropriately normed and standardized tests are not available, the diagnosis of disorders of intellectual development requires the clinician to rely upon greater judgment and the appropriate assessment of comparable behavioral indicators. The ICD-11 also specifies that, if a disorder of intellectual development is associated with a known etiology classified elsewhere, both the diagnosis of intellectual disability (ID) and the known etiology should be described (World Health Organization, 2016).

Consideration of Psychometrics

Each of these schemata operationalize "subaverage intellectual functioning" as being defined by an intelligence quotient score that is "approximately"

2 standard deviations below the mean for that individual's age. The term approximately was purposely chosen because of several factors. The first is that all IQ test have some degree of measurement error, commonly expressed as a confidence interval placed around a given score. For example, the 95% confidence interval for an IQ score of X is X+/−Y points, depending upon the test's standard error of estimate. This means that, if the same test were given several times, you might expect the obtained scores to fluctuate to some degree around the "true" score. It therefore isn't useful to say that an IQ score of 73 excludes the possibility of ID, because repeated testing might find scores of 64, 69, and 71 if the individual's "true" score is 68; all of which are probably fair reflections of that individual's standing, relative to peers. Conversely, repeated measurement might identify scores of 75, 77, or 81, if the individual's "true" score is 80. The wise clinician therefore takes any obtained scored on a psychological test as being approximate and possibly a high estimate, or possibly a low estimate.

Another consideration is the fact that as intelligence tests age, scores obtained through the administration of the test tend to increase approximately 0.3 points per year (Reynolds, Niland, Wright, & Rosenn, 2010). This tendency might result in finding an individual who scored below a "cutoff" established to identify intellectual disability to gradually "grow out of" their categorical eligibility over time. Such a process, in turn, may result in an individual who is involved in death penalty litigation to score above the range of intellectual disability, if an older test is used, as opposed to being protected by the Eighth Amendment's prohibition against cruel and unusual punishment and therefore ineligibility for execution (Reynolds et al., 2010).

The observation that scores on standardized measures of intelligence steadily rise has come to be known as the "Flynn effect," after James Flynn who, documented this phenomenon (Flynn, 1984). Flynn argued that changes in the environment, associated with modernization, increased people's ability to manipulate abstract concepts, which has become a key skill measured by modern intelligence tests. Other arguments have suggested that, as healthcare and education improve, our population as a whole is less likely to succumb to cognition-impacting illness and is exposed to improved methods of education and other factors, all resulting in people "getting smarter," such that individuals who take an intelligence test that was normed some time ago are more likely to obtain a higher score than an individual who took the test shortly after it was first published. The various arguments for and against the Flynn effect, and discussion of this concept, are presented in the October 2010 issue of the *Journal of Psychoeducational Assessment*, for those interested; however, for our purposes, it is sufficient to recognize that specific scores on intelligence tests are estimates of a range of potential scores. Seasoned clinicians recognize that, with each revision of an intelligence test, scores on the more recently developed test tend to be slightly different for an individual, than if they had taken the previously administered task. It is thus important for clinicians to understand the way test scores we use to categorize patients are obtained.

It is generally considered appropriate to consider an individual who obtains an IQ somewhere between 70 and 75 as potentially qualifying as having an intellectual disorder; with this position being consistent with that taken by the American Association of Intellectual and Developmental Disabilities (2017a), as well as the Supreme Court decisions in *Hall v. Florida* (2014). When comparing serial testing of an individual who has had multiple prior evaluations, it is very important to consider which tests have been previously used, how old the norms for that test were at the time, and which current test might best evaluate the given individual referred to you. While some clinicians have a "favorite" measure or prefer an older test because of the nature of the subtests involved, such clinicians need to be able to explain their rationale, defend their choices, and be aware of the impact of a host of variables upon the obtained scores.

Clinicians should also recognize that certain measures of cognitive functioning may be normed/standardized on populations of individuals who are very different from the person in your office. At the most basic level, for example, an individual who had been raised in Canada may not have a good appreciation of United States history and may be unprepared to answer questions that presume such knowledge. Indeed, utilization of American-based testing instruments in other areas of the world raises questions as to the impact of different languages, cultures, and educational systems upon the individual's capacity to obtain a given score. Certain published measures have versions that have been normed on different populations worldwide. Even within the United States, however, there are groups of individuals who are disadvantaged when asked to take standardized testing. Native Americans, Alaskan Natives, and Hawaiian Peoples have long been subject to discrimination, have typically not been included in standardized test development, and have personal and cultural values that are different from the mainstream American student.

Whether by choice or ignorance, therefore, many clinicians who evaluate children and adolescents have been unaware of the cultural factors and values that can have a significant impact upon mainstream society's appraisal of behavior, cognition, and mental health. This chapter focuses upon intellectual disabilities; however, the phenomenon also is found at the highest levels of ability, and in February of 2017, the American Psychological Association reaffirmed diversity in graduate education and encouraged multiple indicators in the review and admissions decisions of applicants to graduate programs in psychology (American Psychological Association, 2017). This resolution was in part secondary to recognition and concern that certain minority applicants to graduate schools were being denied admission secondary to scores on certain high-stakes examinations, which have been found to result in lower scores for such minorities (Gardere, 2015).

Such discrimination also extends to individuals who are born with various craniofacial anomalies or have other acquired conditions which make them "look" different from societal norms. Tragically, our society's history is full of stories of individuals who were thought to be intellectually disabled based on their appearance and were denied opportunities because of the assumptions made by often well-meaning clinicians. This in turn leads to the "Matthew effect," which notes that individuals who have learning disorders often are not provided similar opportunities as non-disabled peers in the processes of gaining new knowledge, such that their standing relative to same-aged peers tends to decline over time (Stanovich, 1986). As an example, the student who has a language-based learning disability in reading may tend to fall farther behind peers in vocabulary development (and therefore score lower on some IQ tests) as they grow older, primarily because much of vocabulary knowledge is acquired through reading and verbal discourse. The primary take-home message, therefore, is that scores that clinicians obtain on various measures of abilities need to be interpreted in terms of multiple factors that can affect how the score is determined. It is essential that clinicians continually question their findings, their belief systems, the accuracy of their tests and measurements, and other factors that may be at work in a given case.

A Change in Emphasis Toward Adaptive Behavioral Functioning

Perhaps the most important change that occurred with the publication of DSM-5 is the recognition that ID severity is more likely associated with deficits in adaptive behavior rather than IQ alone. Clinicians who evaluate individuals with intellectual disabilities must therefore consider other factors, such as the community and environment within which the individual and his or her peers live, as well as factors such as linguistic diversity and cultural differences in behavior. The youngster who has grown up in a rural area, perhaps far from a major city, will have had a much different set of life experiences as compared with the youngster who grew up within the inner city of a large metropolitan area. What is the impact of poverty and educational opportunities upon the developing mind of the young child? The child who is raised in a middle-class, two-caregiver family where there are multiple computers and electronic devices, parents who regularly read to their children, and mealtimes that involve discussion of current events is likely more advantaged as compared with the child whose sole caregiver may be working two jobs, comes home exhausted, and relies upon an older child to care for his or her other siblings. Even a cursory review of the questions asked on many scales of adaptive behavior reveals that competence in the various areas of development requires some level of exposure and opportunity, the absence of which may artificially depress individuals' achievements.

Assessments of cognitive competence must also recognize that individuals with intellectual disabilities have areas of strength. This speaks to the idea that most of us have a profile of strengths and weaknesses in our learning skills, which is helpful in identifying areas within which we can potentially have greater success. This fact nevertheless also means that, just because an individual may have one or two areas of substantially better functioning than the rest of their abilities, it may not negate the presence of an overall disability, which is best measured by the degree of support that individual needs in day-to-day life. How much assistance does the patient need in terms of personal hygiene, choice of weather-appropriate clothing, food purchases and preparation, management of bill paying, assistance with transportation, protection from victimization, etc. Many referrals seem to arise when an individual who has been competently managing most of their life comes up against the requirements of a more advanced life stage. The demands of higher-grade schooling, the onset of puberty, emerging questions regarding who will be the caregiver as aging parents become less able, all can prompt a need for determination of the individual's cognitive and adaptive behavioral competence. We must recognize that an individual's daily functioning is frequently dependent upon the appropriate supports that are consistently provided over time, as they interact with episodic stressors and developmental challenges experienced by the individual who is ever growing older. Intellectual disability clearly implies more than just low IQ.

Categorical Assessment Strategies

Developmental and behavioral testing is considered to be one of the core skills that many child clinicians possess. Whether based on direct observation of the child's ability to perform certain developmental skills, caregiver ratings of competence across different areas of development, or the formal administration of psychometrically sound cognitive tests, many child clinicians attempt to estimate the baseline level of functioning present in a child or adolescent who comes for an evaluation. When using formal testing, certain important considerations need attention. Perhaps the first is the need to ask whether the testing instrument used has a sufficient number of items at the lowest levels of ability, or what is referred to as an "adequate basal." It is instructive to see how obtained estimates of global ability might change based on whether the patient is given credit (or not) for as few as one or two items. When testing a youngster with possible intellectual disability, therefore, it is useful to utilize an instrument that has scores for youngsters much younger than the child who enters your office. Testing a potentially intellectually disabled 6- or 7-year-old may not be accurately accomplished if the norms for the chosen test start at 6 years of age, because the individual may only be able to pass a limited number of items, thereby restricting the sample range of behaviors on which we draw our conclusions. In this case, one might consider utilizing a testing instrument that measures abilities well below the chronological age of the individual you are working with, to be sure to have items that are sufficiently easy and will allow a valid basal of performance to be obtained. Just because a given test is touted as the "gold standard" for measuring certain skills does not mean it is the best choice for your patient.

One must also consider the nature of how a test measures abilities. Is the youngster asked to verbally respond to increasingly abstract questions, which require competent expressive language skills? Or can the youngster obtain a correct score simply by coming up with a single word or two, to demonstrate their knowledge. Is it possible for the youngster to obtain a correct score by pointing, rather than verbalizing? What is the nature of the test materials, and how well do they engage the child's attention and willingness to "play the game" of testing? Younger children who have intellectual disabilities often need modifications of evaluation procedures, with more frequent rest breaks, or the opportunity to seek reassurance by touching base with caregivers, to have a snack, etc. Clinicians should strive to optimize the evaluation environment to maximize the youngster's performance, and all efforts should be made to avoid concluding that a youngster has a lower level of abilities than they actually possess, as a result of factors within the testing environment that are independent of the child's abilities.

When performing a formal evaluation of a child's abilities, one should consider the experiences of the child and whether they have been through similar evaluation procedures previously. Younger children who may still experience some degree of separation anxiety may feel overwhelmed by the sterile testing environment and necessity of interacting with a stranger. It is important to make sure that the clinician takes a sufficient amount of time to allow the child to become comfortable in the situation, ideally in the presence of the caregiver with whom the clinician interacts for a period of time, while the child has the opportunity to take in the environment, get used to the clinician, and start to interact through simple questions and requests of the child. Not all children know how to take tests, and it is sometimes necessary for the clinician to see the child on a couple of occasions before actually administering formal testing procedures. Other children need to be taught the give and take of their responding to requests and tasks, perhaps as simple as starting with a request that the child draw their caregiver a picture. Clinicians can develop positive effort by the child through praise of their effort and cooperation and by accepting initial non-test behavior in an uncritical and accepting manner. Through this process, the child learns to adapt to the testing situation and is more likely to produce optimal performance.

At the other end of the spectrum, adolescents who present for examination may have a history of previous evaluations and testing and arrive with assumptions about what the process in your office will be like. It is therefore helpful to ask about their prior experience with assessment, their feelings about the process, and their willingness to participate. Regardless of the chronological age of the individual, the clinician who respectfully asks permission of their client to join in the evaluation is more likely to achieve successful cooperation and good effort. Reflective listening and validation of the teen's concerns about the process may facilitate cooperation by the patient, and the voluntary offering of insights they may have about their learning challenges. Conversely, the hurried clinician who brusquely tells the youngster to sit down and "let's get started" may find the youngster unwilling to give more than single-word answers or a minimal level of effort. As is discussed in subsequent chapters, it is becoming increasingly clear that the level of engagement and cooperation the clinician can elicit from their clients is a strong predictor of how well they will perform on many of our tests. If in fact the clinician decides that the youngster is giving minimal effort, or is otherwise disengaged, it may be best to reschedule formal assessment for another visit and spend time establishing rapport.

As noted above, current conceptualizations of intellectual disability place an emphasis upon focused assessment of the individual's adaptive behavioral development. The DSM-5 (American Psychiatric Association, 2013) and other categorical schemata seem to have reached agreement as to a tripartite conceptualization of adaptive behavior, variously described as involving conceptual, social, and practical skills. Historically, clinicians were asked to obtain a formal summary score on a psychometrically valid/sound measure of these skills, and much debate ensued when scores from either formal intelligence tests and/or formal measures of adaptive behavior *did not* fall 2 standard deviations below the mean for individuals of similar age. Current conceptualizations have changed, somewhat, and the clinician is now encouraged to document impairment in adaptive functioning that "result in failure to meet developmental and sociocultural standards for personal independence and social responsibility" (American Psychiatric Association, 2013, p. 33). Impairment must therefore be sufficiently impactful that the individual needs ongoing support, across multiple settings and environments. This process emphasizes the necessity of clinical judgment, which is defined as the integration of multiple sources of information, review of academic reports and prior assessments, and extensive interviews with persons who know the individual well. It is not sufficient to simply send a rating scale to a child's teacher or parent and base potentially life-changing decision-making on standardized scores obtained from subscales.

Another consideration is that the assessment of adaptive behavior needs to focus upon what the individual "typically" does and not whether he or she has "ever" performed a certain skill or does so infrequently. Caregivers and teachers, often wishing to paint the most positive picture of a child, will frequently make comments such as "Well, he can do it, sometimes." The clinician is therefore placed in a position of trying to learn more about the frequency with which the individual performs the behavior and the degree of support necessary for the individual on a day-to-day basis. It is often helpful to get input from multiple individuals who know the patient well and to discuss discrepancies between their reports. Often agreement can be reached when specific examples of the concepts questioned are gathered and caregivers are questioned about whether the skills are typically performed without assistance or support.

Dimensional Assessment

The shift in the focus of our evaluations toward a more dimensional perspective has prompted a change from simply getting scores on tests, to the need to delineate and document the abilities and support needs of the individual we are evaluating. The American Association of Intellectual and Developmental Disorders (AAIDD) emphasizes that individuals with intellectual disabilities need a person-centered planning process that helps to identify that individual's unique preferences, skills, and life goals. The needs of individuals with intellectual disabilities change over time, from the preschool years through elementary school, middle school, high school, and beyond. Other considerations include the presence or absence of specific medical conditions or behavioral concerns that require substantial levels of support, regardless of the individual's need for support in other life areas. The AAIDD has developed the Supports Intensity Scales (American Association of Intellectual and Developmental Disorders, 2017b) as a method of quantifying these needs. Individuals knowledgeable of the client's daily function are asked to rate the frequency, daily support time, and types of support needed by an individual, across multiple areas including home living, community and neighborhood engagement, school participation, school learning, health and safety, social activities, and advocacy. Utilization of this process identifies that some individuals with intellectual disabilities have a relatively low level of support needs, while others have needs that are quite demanding.

Most clinicians recognize that the needs of an individual for evaluation and treatment go well beyond the simple identification of whether or not they "fit" a specific diagnosis. Clinicians are faced with multiple questions regarding possible causes for the impairment, the age of onset and first diagnosis, and the current presenting complaints and referral questions. Clinicians need to ask questions including "Who is concerned?" "What are the concerns?" and "Why now?" Some individuals with mild intellectual disability, for example, may not appear to be very different from same-age peers during the early years of schooling. They may develop initial academic skills and keep up with their non-disabled peers until such time that the level of abstraction and language involved in course material exceeds their capacity to keep up. Not infrequently, clinicians will receive referrals for a specific learning disability evaluation in an emerging adolescent only to find that the youngsters learning challenges are more global than specific.

Other individuals with intellectual disabilities learn basic academic skills such as reading decoding but show problems when the process of learning to read transitions into the process of reading to learn. Suddenly, the development of strategies for problem solving (i.e. executive functions) becomes critical for higher-level cognitive processes to emerge. The early adolescent who doesn't understand why his/her peers are suddenly interested in sexuality ("Gross!!!") has many more needs than simply learning strategies to improve reading comprehension. It is therefore important to evaluate the multiple dimensions of impact posed by conditions such as intellectual disabilities and other neurodevelopmental concerns. How does the condition affect that individual? How are they treated by their peers? How does the condition affect the family system within which the individual resides? What are the developmental parameters of importance for consideration in the evaluation process? There are many questions that the clinician will consider at various ages and stages, including the often not talked about issues of sexual development, safety, and independence.

A comprehensive dimensional evaluation of individuals with intellectual and developmental disabilities must therefore take into consideration the etiology of possible impairment. Some causative factors may be treatable, for example, lead poisoning, while others may be associated with other health concerns that will likely need immediate attention. It is becoming clear that many forms of intellectual disabilities, perhaps 50%, have their basis in genetics, as well as acquired neurological injury and insult (Levitas et al., 2016). Other individuals may not have a clear etiology and are lumped into the broad category of "cultural-familial" or "unknown etiology." It is important to consider the etiology, however, because understanding causative factors may point to specific medical interventions that will be needed, may allow consideration of whether the youngster's parents will choose to have another child, and may open doors to available resources and education available through condition-specific national and community organizations. Many specific syndromes also have clear implications for the behavioral phenotype of the disorder. While it is beyond the scope of this book to delve deeply into what is known about the multitude of specific diagnoses, we will discuss examples of the type of questions that can be asked by the clinician, as we perform our consultations. Consistent with the theme of this book, we need to focus upon the perspective and approach of the clinician as the critical factor in determining the adequacy of our services, while recognizing that research findings and information regarding specific conditions can be looked up.

In discussing the concept of a behavioral phenotype, it is becoming clear that certain genetic conditions result in characteristic "footprints" of neurocognitive findings, presumed to be tied to underlying differences in brain development and functioning. Gathering extensive and detailed background medical information is essential when working with all neurodevelopmental disorders and especially those involving global impairment and significant developmental delay. Such information helps us to move beyond classification as the goal of our work toward description of an individual's profile of cognitive and behavioral features, which in turn can help to direct strategies of intervention, appreciation of strengths and assets (rather than just deficits), and a broader understanding of how a genetic pedigree can result in the outcome of the individual. Two individuals who meet diagnostic criteria for an intellectual disability (ID) may have similar levels of global intellectual competence and yet very differing patterns of information processing strengths and weaknesses. This is also true in the profile of their adaptive behavioral functioning, in that some individuals may struggle specifically in social functioning, while others have more difficulties with communication or daily living skills.

As an example of behavioral phenotypes, individuals with Down syndrome can range in their overall intellectual abilities from areas of Borderline/Low

Average ability in some skill sets, to severe and profound levels of global impairment. Down syndrome is the most common congenital disorder among individuals with ID. Core cognitive deficits typically involve language (grammar), working memory impairment, articulation deficits, and impaired intelligibility of expressive language, along with impaired attention and executive function skills development. Conversely, individuals with Down syndrome often demonstrate areas of relative strength in visuospatial skills including spatial awareness, motor coordination, and visual memory, which have implications for their potential for success in vocational training and participation in supported occupational environments.

Contrast this pattern with that observed among individuals who have fragile X syndrome, the most common inherited form of ID. Fragile X syndrome is the term that reflects repeated sequences of the DNA bases cytosine-guanine-guanine (CGG), which in unaffected individuals repeat between 6 and 54 times in a certain area of a gene. When the CGG repetition exceeds 200 times, the condition is referred to as a "full mutation" which interferes with synaptogenesis, causing modifications in multiple brain areas. Males diagnosed with fragile X syndrome are usually more affected than females, although between 50% and 70% of females with full mutations also show cognitive impairments. Individuals with fragile X often show significant features of impaired attention span, impulsivity and hyperactivity, along with language abnormalities, social anxiety, cerebellar ataxia, and other symptoms (Levitas et al., 2016).

Many youngsters with ID do not have a genetic or congenital basis of their impairment, however, and careful review of the history may identify acquired insults to the brain, often associated with mother's health before she became pregnant, adverse events that occur during pregnancy, and complications which impact the perinatal and postnatal time periods. There are many toxins that can impact the developing fetus, loosely referred to as "teratogens," such as high levels of maternal prenatal drug and alcohol use, infections, viruses, and maternal medical treatments (e.g. chemotherapy). The World Health Organization works hard to prevent conditions such as Zika virus-caused microcephaly; however, many more common conditions and the use of various medications by the mother during pregnancy can have tragic consequences.

According to the Centers for Disease Control (2015), statistics from 2015 indicate that approximately 10% of children are born prematurely, defined as reaching a gestational age of less than 37 weeks, and many (8%) of whom are considered to have a low birthweight (less than 5 pounds, 8 ounces). Low birthweight has been found to be predictive of complications in long-term outcomes. Although the quality of neonatal intensive care has improved greatly over the past 30 years, numerous adverse events can still occur, and premature infants are at a much higher risk of developmental disorders than children born at term. When serious problems occur, such as massive intraventricular hemorrhage or severe infection/sepsis, the consequences for the child's developing brain are often catastrophic. Postnatal events can also lead to ID, including severe traumatic brain injury, neurological infections, including encephalitis and meningitis, severe malnutrition, severe neglect and abuse, brain tumors and their treatment, etc. (Armstrong, Hangauer, Agazzi, Nunez, & Gieron-Korthals, 2011).

It is consequently presumed that the differing cognitive and behavioral profiles we identify are reflective of underlying biological factors, and the evaluation process should not stop at the level of global scores such as IQ or standard scores on adaptive behavioral scale. Rather, a description of the levels of strengths and weaknesses and their consistency with published literature on various conditions becomes important. As always, the impact of age must also be considered, as certain symptoms may occur in adolescents but not children, and vice versa.

Questions of Comorbidity

Individuals who have intellectual disabilities are not immune from the impact of other psychiatric disorders and health conditions. Indeed, it has long been recognized that individuals with intellectual disabilities are three to four times more likely to have a comorbid health or psychiatric disorder, as compared to the general population (Murphy, Boyle, Schendel, Decougle, & Yeargin-Allsop, 1998). Not only do such individuals experience similar mental disorders as the general population, they also experience some disorders that are relatively infrequently found in the general population, for example, pica and severe self-abusive behaviors (Fletcher, Barnhill, & Cooper, 2016). The recognition of the extent of comorbidity of psychiatric impairment among individuals with ID has led to the publication of the *Diagnostic Manual-Intellectual Disability: A Textbook of Diagnosis of Mental Disorders in Persons with Intellectual Disability* (DM-ID-2), by the National Association for the Duly Diagnosed (Fletcher et al., 2016). Although the text does not necessarily describe every possible condition the individual with ID may experience, the goal is to recognize that limitations in developmental status should not be used to explain away other potentially treatable conditions.

Based upon an expert consensus model (similar to the DSM), the DM-ID-2 provides a methodology whereby the clinician can thoughtfully evaluate the mental health of individuals with intellectual disabilities. The manual suggests that there are four primary difficulties in performing this process. Perhaps the first consideration is the capacity of the individual to understand diagnostic interview questions asked by the clinician. The concrete nature of thought among some individuals with ID might lead them to not understand implications within presented questions, and they may answer inaccurately when asked questions that require abstract thought or the appraisal of the frequency with which a symptom may appear. A second consideration is whether the psychosocial impact of stress and illness might overwhelm the "cognitive reserve" available for the individual to manage the illness. Many individuals who have neurologically based disorders experience stressors more acutely, and illness can have a greater impact. For example, individuals with Down

Syndrome may develop hallucinations that are reflective of a Major Depressive Disorder with Psychotic Features, while some clinicians may presume that the individual is developing Schizophrenia or Dementia of the Alzheimer's Type. Indeed, the hallucinations may be associated with hypothyroidism or another medical condition that can be treated. At a more basic level, the youngster who has contracted a cold will probably not be able to perform as well on our assessments as they could when they are healthy. Close collaboration with physicians familiar with ID can be invaluable.

Third, one must ask about the baseline frequency of presenting behaviors of concern, which may increase as the patient experiences the stress of going through an evaluation or other situational factors. Psychiatric symptomatology needs to be viewed from the perspective of an understanding of the individual in their day-to-day functioning. Rather than simply focusing upon the behavior at hand, we must comprehensively gather historical information within which to frame presenting symptoms, their pervasiveness, duration, and factors that influence the demonstration of their severity. The assessment of frequency of symptoms is best performed with caregivers who have frequent contact with the patient.

As explained in the DM-ID-2, the physical phenotype of a genetic condition represents the physical features characteristic of that condition. Down syndrome, for example, has a familiar facial set of characteristics that allows one to recognize the condition almost immediately upon interaction with the individual. As science has advanced, the use of laboratory evidence has allowed for the identification of other specific conditions, such as fragile X syndrome, Klinefelter syndrome, Williams syndrome, etc. Individuals who frequently work with intellectual disability can learn to recognize many of the different syndromes based upon facial features of their patients, and referrals for a genetic, endocrinology, and other medical evaluations are necessary to pinpoint the likely underlying biological bases of many conditions. Commonly, it is the presence of a coexisting medical diagnosis such as a heart defect, seizure disorder, or structural skeletal differences that initially brings a child to medical attention, which often leads to a dysmorphology or genetics evaluation, which in turn may result in a referral for a developmental evaluation based upon the frequency of developmental disorders associated with the identified condition. Caution is warranted at this point, however, as much of the literature describing the developmental outcomes of various conditions focuses upon more severely affected individuals, while individuals with mild impairment may not be well represented in the samples studied.

As an example, I recently was asked to evaluate a young lady who had been identified as having a very rare genetic condition. Investigation into what is known about this condition informed me that most diagnosed individuals have severe intellectual and developmental disorders, many with diagnoses of autism spectrum disorders. The young lady I was asked to evaluate, alternatively, scored well within the Average range on measures of verbal intelligence, non-verbal intelligence, and memory. This suggests that there may be others who have the same genetic profile who are not severely impaired—they just haven't been identified or evaluated. It is essential that we keep an open mind, therefore, and take the time to write up or present case studies that are counter to prevailing assumptions at the time.

The DM-ID-2 also describes the behavioral phenotypes of 12 specific intellectual disabilities syndromes, ranging from the familiar Down syndrome and Fetal Alcohol Syndrome, to the less recognized conditions of 22q11.2 deletion syndrome and the tuberous sclerosis complex (Levitas et al., 2016). Clinicians working with ID are encouraged to use the DM-ID-2 as a desk reference, much as the DSM-5.

Ideas Regarding Intervention

Later chapters in this book discuss promising findings from studies of specific interventions tied to certain conditions. Individuals with ID, however, are less likely to grow out of their impairments in cognition and adaptive behavior. The goal of intervention with this population should be to attempt to reduce the burden of the disability, while attempting to increase the individual's participation in society, their access to meaningful personal experiences, and the avoidance or reduction of impact of comorbid health and mental illness. This requires "big picture" thinking and necessarily involves all the factors over which one can exert an impact.

First and foremost, clinicians should advocate for their patients to seek and receive all needed medical care for biological factors impacting the overall health of the individual. It is sometimes hard to find primary care medical providers who specialize in the healthcare of individuals with developmental disorders; however, seeking and identifying such providers can be extremely helpful to the individual and their family. Unfortunately, many individuals with ID are overmedicated with psychoactive agents when the patient is showing agitation and distress secondary to an underlying medical condition. As one example, a youngster who has a tooth abscess but is unable to verbalize what is hurting may behaviorally act up in a manner that appears to caregivers to represent a psychiatric disorder. Only some dentists are comfortable treating developmentally disabled patients, and efforts to identify a specialist in this area can have long-lasting positive consequences for our ID patients. Many other behaviors may reflect untreated medical concerns, including the above-mentioned psychotic symptoms of individuals with significant hypothyroidism. Something as simple as a urinary tract infection can cloud consciousness and create a delirium. Clinicians who work with developmentally disabled patients therefore have an affirmative responsibility to reach out to pediatricians, family practice physicians, and other medical caregivers for their patients and to establish and work to maintain positive communication about our involvement. Unfortunately, clinicians working with neurodevelopmental disorders are often considered to be a "black hole" to primary care providers, who make a referral for an evaluation or treatment and never hear back as to findings or recommendations. Clinicians should routinely make the effort to write a quick letter to our patients' primary care providers to enhance teamwork and recognition of the primary care provider as the leader of an interprofessional team working with the patient.

Similar lines of communication should be opened with the often large number of teachers, tutors, therapists, paraprofessionals, and others who work with the individuals we see. Valuable input to our evaluations can be obtained if sought, and our evaluation findings often provide helpful input for the teaching and therapies provided by these individuals. Rather than operating in an "ivory tower," clinicians should view themselves as only one small part of a comprehensive team of professionals, with whom collaboration and communication is essential and valued by family members. Encouragement of family members to become leaders of their own team also has value, as few are as invested in the totality of a patient's care as are the caregivers.

So how does one provide therapeutic intervention for an individual with an intellectual disability? Many professionals assume that because the patient has limited cognitive abilities, they will not be responsive to our typical arsenal of psychological and other treatments. This assumption may be valid if one thinks only of treatment approaches such as existential psychotherapy or wanting to train an individual to gain insight into the causes of their particular distress. There has nevertheless been clear responsiveness of ID patients to more structured interventions that are administered in a more concrete manner. Indeed, the entire field of Applied Behavior Analysis (ABA) emerged as we learned that through the systematic assessment of the antecedents, purposes and consequences of individual behaviors, we could engineer the environment of the individual so as to modify the frequency of those behaviors. This way of thinking was originally considered to be "behavior modification;" however, this seemed to emphasize changes in the environment only, and it soon became clear that there is a two-way interaction of the individual within his or her environment.

Various behaviors serve different purposes for the individual, and one of the first steps in applying the principles of ABA is to perform a "functional behavioral assessment." Rather than assuming what the purpose of a given behavior might be, the clinician systematically observes the behavior and generates hypotheses as to why both desirable and undesirable behaviors are learned and maintained by the environment. The approach recognizes that, as opposed to classical conditioning, most behaviors serve a purpose for the individual. Thus, classical conditioning might explain why a severely disabled individual might engage in projectile vomiting when taken to a specific treatment room, while operant conditioning likely explains more common behaviors and their development. Although different authorities and organizations use slightly different terminology, behavior typically is thought to serve one of two main functions:

- The behavior allows the individual to get something (attention, tangible goods, pleasant feelings) or
- The behavior allows the person to avoid or escape from something (hunger, embarrassment, punishment)

From this perspective, therefore, behaviors engaged in by the individual with ID serve a purpose and are not random. If we wish to change a behavior, for example, teaching the individual to become toilet trained as opposed to having daily accidents, we must engineer a specific behavioral program that identifies the precursors of the behavior and the consequences for that behavior and then intervene through systematically training and reinforcing the positive steps toward a well-defined goal. The approach is based on the idea that it is easier/better to try to teach a positive skill than it is to try to eliminate a negative behavior. Indeed, one way to think about negative behaviors is the absence of a positive behavior, which if learned would render the negative behavior to be unnecessary. The principles of ABA have a long history of success in working with all children (and pets!).

Current mental health treatment often focuses upon the ideas behind cognitive behavior therapy (CBT), which suggests the idea that it isn't the things of life that are upsetting, it is the way we think about those things. CBT with higher-functioning individuals involves helping them to identify irrational or unhelpful belief patterns that drive automatic negative thinking, which causes distress. With practice, the individual learns to recognize when they engage in upsetting thinking and to substitute more helpful thinking processes, with subsequent reduction in anxiety, depression, etc. What has been found, however, is that children are generally incapable of the self-reflection and abstract thought required by CBT, until they reach a mental age of 8 or 9 years (Kendall, 2004). This has obvious implications for an intellectually disabled youngster, whose mental age may not reach that level, regardless of their chronological age. As such, the use of CBT for persons with intellectual disabilities tends to focus upon training the individual in practicing the use of other-provided self-instruction, positive self-statements, and self-monitoring of unhelpful or challenging behavior. Even if the individual does not understand the philosophical basis for the approach, positive results can be obtained in helping the individual make positive affirmations of competence as a means of enhancing their self-esteem and mood. This type of training is apparent when an ID patient responds to failure on a developmental test by brightly asserting, "I will do the best I can!"

As mentioned above, the use of pharmacological agents is (unfortunately) a frequent first-line intervention effort for individuals with intellectual disabilities. Such interventions nevertheless focus upon treating the comorbid symptoms of intellectual disability and do not address the core cognitive deficits involved. Whereas certain agents, for example, anti-anxiety or antidepressant medicines can be useful in the short term, such treatment approaches should be accompanied by more systematic behavioral interventions, with the goal of ultimately reducing or eliminating the use of medicines. Clinicians also need to be cognizant of the frequently occurring adverse side effects associated with the use of atypical antipsychotic or neuroleptic medications, often involving significant weight gain, sedation, and sometimes serious neurological changes such as tardive dyskinesia. Here again, the identification of a psychiatrist who specializes in working with intellectually disabled youngsters can be of substantial benefit.

A recent trend in working with intellectual disabilities is the recognition and emphasis of what has been termed "person-centered planning" (Armstrong et al., 2011). This approach focuses upon allowing the individual with intellectual disabilities to participate in society to the maximal extent possible, typically through empowering the individual to make choices and decisions that facilitate self-determination. Self-determination theory (Wehmeyer, 2013) emphasizes that individuals should be allowed to make decisions about their own lives, without the pressure or influence of others. In the past, individuals with intellectual disabilities were told what to do or had their lives rigidly programmed by others, whereas current thinking emphasizes the involvement of the individual in freely choosing how to live their life, what programs they wish to attend, and what services they wish to achieve/receive. This approach is based on an assessment of an individual's strengths, responsibility, and freedom to choose. Clinicians involved in the evaluation and treatment of persons with intellectual disabilities must therefore respect and advocate for the ability and rights of individuals with intellectual disabilities to be an active participant in their treatment team. Increasingly, a lifespan perspective is allowing individuals with intellectual disabilities to become married, enjoy sexuality, decline to take medications against their will, and choose the type of residential setting in which they live. Many individuals who, decades ago, would have been presumed to be incapable of living independently, thrive in a supportive environment where autonomy and decision-making are championed and supportive services are limited to areas in which the individual needs active assistance, or during times of crisis. It is important to work to remove barriers to an individual's free choice, which are often based upon archaic or unfounded assumptions.

Conclusions

Our understanding of individuals with intellectual and developmental disabilities has grown substantially over the past 100 years. Advances in genetics and other areas of medicine have taught us the impact of biological factors on the developing brain, and we are increasingly knowledgeable of the differing profiles of strengths and weaknesses associated with different forms of brain impairments. Our focus in assessing ID has gradually shifted away from a global indicator, such as an intelligence quotient on a specific test, to a broader understanding of an individual's capacity to participate in society and the nature of their needs for ongoing support and encouragement. Individuals with ID are important members of our community, have much to offer, and can be a source of joy and wonder in their contributions to our world.

Bibliography

American Association of Intellectual and Developmental Disabilities (AAIDD). (2017a). *Definition of intellectual disability*. Retrieved September 18, 2017, from https://aaidd.org/intellectual-disability/definition#.Wb_wWNOGNTY

American Association of Intellectual and Developmental Disabilities (AAIDD). (2017b). *Supports Intensity Scale*. Retrieved September 18, 2017, from https://aaidd.org/sis#.Wb_2nNOGNTY

American Psychiatric Association (APA). (2013). *Diagnostic and statistical manual of mental disorders* (5th ed.). Arlington, VA: American Psychiatric Association.

American Psychological Association (APA). (2017). *Council meeting minutes*. Retrieved September 18, 2017, from www.apa.org/about/governance/council/index.aspx

Armstrong, K. H., Hangauer, J., Agazzi, H., Nunez, A., & Gieron-Korthals, M. (2011). *The handbook of pediatric neuropsychology* (pp. 537–549). New York: Springer.

Centers for Disease Control and Prevention (CDCP). (2015). *Premature birth*. Retrieved August 9, 2017, from www.cdc.gov/features/prematurebirth/index.html

Edward Thorndike. (n.d.). In *Wikipedia*. Retrieved August 9, 2017, from https://en.wikipedia.org/wiki/Edward_Thorndike

Fletcher, R. J., Barnhill, J., & Cooper, S. A. (2016). *Diagnostic manual—intellectual disability* (2nd ed.). New York, NY: National Association for the Dually Diagnosed.

Flynn, J. R. (1984). The mean IQ of Americans: Massive gains from 1932 to 1978. *Psychological Bulletin, 95*, 29–51.

Francis Galton. (n.d.). In *Wikipedia*. Retrieved August 9, 2017, from https://en.wikipedia.org/wiki/Francis_Galton

Gardere, J. (2015). *Recruiting black males into psychology doctoral programs*. Retrieved August 9, 2017, from www.nationalregister.org/pub/the-national-register-report-pub/the-register-report-spring-2015/recruiting-black-males-into-psychology-doctoral-programs/

Hall v. Florida. (docket number 12–10882) (2014, May 27). *SCOTUSblog*. Retrieved September 17, 2017, from www.scotusblog.com/case-files/cases/freddie-lee-hall-v-florida/

Hallahan, D. P., & Cruickshank, W. M. (1973). *Psychoeducational foundations of learning disabilities*. Princeton, NJ: Prentice-Hall, Inc.

Kendall, P. C., Safford, S., Flannery-Schroeder, E., & Webb, A. (2004). Child anxiety treatment: Outcomes in adolescence and impact on substance use and depression at 7.4-year follow-up. *Journal of Consulting and Clinical Psychology, 72*(2), 276–287.

Levitas, A., Finucane, B., Simone, E. W., Schuster, M., Kates, W. R., Olsszewski, A. K., . . . Danger, N. (2016). Behavioral Phenotypes and Neurodevelopmental Disorders. In R. J. Fletcher, J. Barnhill, & S. A. Cooper (Eds.), *Diagnostic manual—intellectual disability* (2nd ed.). New York, NY: National Association for the Dually Diagnosed.

Lightner Witmer. (n.d.). In *Wikipedia*. Retrieved October 18, 2017, from https://en.wikipedia.org/wiki/Lightner_Witmer

Maulik, P. K., Harbour, C. K., & McCarthy J. (2014). Epidemiology. In E. Tsakanikos & J. McCarthy (Eds.), *Handbook of psychopathology in intellectual disability*. Autism and Child Psychopathology Series. New York, NY: Springer.

Murphy, C. C., Boyle, C., Schendel, D., Decougle, P., & Yeargin-Allsop, M. (1998). Epidemiology of mental retardation in children. *Mental Retardation and Developmental Disabilities Research Reviews, 4*, 6–13.

Museum of Disability History. (2017). *Edward Seguin*. Retrieved September 18, 2017, from http://museumofdisability.org/exhibits/past/pantheon-of-disability-history/edward-seguin/

Reynolds, C. R., Niland, J., Wright, J. E., & Rosenn, M. (2010). Failure to apply the Flynn correction in death penalty litigation: Standard practice of today maybe, but certainly malpractice of tomorrow. *Journal of Psychoeducational Assessment, 28,* 477–481.

Stanovich, K. E. (1986). Matthew effects in reading: Some consequences of individual differences in the acquisition of literacy. *Reading Research Quarterly, 21*(4), 360–407.

Wasserman, J. D. (2012). A history of intelligence assessment. In D. P. Flanagan & P. L. Harrison (Eds.), *Contemporary intellectual assessment* (3rd ed.). New York: Guilford Press.

Wechsler, D. (1946). *Wechsler-Bellevue Intelligence Scale, Form II: Manual for administering and scoring the test.* New York: The Psychological Corporation.

Wehmeyer, M. L. (1992). Self-determination and the education of students with mental retardation. *Education and Training in Mental Retardation,* 302–314.

Wehmeyer, M. L. (Ed.). (2013). *The story of intellectual disability.* Baltimore, MD: Brookes Publishing.

World Health Organization (WHO). (1992). *The ICD-10 classification of mental and behavioural disorders: Clinical descriptions and diagnostic guidelines.* Geneva: World Health Organization.

World Health Organization (WHO). (2015). *Community-based rehabilitation for adults with developmental disorders including intellectual disabilities and autism spectrum disorders.* Retrieved August 9, 2017, from www.who.int/mental_health/mhgap/evidence/child/q16/en/

World Health Organization (WHO). (2016, November 29). *Classifications.* Retrieved August 8, 2017, from www.who.int/classifications/icd/en/

6 Attention and Executive Function Disorders

Children and adolescents often come to the attention of clinicians because someone else is concerned about the child's level of maturity or their readiness for involvement in settings such as school. Because these children often show developmentally immature behaviors, parents are often advised to give them "the gift of time" or another year before they are enrolled in kindergarten or head off to college, and yet lingering concerns remain. Comments that the child "doesn't listen," "daydreams," or is "disorganized" in their activities begin to surface, both in school and when engaged in other activities such as sports teams or other social groups. These are the children who seem more interested in the caterpillar on a blade of grass than in watching the baseball that is being hit to them in the outfield.

The problems these children face do not appear to be secondary to a lack of intelligence or academic competence, and parents will often say that their child pays attention perfectly well when they are engaged in an activity they enjoy, such as playing a video game or watching a movie. Indeed, it is the inconsistency in a child's behavior that seems bewildering to adults in the child's world and leads to a conclusion that if the child *can* do something but *doesn't* always do it, it must be because they are lazy, apathetic, oppositional or choose to not engage. The problem seems to be less about competence and more about performance. This chapter addresses the needs of perhaps the largest group of all referrals for neurodevelopmental evaluations, the children and adolescents who have difficulties with what is commonly diagnosed as an attention-deficit/hyperactivity disorder (ADHD).

Historical Considerations

It may be that the first published discussion of ADHD was by Melchior Adam Weikard, a German physician in the late 1700s, in a medical publication *Der Philosophische Arzt* (Barkley & Peters, 2012). Weikard emphasized the inattentive symptoms of ADHD; however, other healthcare professionals have been aware that there are youngsters who have trouble sitting still, being quiet, and thinking before they act. One of the early descriptions of this behavior occurred in 1848, when Dr. Heinrich Hoffman wrote a story called "Fidgety

Phil." This story was subsequently translated into English and published in the book *Struwwelpeter: Merry Tales and Funny Pictures* (Hoffman, 1848). The opening lines of this poem include:

> Let me see if Philip can
> Be a little gentleman;
> Let me see, if he is able
> To sit still for once at table;
> And Mamma look'd very grave.
> But fidgety Phil,
> He won't sit still;
> He wriggles
> And giggles,
> And then, I declare,
> Swings backwards and forwards
> And tilts up his chair,
> Just like any rocking horse;
> "Philip! I am getting cross!"

George Frederic Still, sometimes referred to as the father of British pediatrics, formalized the condition in a series of lectures to the Royal College of Physicians, in London, in which he described a series of forty-three children who had problems with self-regulation and attention. In one lecture, he noted, "I would point out that a notable feature in many of these cases of moral defect without general impairment of intellect is a quite abnormal incapacity for sustained attention" (Still, 1902).

The idea that these types of behaviors may have a biological basis emerged in the early part of the 1900s, when similar patterns of behavior were observed in children who recovered from an encephalitis outbreak that occurred between 1917 and 1918, and a subsequent influenza pandemic between 1919 and 1920 (Kessler, 1980), which led to the conclusion that the children were showing behaviors that must reflect "brain damage" or what also was called "postencephalitic behavior disorder." Children who had previously shown no symptoms suddenly became hyperactive, impulsive, and distractible following their recovery from their brain infections. However, given that most children who showed the concerning patterns of behavior had no history of brain infection, clinicians in the following years began to suggest that the symptoms we now call ADHD must reflect "minimal brain damage" or "minimal brain dysfunction," terms that found their way into the early diagnostic manuals of psychiatric conditions. Efforts to identify exactly what kind of brain damage or dysfunction was causing the symptoms were unsuccessful, however, and indeed most individuals who are diagnosed with ADHD show no overt symptoms of brain injury or damage.

As the world became embroiled in the World Wars, psychiatrists began to be involved in the healthcare and processing of soldiers, and the emphasis of mental health moved to a primary concern for classification of these individuals, resulting in a modification of the World Health Organization's International Statistical Classification of Diseases (ICD), sixth edition (World Health Organization, 1948), to align with mental disorders recognized primarily in the United States. The first "Diagnostic and Statistical Manual" had as its purpose the differentiation of "organic brain syndromes" from "functional disorders"; however, its focus was primarily upon inpatient psychiatric populations and contained mostly prose descriptions of conditions (Blashfield, Keeley, Flanagan, & Miles, 2014). There were few conditions experienced by children included in these earliest categorical schemata—a fact that changed with the 1968 publication of DSM-II (American Psychiatric Association, 1968), which included categories relevant to outpatient mental health and larger subsets of child and adolescent conditions. ADHD was referred to in this volume as a "hyperkinetic reaction" of childhood, consistent with the view at that time that most childhood disorders were a "reaction" to their progression through stages of psychosexual development and ego identity development.

The term "Attention Deficit Disorder" was first used in the third edition of the DSM, published in 1980 (American Psychiatric Association, 1980). This change in terminology indicated a focus upon problems with attention, in addition to the disruptive behaviors of impulsivity and hyperactivity. Subsequent revisions of the DSM modified the specific diagnostic criteria for ADHD, and in 2013, the fifth and current edition of the DSM was published (American Psychiatric Association, 2013), which continued a tripartite categorization of predominately inattentive, predominately hyperactive-impulsive, and the combined subtypes of ADHD. DSM-5 also increased the number of examples of different symptoms within each category to improve clarity and inter-rater reliability. Four additional hyperactive-impulsive symptoms were added to the list of diagnostic criteria, and the DSM-5 includes examples of behaviors typically shown by older children/adolescents and adults, recognizing the changing and developmental nature of the restlessness component. DSM-5 also included the concept that one could have ADHD "in partial remission" and added severity specifiers of mild, moderate, and severe (American Psychiatric Association, 2013).

Some researchers nevertheless suggest that there is little evidence supporting the differentiation of the subtypes, which are thought to be more similar than different and often show a similar response to medications (Bernfield, 2012). One possible reason for the lack of differentiation among subtypes involves the observed heterogeneity of individuals within the diagnosis. In other words, there are many possible reasons for a person to endorse a given criterion such as "often doesn't seem to listen" and a wide range of symptoms and their severity within the global category of ADHD.

Categorical Diagnosis

Given that DSM-5 defines disorders based on their symptoms and behavioral presentations, the most common approach to the diagnosis of ADHD involves having caregivers and others knowledgeable of an individual's behavior to rate the presence or absence, and possibly the severity, of the various diagnostic criteria. Russell Barkley, in 2006, suggested that all one really needs to make a differential diagnosis of ADHD is a set of behavioral (i.e. observational) rating scales. Barkley suggested that these scales assess the "extended utilitarian zone" in which the diagnosis or disorder can be defined by symptoms that are observable to others (Barkley, 2012, p. 12).

There are indeed many rating scales that purport to document the perception of core symptoms of ADHD, as rated by the patient themselves, their parents or caregivers, and/or their teachers. Yet, behavior rating scales are notoriously unstable and are influenced by who the informants are, by their subjective perspectives, by the specific scale used, and by the way the data from several sources is aggregated (Koziol & Budding, 2012). This conundrum is frequently encountered, clinically. We ask for multiple individuals to complete our questionnaires and inevitably find that the obtained "profiles" are different across the informants. One teacher reports few if any symptoms while another reports multiple concerns at a severe level. One caregiver produces a profile that is inconsistent with another caregiver within the same household. Discussions often ensue as to the motivations of each respondent, and the child/adolescent's self-report is often different from anyone else's. If there is no reliability within the observations of those on whom we depend to provide data for our assessments, is there reliability within the diagnosis itself? If there is no reliability, can the diagnosis be valid? What a mess!

As our understanding of brain development and its functions and impairments increases, we have come to realize that there is likely no single "thing" that is ADHD, and some authors have even suggested that the usefulness of this "label" has come to an end (Wasserman & Wasserman, 2012). Still, research into the characteristics of the disorder must start with some definition of the disorder. We have agreed to use the criteria of DSM-5 to serve the process of diagnosis and to advance research. On some levels, this is helpful, because the U.S. Department of Education, in the fall of 2016, estimated that there were just over 50 million children attending public elementary and secondary schools (National Center for Education Statistics, n.d.), and the American Psychiatric Association has estimated that 5% of children have ADHD (American Psychiatric Association, 2013). Other statistics are much higher, and the Centers for Disease Control reports that 11% of children age 4–17 years of age (i.e. 6.4 million) children have ever been diagnosed with ADHD on parent report forms (Centers for Disease Control and Prevention, 2017). ADHD clearly is something that cannot be ignored. As such, we need to have clear definition of what the symptoms of the condition are and agreed-upon categorical diagnostic criteria for how many of the symptoms are necessary to reach the level of impairment that justifies a diagnosis.

Potential Strategies for Evaluation

Clinical Interview

Chapter 9 covers the process of performing a clinical interview in more detail; however, in the evaluation of ADHD it is important to first identify who is concerned, what the concerns are, and how the behaviors of concern change across situations and circumstances. As opposed to intellectual disability which represents more of a "hardware" problem in learning, ADHD seems to be more of a "software" problem that looks differently at different times.

Caregiver descriptions of ADHD in the younger child often focus upon motor activity and disinhibition. Russell Barkley, in his best-selling book *Taking Charge of ADHD* (Barkley, 2013) describes the condition as a primary disorder of self-control. If one has difficulty "putting on the brakes," one has trouble utilizing rules to govern one's behavior. Disinhibited children live in the moment, blurt things out, and don't think of the consequences of their choices before they make them. The behaviors of such children are often socially challenging and appear to the outsider as being driven primarily by opposition and defiance, sometimes raising concerns among parents and caregivers about whether the child will ever develop a sense of morality.

The interesting thing, however, is that these children are often not poorly behaved in certain other settings, such as the classroom managed by a seasoned teacher who leads a highly structured curriculum. It truly seems that the primary problem for the young child (and sometimes older individuals) who has ADHD is the inability to stop and think, such that they repetitively make impulsive blunders that result in other people becoming upset (rather than their becoming upset themselves). If the environment provides higher levels of structure, explicit rules, prompts for good behavior, and models of such behavior in peers, the child seems to be able to "keep it together" and stay out of trouble.

After school, however, and in the frequently less structured environments of the home, aftercare, or free play, the disinhibited child shows his or her true colors and often has a greater level of difficulty. What is important to recognize is that these children generally do not lack a moral compass, and when questioned, they can tell you the difference between right and wrong or the rule that they should have followed had they stopped to think about it. The failure to put on the brakes nevertheless results in these children regularly getting into trouble before they stop to realize what they have done, with parents in exasperation repeating, "I've told you 1,000 times. . . ." Most commonly this type of child is a boy, although Kathleen Nadeau describes girls with similar characteristics that she refers to as "tomboys." Some of these girls are also disinhibited, frequently hyperactive, and prone to more risk-taking activities than other girls, but they are different from boys with similar characteristics in that they are generally more cooperative at home and may work harder to please parents and teachers (Nadeau, 2017).

At about the same time that Barkley was discussing his model of disinhibition as the primary deficit in ADHD, Thomas Brown forwarded a model that emphasized that most ADHD-related impairments were in the realm of executive functions (Brown, 2013). While both authors acknowledge the biological underpinnings of the various difficulties, Brown emphasized that the primary difficulties experienced by individuals who have ADHD are in the areas of organization, prioritizing, and activating to work. Brown emphasized attention as defined by the ability to focus, sustain, and shift one's focus; the ability to regulate one's alertness; and the capacity for sustained effort and processing speed. Finally, Brown pointed to challenges in the emotional regulatory skills needed to manage frustrations and modulate emotions, as well as the cognitive regulation needed to utilize working memory and to recall information from memory. Thus, as opposed to focusing upon the symptoms traditionally described as fitting within the hyperactive-impulsive subtype of ADHD, Brown began to emphasize the inattentive symptoms and the fact that these were the core difficulties children and adolescents experience, particularly as the demands of the environment increase toward later childhood and as one enters adulthood. This does not invalidate the concept of ADHD; it emphasizes the dynamic nature of neurodevelopmental disorders.

Questionnaire-Based Assessment

Next to a symptom based diagnostic interview, the second most commonly performed evaluation procedure in the diagnosis of ADHD is the provision of a behavior checklist that the caregivers are asked to complete. This is typically the default strategy of pediatricians, family practice physicians, and other primary care health providers. Many of these checklists and questionnaires are freely available and serve to give some indication of the frequency and severity of the most common manifestations of the condition in question. Perhaps the most commonly used tool in pediatric practices is the first edition (2002) of the Vanderbilt Assessment Scales, which can be downloaded for free from the National Institute for Children's Health Quality (NICHQ), if the NICHQ is credited as the original source (National Institute for Children's Health Quality, 2002). There are also other, primarily research oriented tools such as the Swanson, Nolan and Pelham Questionnaire (SNAP), with these questionnaires having the benefit of having been used over extended periods of time in multiple research investigations. As is the case with many methodologies nevertheless, the free versions of these and other questionnaires are being replaced by revised questionnaires for which one needs to purchase their usage. The Vanderbilt Scales, for example, have now become a part of a more comprehensive toolkit for caring for children with ADHD, which is sold by the American Academy of Pediatrics (American Academy of Pediatrics, 2017), while the SNAP questionnaires are now licensed through DefiniPoint. com (DefiniPoint, 2017).

Other commercially available questionnaires include the Behavior Assessment System for Children (Reynolds & Kamphaus, 2015); the Conners Comprehensive Behavior Rating Scales (Conners, 2008); the Child Behavior Checklist (Achenbach, 2001); the Barkley Home Situations Questionnaire (Barkley, 1997); and several more. Each of these questionnaires are useful in that they not only rate the presence or absence of symptoms of ADHD, but they provide indications of the severity of impairment and screen for other common child and adolescent adjustment disorders that are frequently comorbid with ADHD, such as oppositional-defiant disorder, anxiety, depression, etc. Like most categorical diagnoses, ADHD is rarely found in isolation and comorbidity is the rule, rather than the exception. Most of the above questionnaires also are provided in forms that can be completed by parents/caregivers, teachers, and self-report on the part of the child/adolescent. Gathering multiple perspectives on rating scales that rank symptom presence and severity as compared with age- and gender-specific normative data can be of great help in assisting the evaluator determine the nature and extent of distress with which the youngster presents.

In addition to these rather broad questionnaires, there are also more specific questionnaires focused upon the concept of executive functions. The Behavior Rating Inventory of Executive Functions (Gioia, Isquith, Guy, & Kenworthy, 2015); the Comprehensive Executive Function Inventory (Naglieri & Goldstein, 2013); and the Barkley Deficits in Executive Functioning Scale (Barkley, 2011) are all useful in specifically asking questions about the day-to-day manifestation of executive function deficits within an ecologically valid strategy. It will be recalled that many of the executive function impairments that are commonly attributed to ADHD also exist in other psychiatric categorical diagnoses, and these scales can be useful to reflect the dimensions of executive functions that are observable in the daily life of the child/adolescent with several different diagnoses.

Direct Testing of Attention

An argument could be made that, if we are attempting to diagnose the presence of an attention disorder, we should administer direct cognitive measures of the construct of attention. This is the rationale behind the common use of computerized measures of attention to determine symptom presence and severity. These measures ask the patient to focus their attention on either an auditory or visual stimulus (or both) which is presented in a controlled fashion over an extended period of time. The patient is asked to respond to one form of stimulus and to not respond to others. Measurement of the speed of responsiveness, errors of incorrectly responding, errors of not correctly responding, and the overall variability of the patient's performance over time can be compared with normative data for how the average individual of that age and gender might perform. Some of these instruments provide a clinical cutoff score that purportedly differentiates individuals who are more similar to clinically diagnosed ADHD patients versus a control group, giving the impression that performance on these tests is diagnostic of the condition.

Unfortunately, diagnosis is not that simple, and the authors of the tests caution clinicians not to base decisions solely upon the scores obtained. Indeed, disorders of attention as measured by continuous performance tests may actually reflect another causative factor, such as an individual who has a sleep disorder (and has multiple lapses in daytime alertness as a consequence) or perhaps even certain forms of a seizure disorder. Indeed, Barkley is adamant that "the majority of individuals with ADHD are not impaired on neuropsychological [executive function] tests, even if groups of ADHD cases differ in mean scores from control groups on many such tests" (Barkley, 2012). We should remember that ADHD is a behavioral disorder and not necessarily a defined cognitive disorder. As will be seen, however, a shift in perspective may change this line of thinking.

Dimensional Diagnosis

Our gradually refined understanding of how the brain and behavior are related has led to a shift in the way various neurodevelopmental conditions are conceptualized. Some of our theoretical advances are based upon psychological models, some on models of neurological organization and function, and some based upon conceptual shifts at the highest levels of science. Changing perspectives, in turn, have led to changing models on how the assessment of ADHD should be performed.

The Integration of Psychological and Biological Models

Many individuals who have been diagnosed with ADHD seem to be capable of performing assigned tasks and chores but infuriatingly do not. These are the youngsters the parents describe as "lazy," "apathetic," or "unmotivated." In England, Edmund Sonuga-Barke has been studying this phenomenon and brings to our attention the differentiation between executive functions as cognitively based aspects of ADHD, on the one hand, and the motivationally based components of ADHD that implicate altered reward processes, on the other. Sonuga-Barke identifies a "delay aversion" subtype of ADHD in which one's motivational style is characterized by attempts to escape or avoid delay (Sonuga-Barke, 2003). This is similar to other recent suggestions that one subtype of ADHD may represent an "intention" disorder rather than an "attention" disorder and may related to the functions of a specific area of the brain, the nucleus accumbens.

Durston, van Belle, and de Zeeuw (2011) has expanded this concept by suggesting that ADHD represents dysfunction in any of three neurobiological circuits that differentially affect cognitive control, reward processing, and affective timing/one's ability to build temporal prediction. While thinking has previously localized ADHD as a "frontal lobe" dysfunction, Durston's model goes beyond this idea to include the cerebellum, within a broader model of cortical-subcortical connectivity. Indeed, timing and speed have started to find their ways into thinking of several researchers in ADHD, and the January 2014 edition of the *Journal of Abnormal Child Psychology* was entirely devoted to the concept that a "sluggish cognitive tempo" might represent yet another subtype or form of ADHD. Also, as research into the functions of the basal ganglia (a subcortical area of the brain) progresses, we are learning of concepts such as "time discounting" and "intolerance of uncertainty" (King, Shin, Taylor, Mattek, Chavez, & Whalen, 2017), representing our growing appreciation of the fine distinctions between specific dimensions of behavior. In sum, dimensional models of ADHD are moving beyond description and the determination of whether one "fits" a behavioral category, to more of an understanding of the underlying biobehavioral mechanisms driving behavior.

The Human Connectome Project (n.d.) represents one example of the new approaches to understanding the brain. This collaboration between the University of Southern California's Laboratory of Neuro Imaging and the Martinos Center for Biomedical Imaging at Massachusetts General Hospital has as its goal the construction of a map of the complete structural and functional neural connections of the brain. While producing spectacular images of the major brain pathways, this project hopes to map the essential circuits of the brain, to allow us to explore the cells of various areas of brain and the functions that depend upon those cells. What becomes abundantly clear is that a problem in one section of a circuit has far-reaching consequences and implications for other sections of that circuit. We are therefore turning our attention away from specific locations or areas of the brain, to the study of behaviors and skills that are reflective of complicated circuits and networks of brain "wiring."

Such brain science is helping us to understand the interacting influence of multiple networks. For example, a "ventral attentional network" has been shown to be involved in our processing of object shapes and forms which helps us to understand the "what" aspects of our world. On the other hand, a "dorsal attentional network" has been identified as being involved in object location and helps us to process "where" and "how" aspects of what we do. Additionally, and relevant to ADHD, initial work focusing upon a "default network" seems to suggest that we have differing levels of activity depending upon whether we are engaged in active processing of information in a goal-directed manner or, conversely, are in neutral or at rest. Koziol, Budding, and Chidiekel (2013) have in fact suggested that the brain's failure to inhibit this default network may be at the core of ADHD.

Next, as if understanding the structural components of the brain is not difficult enough, psychiatry reminds us that the brain operates on the basis of electricity and chemistry. One of the true miracles of medicine has been the discovery that stimulant medications can effectively treat the symptoms of the vast majority of individuals who have been diagnosed with ADHD. Medications such as Ritalin and Adderall have become some of the most frequently prescribed medicines in child and adolescent mental health. Stephen

M. Stahl, in *Stahl's Essential Psychopharmacology* (Stahl, 2013), nevertheless clarifies that many of the individual symptoms assigned to specific diagnoses, such as ADHD or Bipolar Disorder, actually cut across multiple psychiatric disorders that share impairment in the various executive dysfunctions. From Stahl's perspective, ADHD is not comprised of two subtypes but various combinations of four subtypes as well as the influence of comorbid conditions. Stahl relates the symptom clusters within ADHD to inefficient information processing in the brain circuits connecting frontal regions through subcortical structures such as the basal ganglia and thalamus, returning to the prefrontal lobes in a "feedback loop." Thus, symptoms of hyperactivity are related to the prefrontal motor cortex; symptoms of impulsivity are tied to the orbitofrontal cortex (OFC), troubles with selective attention are localized to the dorsal anterior cingulate cortex (ACC), and troubles with sustained attention and problem solving are associated with the dorsolateral prefrontal cortex (DLPFC). While such vocabulary seems obscure to the clinician who has not studied neuroanatomy and neuropsychology, Stahl's concepts suggest that there are brain "neighborhoods" that drive how a child or adolescent presents in daily life. The student who has trouble sustaining mental effort, seems disorganized, and has trouble finishing tasks is likely to have trouble in the DLPFC, while in contrast the student who makes careless mistakes, doesn't attend to details, doesn't listen, loses things, and seems distracted and forgetful is more likely to have troubles in the ACC. Hyperactivity is also viewed as distinct from impulsivity.

Stahl's model is important in recognizing that the symptoms of ADHD are not only tied to different brain regions but that different chemical processes are likely at work. Stahl suggests that one can have symptoms of ADHD because of poor "tuning" of the circuits feeding these brain regions. The brain's circuitry operates on the basis of electrical transmission of impulses down nerves to the point where they attempt to communicate with other nerves—the so-called "synapse." Communication at the synapse occurs chemically, i.e. the electrical signal that arrives at the end of the nerve's axon causes bubbles of various chemicals, neurotransmitters, to move to the surface of the nerve ending and release its "messengers" into the gap between the two nerves. As the messenger chemical floats across to the receiving neuron, various channels open to accept the messenger, which causes the receiving nerve to react in certain ways that either facilitate or inhibit communication and firing of the nerves downstream, within the circuit. In the case of ADHD, the two chemicals that seem to be most important are norepinephrine and dopamine. Stahl explains that from a biochemical perspective, ADHD is a disorder reflecting inefficient "tuning" of the prefrontal cortex by dopamine and norepinephrine. The concept of tuning refers to the fact that optimal functioning of the brain relies upon a balance between not enough and too much firing of the neurons containing these chemicals. Imbalances in norepinephrine and dopamine within certain circuits cause inefficient information processing and results in the symptoms of ADHD tied to the specific region of the brain in which the abnormality occurs. Thus, norepinephrine at modest levels can improve prefrontal cortical functioning by stimulating certain nerves but leads to impaired working memory when too much norepinephrine is involved. Similarly, low to moderate, but not high, levels of dopamine stimulation can be beneficial, and the key seems to be an optimal balance of neither too much nor too little stimulation.

Direct, "Objective" Testing in ADHD

While understanding the emerging science of ADHD is interesting and will direct the future of assessment and intervention, clinicians at the current time must still have methods of direct testing of the most common areas of impairment experienced by individuals with ADHD. It is become increasingly clear that ADHD is less a disorder of competence and more disorder of performance. Barkley (2012) suggests that this distinction roughly follows "back of the brain" as opposed to "front of the brain" functions, and he emphasizes that traditional tests of cognitive abilities such as intelligence and academic achievement (which measure more posterior brain functions) have little value in ADHD assessment. We are thus tasked with the goal of deciding upon what measures can be used to evaluate what have come to be called the "executive functions." These are the self-regulatory capabilities which allow us to utilize our intelligence in managing the requirements of day-to-day living and problem solving.

One set of executive functions rely upon the concept of inhibition. The individual who is disinhibited, who does not think before they act, or who blurts out comments that they might have reconsidered if given time to think are all examples of the kind of difficulties associated with inhibitory control. Dating back to the work of Vygotsky, developmental psychologists have learned that socialization involves the development of internal rules for our behavior (Flavell, 1992). The hungry toddler who reaches for the cookie jar is repeatedly exposed to the patient mother's explanation that having a cookie will spoil his appetite for dinner and that he must wait. Rather than having the immediate gratification of eating a cookie, therefore, the toddler learns that mother's approval or disapproval is dependent upon following mother's rules. With repeated exposure, over time, even when mother is not present, the child remembers mother's voice and learns to self-inhibit the impulse to reach for a cookie. Vygotsky suggests that this is the product of the internalization of language and suggests that such internal "self-talk" is the origin of what we ultimately describe as "thinking." We have conversations in our head in which we imagine discussions back and forth with other people, consider alternatives and varying perspectives, and gradually learn that our behavior leads to the best outcome when we comply with socially accepted norms. We develop rule-governed behavior. Learning to "put on the brakes" is an essential component of growing up and must be achieved to a certain level prior to entering daycare, preschool, and certainly by kindergarten. Remembering the "rules" for various situations allows us to engage on a social level and to be accepted by various individuals, groups, and settings. If we stray too far from the rules for acceptable behavior, corrective feedback is given to return us to the correct path.

Another component of the "hot" executive functions involves emotional regulation. As an infant, one of our few ways of communicating our needs is through crying, yelling, and otherwise demonstrating our distress. Behavioral action in the service of communication continues through the toddler years, as exemplified by the temper tantrums of a young child who does not get their way. With time and hopefully contingent and differential responsiveness on the part of the parent, the child learns that certain methods of communicating their needs work better than others. Parents teach children to "use your words" and will send children to "time out" to allow the child the opportunity to learn emotional self-regulation and how to calm down. Many clinicians therefore include emotional regulation within the broad category of executive functioning and suggest that self-control involves an interaction between the frontal lobes of the brain and more subcortical, limbic structures.

As opposed to the above emotional and behavioral self-regulatory abilities, cool executive functions reflect one's ability to utilize *cognitive* processes in the service of problem solving. If one defines intelligence and information processing as a "back of the brain" capacity, it is the front of the brain that governs the utilization of one's intelligence for specific purposes. Many students struggle with these processes as they progress through school. It is common for children who previously had few difficulties with behavioral regulation or emotional management to first come to the attention of clinicians around the entrance to middle school, as they must utilize executive functions to read longer passages of text, to write papers, and to give oral presentations. Even the brightest of students will fail in these pursuits if they don't know how to organize their thoughts, sequence their ideas, and express them in a coherent manner. The cool executive functions are therefore involved in the demonstration of our knowledge and in performance rather than competence.

From the perspective of how we should measure these skills, one can break the cool executive functions down into subcategories. The first involves a broad concept of attention, which really encompasses multiple, separate, and different processes. If someone says, "Pay Attention!" they may be referring to your failure to disengage from some activity to focus upon new information. Pay attention may also refer to an inability to differentiate between important versus unimportant information in the material that is presented to you. The term "attention span" is sometimes used to refer to how much information one can manage at any one time, whereas divided attention refers to one's ability to rapidly switch between two different areas of focus. Scanning attention is the process of systematically reviewing larger quantities of information while searching for a specific target, while sustained attention relates to one's ability to stick with a task over an extended period of time, while resisting distraction.

If one can initially orient their attention and focus upon what is being asked of them, back of the brain processes that include perception, visuospatial integration, language processing, and comparison of new information with our stores of previously learned knowledge can then occur. Still, we have a limited capacity to process new information. Most researchers agree that we can hold between five and nine "chunks" of information in our short-term memory. This is why we break telephone numbers into groups of three and four numbers or why Social Security numbers consist of groups from two to four numbers in length. Most people simply can't remember much more information in any one chunk. If we are asked to hold and mentally manipulate sequences of information in our immediate awareness, for us to reach the goal of solving a presented problem, we are next discussing what is referred to as "working memory." Remembering multiple-step directions becomes essential as parents train us to perform sequenced steps of operation. Remembering what a teacher just said allows us to summarize in written form our "notes" that will allow us to study later and remember new information. Holding a vision of what a completed project would "look like" in our mind helps us to persist in our efforts to solve tasks that may involve multiple steps, such as cleaning our bedroom or writing a several-page essay.

Clearly, the necessity of holding sequences of information in one's mind as one works their way through a problem makes it more difficult. Parents will often smile if you ask them what their 6-year-old might accomplish if you ask them to "Take your plate to the sink, go put on your pajamas, brush your teeth and come out to say goodnight!" We simply have a limited capacity for processing much more than a limited amount of information at any one time, and this capacity seems to be even more limited in some individuals, including those diagnosed with ADHD.

If we assume that the child can hold information in their immediate awareness, they must next develop a coherent plan of attack for how to go about the task. This involves the development of a strategy, the consideration of alternative approaches, and weighing the relative strengths and weaknesses of each option. Having chosen a strategy, the child must next initiate the utilization of the given plan or strategy and monitor how well it is working. If the plan is working, the child needs to persist in their efforts, stick with it, and finish the task. If the plan is not working, alternatively, the child needs to recognize this fact, stop what they are doing, and shift their strategy to something that is hopefully more effective. Many individuals are highly intelligent, but when it comes to performing some form of focused task, they come across as "scattered" and absent-minded. They seem to have good ideas but never seem to get anything accomplished. Alternatively, they jump into the use of a certain kind of strategy which clearly doesn't work, and yet they struggle to recognize this fact and continue to persist in doing things that are ineffective.

Returning to the role of the examiner, as one might expect, the evaluation of hot and cool executive functions requires different strategies. We have devised certain tasks for which we have obtained normative data as to what is typical or "average" for an individual of a given age and in some cases gender. We can thus measure how much information a person can hold in their working memory and decide if it is equivalent to, stronger than, or deficient relative to similar age peers. We have computerized tests that can determine how well one can sustain one's attention on long and boring activities, and we have elaborate problem-solving assessment methodologies that can determine our efficiency, flexibility, and speed of problem solving.

What is increasingly becoming recognized, however, is that a task that measures a certain kind of executive function the first time is administered, does not measure that same skill set the second time the individual is exposed. Thus, for example, we may attempt to observe how systematic and organized a person's problem-solving strategies are by giving them a complex drawing to copy. We might then evaluate their working memory and memory-encoding skills by asking them to redraw that drawing after the model has been removed, both immediately and after period of delay. But what if you have been through a previous evaluation where this drawing test was administered, and when it is presented again, you think, "Oh, I remember this!" When this happens, the task is not novel and measures executive functions to a lesser degree. Are you measuring the same capability, or has the individual developed an internal representation of the task that facilitates their performance the second time? An analogy can be found in cooking. If one attempts to fry an egg but either burns or over cooks the egg because the heat is too high, the next time around, we might remember to have the heat setting lower. When we evaluate such learning, or if one is given multiple opportunities to perform a given task, we need to pay attention to how an individual's performance changes with each repeated exposure.

Another important consideration for individuals who perform evaluations of ADHD is that many commercially available psychological tests do not measure what it seems that they should measure, based upon the name of the test. If one takes, for example, the concept of "working memory," several broad scale intellectual assessment tests have working memory subscales. The Wechsler scales, for example, measure working memory through performance upon several subtests, such as a digit span forward task, a digit span backwards task, a digits sequencing task, and a picture span task (Wechsler, 2014). Scores from these individual tests are integrated and produce an overall working memory "index." The problem is that each of these individual subtests measure different cognitive variables. Digits forward, which asks you to hold increasingly long strings of numbers in your immediate memory and to then repeat the sequence when asked, is a very different task from digits backwards, where one must hold increasingly long sequences of digits in mind but then repeat them in reverse order from that presented. Digits backward seems to be a stronger measure of working memory then digits forward; however, the tradition over the years has been to report combined scores from the subtests as if they represented a unitary variable.

Another consideration is that a set of tasks described as reflecting a certain cognitive skill such as "processing speed" are typically very different from one test to another. One kind of test may measure processing speed by how quickly one can learn a number-symbol coding scheme and demonstrate that knowledge through drawing using paper and pencil. Another task of processing speed might involve searching for a target symbol within rows of distractor symbols. Yet another processing speed task might measure how quickly one can name pictures of objects. It is not uncommon, therefore, for a student that one is evaluating to obtain a processing speed index score that is within the Average range on one test instrument, but below average on a different test that is also labeled a measure of processing speed. It is incumbent upon the evaluator to understand exactly what the tests that we administer measures and how different tools evaluate different aspects of what might erroneously presumed to be a single dimension of cognition or behavior. Indeed, some authorities are increasingly raising concern that the entire concept of "executive functions" is losing its usefulness, much as categorical diagnoses like ADHD are becoming less useful.

Despite the controversy, it seems clear that an effort to evaluate performance, rather than competence, is an important component of evaluating difficulties with self-regulation and self-control. Athletic coaches refer to this as how coachable an athlete is. In athletics, coaches first tell the athlete what they will do, demonstrate the skill, have the athlete practice the skill, and repetitively provide opportunities for honing the skill with the goal of eventually turning it into "muscle memory." Cognitive activities can take the same course, with repetitive exposure resulting in more efficient problem solving, modification through the experience of success and failure, and adjustment according to the situation and the problem presented. The measurement of executive functions is therefore not a robotic process. Indeed, some of the executive functions have as yet managed to escape our ability to reliably measure them in any objective fashion. To state that someone has an executive function disorder, such as ADHD, therefore becomes complicated.

There are dimensions of impact of any condition, and we must ask how the specific symptoms of concern impact the individual on a day-to-day basis. It is also important to consider how the symptoms impact the family system and what changes in interaction patterns, family roles, and interpersonal boundaries were necessitated by the fact that the individual has a symptom. If two children in the family seem to have no difficulty waking up in the morning, getting dressed, and being ready to leave by the time the school bus arrives, but a third child seems incapable of remembering the sequence of these activities from day-to-day and requires more of the caregiver's time and energy, there will develop a natural shift in the balance of interpersonal relationships within the family. If this child is then chronically late and not ready to leave for school, how does that impact the other siblings and/or other caregivers?

Perhaps one of the most important roles in evaluator can take, therefore, is to help to differentiate for the individual and family system whether an individual cannot perform skills needed at a given age and in given situations, as distinct from the case in which the individual has the skills but doesn't perform them on a consistent basis. It is often quite exasperating for parents to recognize that the youngster can do things when it is of interest to them or they are motivated to perform the task, but then doesn't do the thing when it is expected, independently and without parental supervision.

Potential Strategies for Intervention

The specific strategies one can use to intervene with ADHD and other executive function disorders will depend upon the clinician's differentiation of whether the behaviors of concern reflect "can't" versus "doesn't" versus "won't." If one concludes that an individual can't perform a desired skill, then we need to teach that individual how to perform that skill. Remember that many caregivers view children's failure to perform certain skills as willful and oppositional. It is easy to have a knee-jerk reaction to what we view as a "negative" behavior by becoming frustrated, angry, and upset with the child. Before we jump to the conclusion that their failure to perform the activity is an act of disobedience, however, it is important for us to break down the skill into its individual components and evaluate whether the child can in fact perform the steps required. A child who has trouble getting dressed in the morning may have difficulties with fine motor control that leads to troubles with buttons, zippers, shoelace time, etc. If this is the case, then we need to identify which specific skills need assistance and systematically go about training the needed skills or bypassing the problem, for example, by providing shoes with Velcro fasteners.

For the middle school student who has great difficulty writing essays and term papers, we need to know where the problem lies. Is it in their understanding of the presented task, the identification of information to be presented in the paper, the formulation of their ideas about that information, the organization of the facts in a systematic manner, the process of handwriting or typing the ideas, or the awareness of the necessity of planning ahead and breaking the larger task into smaller components, with timelines for their completion? The student who has not completed their written work on Thursday night, when it is due on Friday morning, clearly has a problem. What is not clear is where the difficulty lies and what assistance that student might need.

It is beyond the scope of this book to provide systematic strategies for assessment of and intervention into the numerous components of the self-regulatory difficulties experienced in ADHD. There are, nevertheless, excellent guidebooks toward the process, such as Peg Dawson and Richard Guare's *Executive Skills in Children and Adolescents: A Practical Guide to Assessment and Intervention* (Dawson & Guare, 2010). This manual systematically provides guidance on the assessment of executive skills, and how to link assessments to the processes of intervention, and offers specific intervention strategies to promote executive skills development in various common areas of difficulty. Ideas about how to teach executive function skills emerged from rehabilitation work with traumatic brain injuries and the recognition that certain acquired neurological conditions result in an individual no longer knowing how to do things which most people seem to have no trouble with (Ylvisaker & Feeney, 1998).

When one is attempting to teach executive function skills, one must first break larger skill sets into smaller and specific skills. We next must establish a procedure or methodology for teaching the skills involved and provide initial prompting and supervision of the youngster in the performance of these activities. We have learned from social learning theory, however, that effective learning requires strategies to ensure generalization of skill learning and strategies to ensure maintenance of the new behavior(s). We thus should identify prompts that will assist the youngster in remembering the steps to take, structure to allow the youngster to recognize the progress they are making as they complete each successive step, and provide feedback to help improve performance of the child as they work their way through the task. Initially we need to praise and reinforce each step along the way, gradually fading both prompts and rewards as the behavior becomes more habitual. Next, we need to chain individual behaviors into sequences of behavior, again with prompts, reminders, and reinforcement until the sequence of behavior can be completed independently, without supervision. Most of the executive function skill sets can be taught, if a sufficiently explicit, systematic, and focused approach is utilized.

Some of the concerns we face, however, reflect less of a skill deficit and more an indication of a biological substrate for the symptom. It has long been recognized that telling an individual who has clinical depression to "cheer up!" simply doesn't work. If our evaluation is to be useful for our patients, we must be scientific in our appraisal of the efficacy of the recommendations we make. This leads to the concept of "evidence-based" intervention, and clinicians need to be aware of scientific research that investigates whether a specific strategy or intervention "works." In the case of ADHD, for example, there is clear evidence that the use of stimulant medications is highly effective in managing symptoms in the vast majority of individuals. It is also clear, however, the simply asserting that a stimulant medicine would be helpful for ADHD is insufficient. There are multiple stimulant preparations, with multiple different pharmacological mechanisms and pharmacokinetic profiles, the understanding of which is highly complex (Shier, Reichenbacher, Ghuman, & Ghuman, 2013).

Over the years, probably the most commonly utilized medication is methylphenidate, originally marketed as Ritalin. This medication has its impact through a process of blocking the reuptake of a specific neurotransmitter, dopamine, into the presynaptic terminal at the point where brain circuitries communicate. Methylphenidate also seems to block the transporter for norepinephrine but does not seem to result in an impact upon the vesicular monoamine transporter (VMAT) in the presynaptic terminal. The amphetamine class of medications, such as Adderall, also block the transporters for norepinephrine and dopamine but do so in a different manner than methylphenidate (see Stahl, 2013, for more information). Both methylphenidate and amphetamine seem to be highly effective when dopamine and norepinephrine levels are too low in the prefrontal cortex of the brain; however, as already discussed, having too high a level of these neurotransmitters is also problematic. It is important to recognize that different preparations of stimulant medicines have different timelines of impact, such that some seem to have a rapid onset and don't last very long, some have a steady onset and withdrawal but with essentially equivalent impact levels throughout the day, and some preparations have a slow onset but a greater level of impact later in the day.

Medication treatment for ADHD can also take a different approach, such as the use of non-stimulant medications. The norepinephrine reuptake inhibitor atomoxetine (Strattera) is increasingly being utilized in the management of ADHD. Likewise, comorbid conditions may require a combination of medications such as a stimulant combined with guanfacine (Intuniv) or clonidine. The take-home message is that, for many individuals, the self-regulatory difficulties which we describe as ADHD reflect underlying brain circuitries and a lack of fine tuning of nerve circuits. Medication treatment for ADHD is, according to current evidence, the most effective means of treating this biological dysfunction. Medication is not, however, a "one-size-fits-all" process, and clinicians will benefit from building a relationship with a physician expert in understanding these issues. It is gratifying to have a follow-up appointment with a family who, following a recommendation to speak to their physician about a trial of medications, comes back with smiles and says, "He's a new child!"

It is also clearly the case that ADHD and other self-regulatory disorders do not occur in isolation and that an essential component of managing these disorders is the education, involvement, and support of the individual's family. For many individuals, the diagnosis of these conditions is a life-changing event, which can take some getting used to. I find it useful to refer individuals to support sources, whether online, through reading, or through attendance at family support network organizations. The organization Children and Adults with Attention Deficit Disorder (www.ChADD.org) not only has a website that presents useful, scientifically verified information and recommendations/ strategies, it also has a nationwide network of support group meetings, typically organized around a monthly get-together where some professional within the community gives a presentation and attendees benefit from contact with other individuals in a similar situation, establish networks of support, share ideas, etc. This is not the only organization to offer this service, and there are certainly other website-based support programs and sources of information, for example, www.additudemag.com, www.adda.com, among others. It is important for clinicians to be familiar with these organizations and websites and to verify that the groups are substantially research based, free from commercial influence, and indeed helpful. Here, the website www.infoaboutkids. org can be useful in its review of multiple internet sites focused upon children. Bibliotherapy is also very helpful for many individuals. Reading the stories of other individuals who have gone through similar life experiences to your own allows for a sense that one is not alone and that there is hope through learning about knowledge gained by others.

Finally, the individual who is the recipient of our focus and diagnosis needs to be an important and active member of the treatment team. Increasingly there are materials available that help to explain ADHD to youngsters of different ages, in a format and methodology that is accessible to their level of development. Normalization of the child's experience, combined with an explanation as to why they may have trouble sitting still, perform impulsive actions, or can't seem to remember to turn in their homework, can be uplifting and reassuring and help to minimize secondary concerns of anxiety, depression, somatic aches and pains, and plummeting self-esteem. It is important to recognize the spectrum of executive function disorders is not based primarily in psychological conflict and that therefore psychotherapy is typically of limited use or benefit. Nevertheless, some individuals will benefit from focused psychotherapeutic interventions geared to specific needs that that individual may have. Appropriate assertiveness training, learning progressive muscle relaxation and deep breathing techniques, and using positive self-statements and affirmations can all be useful in helping the youngster to realize that ADHD is only one part of themselves. Social skills education can be helpful but should occur in an ecologically valid setting, such as group interactions or other structured activities. It is probably less helpful to teach individual skills in isolation, as most individuals with ADHD know what they should do, they just don't do it. Preventive self-esteem activities such as involvement on athletic teams, theater groups, or religious and non-religious support groups can all be helpful.

Conclusions

Neurodevelopmental disorders are not "things" and alternatively represent strengths and weaknesses within a functioning brain. The ability of the brain to efficiently perform a given task seems to change rapidly, depending upon the nature of the task, the demands placed upon the brain, and the organism's capacity for regulation of the underlying brain functions and circuitries. ADHD represents a broad category of potential impairment, and there are many more than two subtypes. From this point of view, categorical diagnosis becomes even less tenable, as one must not only ask if the child or adolescent meets the diagnostic criteria of some taxonomy, but more importantly we must perform an assessment that helps to tease apart the various components of the individual's struggles. A dimensional approach can help to explain, and not just label, a condition. It is more important to describe than to categorize, as what the individual and their family will do next depends in large part upon understanding what the problem is at a level that directs treatment.

The diagnosis of ADHD and other executive function disorders is complex and likely needs to go beyond the simple use of a checklist. Clinicians need to rule out alternative causes, document areas of strength and weakness, and devise treatment plans for which there is published research from well-designed studies. ADHD is very common in our population, and although some claim that the condition is over-diagnosed, it is likely that in fact the opposite is true. Still, many in mental health are quick to suggest that individuals' difficulties with managing daily demands is the result of personality inadequacies or adjustment problems, rather than considering that the challenges may be beyond an individual's conscious control. We should take care to not blame our patients and instead maintain our questioning stance of asking what, where, when, and how before we jump to why.

Bibliography

Achenbach, T. M. (2001). *Manual for the ASEBA school-age forms and profiles*. Burlington, VT: University of Vermont, Research Center for Children, Youth and Families.

American Academy of Pediatrics (AAP). (2017). *Caring for children with ADHD: A resource toolkit for clinicians*. Retrieved August 9, 2017, from https://shop.aap.org/Caring-for-Children-with-ADHD-A-Resource-Toolkit-for-Clinicians/

American Psychiatric Association (APA). (1968). *Diagnostic and statistical manual of mental disorders* (2nd ed.). Washington, DC: American Psychiatric Association.

American Psychiatric Association (APA). (1980). *Diagnostic and statistical manual of mental disorders* (3rd ed.). Arlington, VA: American Psychiatric Association.

American Psychiatric Association (APA). (2013). *Diagnostic and statistical manual of mental disorders* (5th ed.). Arlington, VA: American Psychiatric Association.

Attention-Deficit/Hyperactivity Disorder (ADHD). (n.d.). Retrieved August 28, 2017, from www.cdc.gov/ncbddd/adhd/data.html

Barkley, R. A. (1997). *Home situations questionnaire*. New York: Guilford.

Barkley, R. A. (2011). *Barkley deficits in executive functioning scale*. New York: Guilford.

Barkley, R. A. (2012). *Executive functions: What they are, how they work, and why they evolved*. New York: Guilford.

Barkley, R. A. (2013). *Taking charge of ADHD*. New York: Guilford.

Barkley, R. A., & Peters, H. (2012). The earliest reference to ADHD in the medical literature? Melchior Adam Wikard's description in 1775 of attention deficit (Mangel der Aufmerksamkeit, Attentio Volubilis). *Journal of Attention Disorders, 16*, 623–630.

Bernfield, J. (2012). ADHD and factor analysis: Are there really three distinct subtypes of ADHD? *Applied Neuropsychology: Child, 1*, 1–5.

Blashfield, R. K., Keeley, J. W., Flanagan, E. H., & Miles, S. R. (2014). The cycle of classification: DSM-1 through DSM-5. *Annual Review of Clinical Psychology, 10*, 25–51.

Brown, T. E. (2013). *A new understanding of ADHD in children and adults*. New York: Routledge.

Centers for Disease Control and Prevention (CDCP). (2017, November 13). *Attention- deficit/hyperactivity disorder: data & statistics*. Retrieved January 4, 2018, from www.cdc.gov/incbddd/adhd/data.html

Conners, C. K. (2008). *Conners comprehensive behavior rating scales manual*. Toronto, Ontario, Canada: Multi-Health Systems.

Dawson, P., & Guare, R. (2010). *Executive skills in children and adolescents* (2nd ed.). New York: Guilford.

DefiniPoint.com. (2017). *Swanson, Nolan and Pelham Questionnaire (SNAP)*. Retrieved August 9, 2017, from www.attentionpoint.com/x_upload/media/images/snap_description_with_questions-1.pdf

Durston, S., van Belle, J., & de Zeeuw, P. (2011). Differentiating frontostriatal and fronto- cerebellar circuits in Attention-Deficit/Hyperactivity Disorder. *Biological Psychiatry, 69*, 1178–1184.

Flavell, J. H. (1992). Cognitive development: Past, present and future. *Developmental Psychology, 28*(6), 998–1005.

Gioia, G. A., Isquith, P. K., Guy, S. C., & Kenworthy, L. (2015). *Behavior rating inventory of executive functions* (2nd ed.). Lutz, FL: PAR.

Hoffman, H. (1848). *The English struwwelpeter, or pretty stories and funny pictures.* Retrieved August 9, 2017, from https://archive.org/stream/englishstruwwelp00ho ffrich/englishstruwwelp00hoffrich_djvu.txt

Human Connectome Project. (n.d.). Retrieved October 18, 2017, from www.humanconnectomeproject.org/informatics/relationship-viewer/

Kessler, J. W. (1980). *Handbook of minimal brain dysfunction: A critical view.* New York: Wiley.

King, M. J., Shin, J., Taylor, J. M., Mattek, A., Chavez, S., & Whalen, P. (2017). Intolerance of uncertainty predicts increased striatal volume. *Emotion, 17*(6), 895–899.

Koziol, L., & Budding, D. (2012). Requiem for a diagnosis: Attention Deficit/Hyperactivity. *Applied Neuropsychology: Child, 1*(1), 2–5.

Koziol, L., Budding, D., & Chidiekel, D. (2013). *ADHD as a model of brain-behavior relationships.* New York: Springer.

Nadeau, K. G. (2017). *Is your daughter a daydreamer, tomboy or "chatty Kathy"?* Retrieved August 9, 2017, from www.addvance.com/help/women/daydreamer.html

Naglieri, J. A., & Goldstein, S. (2013). *Comprehensive executive function inventory.* North Tonawanda, NY: Multi-Health Systems.

National Center for Education Statistics (NCES). (n.d.). *Fast facts.* Retrieved October 18, 2017, from https://nces.ed.gov/fastfacts/display.asp?id=65

National Institute for Children's Health Quality (NICHQ). (2002). *NICHQ Vanderbilt assessment scales.* Retrieved August 9, 2017, from www.nichq.org/resource/nichq-vanderbilt-assessment-scales

Reynolds, C. R., & Kamphaus, R. W. (2015). *Behavior assessment system for children* (3rd ed.). San Antonio, TX: Pearson.

Shier, A., Reichenbacher, T., Ghuman, H. S., & Ghuman, J. K. (2013). Pharmacological treatment of Attention Deficit Hyperactivity Disorder in children and adolescents: Clinical strategies. *Journal of Central Nervous System Disease, 5*, 1–17.

Sonuga-Barke, E. (2003). The dual-pathway model of AD/HD: An elaboration of neuro- developmental characteristics. *Neuroscience and Biobehavioral Reviews, 27*, 593–604.

Stahl, S. M. (2013). *Stahl's essential psychopharmacology: Neuroscientific basis and practical applications* (4th ed.). New York: Cambridge University Press.

Still, G. F. (1902). The Goulstonian lectures: On some abnormal psychical conditions in children. *Lancet, 159*, 1008–1013.

USC Mark and Mary Stevens Neuroimaging and Informatics Institute. (2017). *Human connectome project.* Retrieved August 9, 2017, from www.humanconnec tomeproject.org

Wasserman, T., & Wasserman, L. D. (2012). The sensitivity and specificity of neuropsychological tests in the diagnosis of Attention-Deficit/Hyperactivity Disorder. *Applied Neuropsychology: Child, 0,* 1–10.

Wechsler, D. (2014). *Wechsler Intelligence Scale for Children* (5th ed.). Bloomington, IN: Pearson.

World Health Organization (WHO). (1948). *The ICD-10 classification of mental and behavioural disorders: Clinical descriptions and diagnostic guidelines.* Geneva: World Health Organization.

Ylvisaker, M., & Feeney, T. J. (1998). *Collaborative brain injury intervention.* San Diego, CA: Singular Publishing Group, Inc.

7 Developmental Social Neuroscience and the Autism Spectrum of Disorders

Historical Considerations

The most rapidly growing diagnosis in developmental neuroscience is that of the autism spectrum disorders (ASD). Individuals with autistic-like features and behaviors have existed throughout history and certainly before the term "autism" was formally adopted. In the late 1700s, a 12-year-old child who had grown up in the woods of the south of France, apparently having been without human contact for many years, was found and described as having an absence of speech, peculiar food preferences, and numerous scars on his body. It appeared that he had lived in the wilds for most of his life and was quite content to have done so. Initial efforts to civilize the boy, who became known as Victor, ultimately resulted in his being adopted by a young medical student, John Marc Gaspard Itard. Itard believed that two features separate humans from animals: the capacity to use language and the capacity for empathy (Itard, 1802). Itard attempted to teach Victor to use language and to communicate human emotions; however, he was minimally successful. Ultimately, Victor's story became dramatized in François Truffaut's 1970 film *L'Enfant Sauvage* (The Wild Child).

The word "autism" was coined by a Swiss psychiatrist, Eugen Bleuler in 1910 and was used to define one set of the symptoms of schizophrenia. Bleuler described the "autistic withdrawal of the patient into his fantasies, against which any influence from outside becomes an intolerable disturbance" (Kuhn, 2004). The more modern sense of the word "autism" nevertheless derives from the work of two physicians, Hans Asperger and Leo Kanner. Kanner first used the label of early infantile autism in 1943, when he published a paper describing eleven children who had significant developmental difficulties, including withdrawal from others and insistence on routines and sameness (Kanner, 1943). Kanner had emigrated from Germany to America and was working at Johns Hopkins University, and his works were written in English. Asperger, working at roughly the same time in Austria, was less well known primarily because his writing was in German. Additionally, while Kanner worked with individuals who had fairly significant intellectual and developmental disabilities, Asperger's work was primarily with higher-functioning individuals who nevertheless demonstrated "a lack of empathy, little ability to form friendships, one-sided conversations, intense absorption in a special interest, and clumsy movements" (Attwood, 1997).

Research in the 1950s and 1960s began to focus upon more specific diagnoses of childhood developmental difficulties, and more rigorous scientific approaches were applied to the study of psychopathology. In 1959, the British government passed the "Mental Health Act," which led to large-scale closure of institutions for individuals who were thought to have mental abnormalities (The National Archives, 1959). As these individuals were returned to the community, awareness and recognition of the range of impairments among the population increased. In 1961, Victor Lotter completed the first epidemiological study of autism in a county in England, suggesting that autism occurred at a rate of 4.5 per 10,000 children (Lotter, 1966). This incidence statistic is contrasted with the current estimates from the Centers for Disease Control that about 1 in 68 children has been found to have an autism spectrum disorder (Centers for Disease Control and Prevention [CDC], 2017). Worldwide recognition of the frequency of autism and other psychiatric conditions can therefore be dated back to the 1960s, at which time a greater emphasis began to be placed upon the development of agreed-upon behavioral criteria for numerous childhood disorders. The reader who is interested in this history is referred to Bonnie Evans' paper: "How Autism Became Autism" (Evans, 2013).

By 1979, Lorna Wing and Judith Gould performed another epidemiological study in which they emphasized the necessity of differentiating between intellectual disabilities and social impairments (Wing & Gould, 1979). Their defining characteristics of autism followed Folstein and Rutter's definition of the key features, including the absence or impairment of social interaction; the absence or impairment of the development of verbal or non-verbal language; and/or the presence of repetitive, stereotyped activities of any kind (Folstein & Rutter, 1977). Wing, a psychiatrist whose own daughter, Susie, had been diagnosed with autism, also began discussing the concept of a "spectrum" of subcategories within the broader category of autism. Wing referred to three different subtypes based upon the quality of their social interaction, which she and Gould differentiated into the aloof group, the passive group, and the "active but odd" group (Wing, 1997).

Categorical Diagnosis

As with other neurodevelopmental disorders, efforts to categorize the diagnostic criteria for ASD, upon which agreement could be reached within the World Health Organization and the American Psychiatric Association, resulted in the initial differentiation of specific subtypes of autistic disorders. While the DSM-III (American Psychiatric Association, 1980) category of Infantile Autism was felt to be highly specific, it also was considered overly stringent, to not sufficiently encompass developmental change, and to focus primarily on the infantile stages of behavioral abnormality (Cohen, Volkmar, & Paul, 1986). DSM-III-R (American Psychiatric Association, 1987) broadened the diagnostic criteria to encompass the broad spectrum of autism over the lifespan, but was considered overly broad. DSM-IV (American Psychiatric Association, 1994) closely matched international consensus as detailed in the ICD-10 (World Health Organization, 1992) and included multiple subtypes (Autistic Disorder, Asperger's Disorder, Rett Syndrome, Pervasive Developmental Disorder, etc.).

Substantial effort was devoted to determining the boundaries between the various subcategories and ways to differentiate between the subtypes within the broader category. Asperger's disorder, for example, was thought to reflect relatively stronger levels of left brain hemisphere competence particularly in language skills, combined with difficulties in visual-spatial information processing, whereas autism was thought to reflect more pervasive developmental impairments, particularly involving language. Individuals with Asperger's were often thought to be much more intelligent and to have fewer adaptive behavioral challenges, while individuals with autism were thought to be more cognitively impaired and to need substantially higher levels of support. Despite these arguments, it eventually became clear that the variable of intellectual ability was independent of the core features of autism, although some writers differentiated between "high" and "low" functioning autism. DSM-5 consequently adjusted its diagnostic criteria to focus upon the existence of primary and persistent deficits in social communication and social interaction, which occur across multiple contacts and, secondarily, the presence of restricted, repetitive patterns of behavior, interests, or activities (American Psychiatric Association, 2013).

The current DSM-5 also returns to the broader concepts discussed by Wing and now refers to the Autism Spectrum of Disorders (ASD) (Wing, 1997). Diagnostic criteria include three subcriteria for deficits in social communication/interaction, all of which are required. These include deficits in social-emotional reciprocity; deficits in non-verbal communicative behaviors used for social interaction; and deficits in developing, maintaining, and understanding relationships. A range of severity qualifiers is added based upon degrees of impairment in each area. Within the restricted and repetitive patterns of behavior criteria, at least two out of four subcategories of impairment need to be documented in the areas of stereotyped or repetitive motor movements, use of objects or speech; insistence on sameness, inflexible adherence to routines, or ritualized patterns of verbal and non-verbal behavior; highly restricted, fixated interests that are abnormal in intensity or focus; and/or hyper- or hyporeactivity to sensory input or unusual interest in the sensory aspects of the environment. Qualifying characteristics also need to specify whether the symptoms were with or without accompanying intellectual or language impairment, whether they are associated with a known medical or genetic condition or environmental factor, whether they are associated with another neurodevelopmental disorder, and whether there is the presence of catatonia. Severity levels range from "requiring very substantial support" to "requiring support," with a middle category of "requiring substantial support" (American Psychiatric Association, 2013).

Given the delineation of these diagnostic criteria, consensual diagnostic strategies have begun to emerge. It has become common that most children with ASD are first identified by primary care physician screening. The Centers for Disease Control suggests but does not endorse multiple tools for pediatric autism screening, including the Ages and Stages Questionnaire (Ages & Stages Questionnaire, 2017); the Communication and Symbolic Behavior Scales (Wetherby & Prizant, 2002); the Modified Checklist for Autism in Toddlers-revised (Robins, Fein, Barton, & Green, 2001); and other screening tools that focus upon the symptoms of autism in toddlers and young children (CDC, 2017). If the outcome of this screening process suggests the possible presence of ASD, the CDC recommends a more comprehensive evaluation be performed by a child development professional.

Neurodevelopmental clinicians who receive such referrals typically consider a broad battery of assessment, designed to document developmental function and to rule out other possible causes of presenting symptoms. Such evaluations may include a hearing screening and a speech/language assessment. A broad battery of developmental or cognitive testing would consider overall intellectual status, the identification of information processing strengths and weaknesses, and the measurement of the child's development of adaptive behavioral skills. A more in-depth description of the child's behavior, provided by caregivers, involves the gathering of specific data regarding the presence or absence of the specific symptoms of ASD.

The CDC notes that no single tool should be used as the basis of the diagnosis of ASD and requires at least two sources of information, including parent or caregiver report as well as direct child observation. Examples of tools that could be utilized to specify symptoms of ASD include the Autism Diagnostic Inventory-Revised (ADI-R) (Lord, Rutter, & Le Couteur, 1994); the Autism Diagnostic Observation Schedule-Generic (ADOS) (Lord, Rutter, DiLavore, Risi, Gotham, & Bishop, 2012); the Childhood Autism Rating Scale (Schopler & Van Bourgondien, 2010); and the Gilliam Autism Rating Scale, 2nd Edition (Gilliam, 2014) among others. These types of tools tend to include diagnostic algorithms or suggested "cutoff" scores, which clinicians can utilize to decide whether the individual "meets" the number and level of symptoms required by the diagnosis. Other tools developed from these strategies take a similar approach, such as the Social Communication Questionnaire (Rutter, Bailey, Berument, Lord, & Pickles, 2003), which asks caregivers to rate a relatively smaller sample of behavior by severity and offers a cutoff score that is thought to have sufficient sensitivity and specificity to warrant its use in diagnosis.

As with all tools used in categorical diagnosis, however, substantial scientific debate has emerged as to the appropriateness of various tools for various purposes, the utilization of specific tools with individuals who are not within or similar to the standardization sample and subpopulations of individuals for whom sensitivity and specificity may be lower. Thus, for example, the ADOS has achieved something close to royalty status as the "gold standard" for the diagnosis of autism. Some clinicians are nevertheless being trained to administer the ADOS in a somewhat robotic fashion, without a comprehensive understanding of the research into the use of this tool or the subtleties of scoring items on the scale. These individuals use the scores obtained from this tool as incontrovertible evidence as to whether a child meets criteria for autism or not. What is becoming clear, however, is that certain subgroups of individuals with autistic symptoms may not "qualify" for services based upon the ADOS, given the fact that not all individuals show all the categorical symptoms at a sufficient level of severity.

As an example of the difficulty associated with categorical diagnostic procedures, the role of intellect upon the manifestation of autistic symptoms is found to be substantial and often impacts the level of impairment an individual might experience and the age at which diagnosis occurs. ASD is found across the spectrum of cognitive abilities, from severely intellectually disabled individuals all the way to doctoral-level professionals in advanced fields such as medicine, engineering, law, and other areas of scientific work. Investigation into the similarities and difference between age- and IQ-matched males and females diagnosed with "high-functioning" autism has also suggested that there may well be a differing developmental course between the genders and that adult outcomes of ASD may look quite different, depending upon the measurement tool used and whether symptoms are derived from self-report versus parental report.

Research performed within the Autism Research Centre at the University of Cambridge has evaluated individuals with High Average intellectual abilities and documented that male and female adults with ASD had comparable levels of childhood autistic symptom severity. In adulthood, however, females were found to have fewer socio-communication symptoms on the ADOS but more lifetime difficulties with sensory issues. Most importantly, however, was the finding that only 20.7% of females were correctly classified by the ADOS as being on the autism spectrum, while 57.6% of males were thus categorized, despite all having scored above cutoff scores on parent report of symptoms of ASD on the Autism Diagnostic Inventory-Revised (reflecting childhood presentations) (Lai et al., 2011).

Another review of 5,723 individuals' records contained in 4 research datasets found that sex differences in the behavioral characteristics of children and adolescents diagnosed with ASD was highly dependent upon cognitive (especially verbal) abilities. Younger females with limited/phrase speech were relatively more severely affected than males, while those with fluent speech had better social skills than males (Howe et al., 2015). This suggests that girls with higher-functioning ASD may be "missed" when they are younger, should they have relatively stronger verbal communication/language skills. Although the authors of the ADOS have recognized the need for continued research into the diagnostic algorithms for this tool (Hus & Lord, 2014), emerging findings point to the necessity of examining the entire cognitive and behavioral profile of children with neurodevelopmental disorders and the avoidance of "favorite" or "gold standard" diagnostic tools used in relative isolation. ASD findings from neuroimaging studies, for example, document that the different symptoms of ASD are associated with different regions of the brain and that a broad assessment strategy is indicated (Anderson & Beauchamp, 2012), while ongoing genetic studies are identifying multiple polygenic interactions, rather than a single-gene, Mendelian transmission.

Dimensional Diagnosis

If one accepts the premise of this book that emphasizing the boundaries between categorical diagnoses is less useful than broadening an understanding of the multiple dimensions that are involved in the human condition, one can begin to take a different approach in the evaluation and treatment of ASD. Different models have been presented and contrasted, including the medical model of disability, as opposed to the social model of disability and as opposed to the concept of neurodiversity. Within a medical model, it is assumed that, to some degree, an individual is disabled because of various levels of impairment. From this perspective, therefore, disabilities are inherently negative conditions which need to be cured or at least treated. A social model, alternatively, suggests that a person with impairments only becomes disabled because of society. In other words, disabilities are the product of a failure of society to accommodate an individual's impairments and not necessarily an indictment of individuals themselves. The neurodiversity movement is in part based upon the social model but adds the consideration that an individual may not perceive their characteristics to represent impairments. Individuals within the neurodiversity movement suggest that they are different, not deficient, and that "neurotypicals" have the burden of accepting their differences and managing any discomfort they may experience, consequently. Individuals within the neurodiversity model therefore assert that they do not need to be treated or cured and that any interventions which are sought should be the choice of the individual, not imposed by others.

As an example, many individuals with ASD experience times in which they feel anxious. Strategies to reduce anxiety, possibly to include direct interventions in the form of medication or psychotherapy, may sometimes be warranted for a specific period of time. Alternatively, the fact that an individual has a narrow range of interests in which they have an intense fascination is not a problem that needs to be fixed or treated. Many higher-functioning individuals with ASD have extensive knowledge about a limited number of things; however, remembering the names and details of all members of a specific category of interest is not really a disabling characteristic. This argument is consistent with the idea of "identity-first" thinking, meaning that neurological differences do not necessarily reflect impairment, nor should they be viewed as positive or negative. They are simply aspects of an individual's identity, and one should not be called "autistic" but rather "a person with autism."

This line of thinking also results in consideration of whether ASD represents a discrete disorder or, alternatively, a continuum of characteristics/symptoms which exist in all persons. From this perspective, diagnosis is only warranted when impairment reaches a sufficient level of severity. Support for this line of thinking is provided by Constantino and Todd's study in which 788 pairs of twins between the ages of 7 and 15, randomly selected from participants in a large epidemiological study, were characterized by parental completion of the Social Responsiveness Scale for each of the twins (Constantino & Todd, 2003). Findings from this study indicated that ASD-related behaviors were continuously distributed and moderately to highly heritable. The study did not find sex-specific genetic influences and emphasized that the social deficits characteristic of ASD are quite common within the general population. This is not surprising in that common experience reveals some people to be more outgoing and social, while others are less so. Diagnosis of impairment therefore depends upon where one makes a cutoff between the numbers and severity of symptoms as differentiating "affected" from "unaffected" persons.

Recognition that there are dimensions of social behavior allows one to begin to consider the developmental and neuroscience dimensions of what it means to be social. Miriam Beauchamp and Vicki Anderson have proposed a theoretical model for the study of developmental social neuroscience, which they hope will assist in understanding social abilities in both typical children as well as those who are either at environmental or biological risk. Their sociocognitive integration of abilities (SOCIAL) model (Beauchamp & Anderson, 2010) incorporates the biological underpinnings and socio-cognitive skills that underlie social function (attention/executive function, communication, socio-emotional skills), as well as the internal and external (environmental) factors that mediate these skills.

The SOCIAL model, more extensively explained in the book *Developmental Social Neuroscience and Childhood Brain Insult* (Anderson & Beauchamp, 2012), acknowledges the importance of both typical and atypical development and the biological and environmental risks which contribute to the outcome. The model recognizes that there are multiple brain regions which contribute to a social brain and that the various components of developmental social difficulties may reflect differing contributions of each brain area. This model also recognizes that social difficulties are not restricted to the autism spectrum and are often found in children who experienced neurological insults associated with prematurity, traumatic brain injury, genetic disorders, etc. Autism therefore represents one "portrait" of impairments in social cognition, while also recognizing that atypical social behavior only reflects one component of the differences demonstrated by people with ASD. The model suggests that multiple foci of attention need to be directed to different components of the individual who presents with social challenges, including a comprehensive assessment of the individual's attentional control, executive functions, effort control, perception of facial expressions; their understandings of the beliefs, intentions, desires, and emotions of others; their capacity for emotional regulation; their overall intellectual and verbal abilities; and their specific communication skills. Adopting this strategy of thinking about developmental social disorders therefore broadens our assessment from one focused upon meeting DSM-5 criteria for a certain diagnosis, or not, to a more comprehensive assessment of the individual as a person.

The dimensional models that we are discussing have been embraced by the National Institute of Mental Health. In 2012, NIMH launched the Research Domain Criteria (RDoC) project (National Institute of Mental Health [NIMH], 2017). This effort was the result of growing awareness that a narrow, categorical approach to the diagnosis of mental health disorders fails to account for emerging research proving the heterogeneity of symptoms aggregated under various diagnostic "labels." The RDoC strategy is based on an approach to mental disorders that will try to incorporate multiple dimensions of evidence, including behavior, thinking, neurobiological measures, and genetics. A prime driver of this approach was emerging neuroimaging technologies, which have helped to identify the ways in which individuals with a given "label" might have differing neural circuitries, reflective of the differing behavioral symptoms. This approach has recently led to a remarkable study in which fifty-nine 6-month-old infants with a high familial risk for ASD underwent functional connectivity magnetic resonance imaging that correctly identified which children would subsequently receive a research clinical best-estimate diagnosis of ASD at 24 months of age (Emerson et al., 2017). As opposed to relying strictly on behavioral assessments, therefore, high levels of both sensitivity and specificity were documented through the use of a neuroimaging approach to the identification of children who would ultimately be found to have ASD. This form of early identification has tremendous potential for early intervention, which may then potentially capitalize upon brain plasticity and the application of evidence-based treatments for the core deficits that characterize the dimension.

The RDoC model considers the role of multiple dimensions of mental health functioning, including negative valence systems, positive valence systems, cognitive systems, social processes, and arousal and regulatory systems (NIMH, 2017). Within the social processes dimension, subcategories of analysis address issues of affiliation and attachment, social communication (reception and production of facial and non-facial communication), and one's perception and understanding of oneself (agency and self-knowledge), as well as the perception and understanding of others (agency, action perception, and understanding of mental states). This subdivision of social processes therefore asks whether subcomponents of many of the criteria used to diagnose ASD might have differing molecular, cellular, neurocircuitry, behavioral, etc. mechanisms, all of which may contribute to a better understanding of how autistic behaviors develop, as well as how they might be treated.

What seems to be missing from the RDoC approach, however, is an analysis of the "other" criteria often required in the diagnosis of ASD. Restricted and/or repetitive patterns of behavior are considered a necessary component for DSM-5 diagnosis; however, recent work also questions the validity of this necessity, in that some individuals with ASD (the often high-functioning younger girls) are less likely to have such behaviors, whereas alternatively the presence of non-purposeful stereotypic movements and other restrictive and repetitive patterns of behavior are found among individuals who do not have the social communication components of ASD (Mahone et al., 2016). Such children may demonstrate unusual motor stereotypies, such as repetitively banging their forehead on their pillow, running around and making unusual hand movements, and yet at other times seem fully engaged in reciprocal social interaction and can be quite affable.

The National Autistic Society in England, continuing the work of Lorna Wing, further emphasizes differentiation of the often subtle subtypes of autism. One example is the concept of Pathological Demand Avoidance (PDA) syndrome (Pathological Demand Avoidance, 2017), in which typically passive infants begin avoiding ordinary life demands and begin to show panic and anxiety when the demands placed upon them by others gradually increase. These youngsters often show a surface level of sociability but have difficulties with social identity, mood lability and impulsivity, and sometimes language delay. These children seem to do well as long as everything goes their way but may become dyscontrolled to a fairly extreme level, with extreme temper outbursts and emotional dysregulation, when pushed outside of their comfort zones. Pathological Demand Avoidance was first identified in the 1980s by Elizabeth Newson, whose work is being continued by Phil Christie, with research now spearheaded by the Pathological Demand Avoidance Society (Pathological Demand Avoidance, 2017). Clinicians in the United States and other areas the world are increasingly becoming familiar with the PDA concept; however, the failure of DSM-5 and ICD-11 to recognize the condition, through circular logic, often causes clinicians to dismiss the possibility of its existence, thereby restricting progression of scientific understanding and knowledge.

A final consideration of the concept of ASD involves the interaction of intellectual ability with developmental progression. More intelligent children can often learn to "hide" their social challenges during the early years but become less able to fit in as normative developmental social groups emerge. Often the middle school years can be a time in which individuals who don't read the subtleties of group interaction, or who don't understand the abstract nature of teasing and non-literal language, suddenly seem to be very different from their peers. While many can continue to get by through withdrawal and isolation, others become the target of bullying and peer ostracism, sometimes with quite negative psychosocial consequences. Clinicians may be sent referrals for an assessment of learning disabilities, only to quickly recognize that the learning disorder is social in nature. Yet other adolescents first encounter their social limitations as they reach adolescence and are confronted with flirtations, sexuality and dating. There is a growing population of young adults with ASD, whose needs are only just being recognized.

Evaluation Strategies

As with all neurodevelopmental disorders, a comprehensive evaluation of developmental social disorders must start with an extensive and comprehensive documentation of historical information. Extended family members' behavioral characteristics may point to a genetic component to the presenting condition, and primary care physicians will often request a genetics study to determine whether specific genetic disorders/conditions might be present that are highly comorbid with ASD. Genetic diagnoses often raise thorny ethical issues but may also lead to the identification of needed biomedical interventions early on in development. It is also critical that the diagnostic process occur as soon as any concerns are identified, and clinicians must avoid well-meaning platitudes that the individual is "just a boy" or that we should "wait and see." Caregivers who present with concerns for their child's behavior and development should always receive respectful attention and consideration of possible factors leading to their concerns.

Especially as we are learning that some features of developmental social disorders can be identified as early as within the first year of life, clinicians should routinely ask caregivers about the quality of their social interactions with their child. Familiarity with the early signs of ASD and the dimensions of possible impairment allows one to gently inquire about a child's development, while remaining sensitive to the possibility that ASD has never crossed the mind of the caregiver. Seasoned clinicians often "sense" the presence of diagnostic conditions upon first meeting a patient; however, it is important to avoid "jumping to conclusions" before gathering sufficient information. As with other conditions, therefore, the first questions should take the form of *what* are the concerns, *who* has the concerns, and *when* did the concerns begin to emerge. Keep in mind that higher-functioning and more intelligent individuals, perhaps especially females, may not demonstrate concerning traits until they are older.

Along with the clinical interview, a comprehensive diagnostic evaluation should request historical data in the form of medical records, school records, and notes/evaluations from other professionals who may have already seen the child. Teacher comments and notes on school progress reports often hint at areas deserving more thorough questioning. The observations of teachers and others who interact with larger groups of youngsters, and therefore observe the patient in social situations, often have a differing perspective from that of parents, who may have limited observation of their child in such settings. Siblings, too, often have a perspective that is worth asking about, as some will express frustration over the patient's social challenges while others will take a protective role.

Objectification of the assessment necessarily involves the use of standardized assessment technologies, and there is a growing arsenal of tests which evaluate the attention, executive function, intellectual, and language profiles of patients who come to our offices. As discussed previously, however, clinicians must be careful to not assume that the name of the test reflects its usefulness in the evaluation of ASD. Tests of social language and problem solving can be very helpful in learning how the child sees the world and their capacity to put themselves in the shoes of another. Posing social dilemmas and asking how the child would resolve the conflict point to the child's social reasoning and awareness of issues such as social judgment, social referencing, and mutual benefit in problem solving. Some children have significant difficulties with non-literal language and metaphors, and there are increasing numbers of psychometric tests that evaluate components of these factors.

Nevertheless, we currently have a limited arsenal of ecologically valid tools to use in the evaluation of the Social Processes dimension of RDoCs. The August 2016 report of the National Advisory Mental Health Council Workgroup, entitled "Behavioral Assessment Methods for RDoC Constructs" (NIMH, 2016), concluded that there is an extensive need for the development of such measures and pointed to the potential of new technologies in assessment for which research to establish the psychometric properties, norms, developmental processes, etc. will have to emerge. Dimensional assessment must therefore accept that there is no single or specific "test" clinicians can rely upon in evaluating many of the components of social competence. At this point, the tools available through the University of Cambridge's Autism Research Centre (Autism Research Centre, 2017) hold promise, but as noted on their website, these tests have been developed primarily for research, and no single measure should be used to indicate that a person has autism.

Interventions

Given the limitations in our arsenal of assessment tools, the question therefore arises as to how our assessment of ASD can lead to interventions. One perspective is that we should answer the questions of how the individual is affected, how the family is affected, the nature of the individual's interaction with peers and society, and whether there are specific needs for skills training or education. The Autism Evidence-Based Practice Review Group, from the University of North Carolina (Wong et al., 2014), recently reviewed available research regarding educational and therapeutic services in an attempt to determine which approaches have sufficient support to be termed "evidence based." A distinction was made between broad-based "Comprehensive Treatment Models" as opposed to "Focused Intervention Practices." The Comprehensive programs tended to be organized around a conceptual framework, had manualized procedures, involved substantial numbers of hours per week and tended to last several years, during which multiple outcomes were targeted (Odom, Boyd, Hall, & Hume, 2010). In contrast, focused intervention practices tended to address specific/single skills or goals of a student. The interested reader is encouraged to review this report, as it ties specific, evidence-based practices to areas of need (e.g. joint attention, play) as well as the specific age ranges (e.g. 0–5, 6–14, etc.) for which various strategies may be most effective.

Evidence-based interventions, either alone or in a comprehensive package, are important because they focus upon the specific needs of the individual child and have as their goal the enhancement of skills in identified areas of weakness. This approach therefore emphasizes the developmental dimension with a goal of enhancing the child's toolkit of resources with which to cope with the lifelong condition of ASD. The goal is to maximize abilities in areas of need and to help the child and adolescent to reach an optimal outcome. In most cases, this will require coordination of services across the multiple environments where support services need to be delivered, along with a recognition that some impairments may need to be bypassed or accommodated. Biological support in the form of symptom-focused medications will often be a component of this plan but likely will not address the core basis of the ASD.

Some children are fortunate to have caregivers who take charge, learn and research, and actively seek out services. Having a child with a disability often means multiple providers invading one's privacy, long hours spent driving to appointments, searching for parking spaces, and spending the money that might have gone to something fun. Rejection and confrontation by insurance companies, social service agencies, governmental bodies, and school districts can try the patience of the best-adjusted parent and can become a tipping point for caregivers who themselves have times of trouble coping. Clinicians working with neurodevelopmental disorders in general, and ASD specifically, must realize that the family is the patient, not just the child or adolescent. Suggesting that families consider local support groups and national organizations of parents can be very helpful in reducing the sense of being alone.

Parents who come to grips with the realization that their child has a severe disability frequently experience what Simon Olshansky (1962) termed "chronic sorrow" to refer to the long-term experience of periodic sadness they face as their child grows older. Some parents may never fully recover from the news of their child's diagnosis and repeatedly experience grief as they are confronted with yet another example of how their child is different. Clinicians must therefore be kind, must take the extra time needed, must strive to put their own needs aside, and make the extra step that is often needed. Grief hits at unexpected times, such as when the parent is at a stoplight and sees gleeful children playing group games or a young couple holding hands as they stroll along. The toll of raising a child with developmental difficulties is not just on a physical exhaustion level; it doesn't end with seeking the best care or advocating at the highest level. It is often in the quiet times, when the questions that have been repeatedly pushed out of conscious awareness resurface—the questions of "What if?" and "Why my child?

Conclusions

Developmental social disorders are in many ways the poster child of dimensional thinking. Science has struggled to understand the child who doesn't easily conform to the behavioral and interpersonal expectations of society. Initially we examined the children who were clearly "abnormal" and severely impaired; however, we are now increasingly aware of the nuances of social interaction and find differences among even the most highly intelligent and academically skilled. Far from wanting to pathologize such differences, modern clinicians seek to understand what it means to be different and how science can help those who experience distress to feel better, without needing to "fix" the underlying profile of an individual's strengths and weaknesses. Developmental social neuroscience embraces this challenge through dimensional analysis of an organism's interaction with its social environment.

Bibliography

Ages & Stages Questionnaire (2017). Brooks Publishing Co. Accessed September 17, 2017 from http://agesandstages.com/

American Psychiatric Association (APA). (1980). *Diagnostic and statistical manual of mental disorders* (3rd ed.). Arlington, VA: American Psychiatric Association.

American Psychiatric Association (APA). (1987). *Diagnostic and statistical manual of mental disorders* (3rd ed., text revision). Arlington, VA: American Psychiatric Association.

American Psychiatric Association (APA). (1994). *Diagnostic and statistical manual of mental disorders* (4th ed.). Arlington, VA: American Psychiatric Association.

American Psychiatric Association (APA). (2013). *Diagnostic and statistical manual of mental disorders* (5th ed.). Arlington, VA: American Psychiatric Association.

Anderson, V., & Beauchamp, M. H. (Eds.). (2012). *Developmental social neuroscience and childhood brain insult.* New York: Guilford.

Attwood, T. (1997). *Asperger's Syndrome: A guide for parents and professionals* (p. 11). London: Jessica Kingsley Publishers.

Autism Research Centre (ARC). (2017). *Downloadable tests.* Retrieved August 9, 2017, from www.autismresearchcentre.com/arc_tests

Beauchamp, M. H., & Anderson, V. (2010). SOCIAL: An integrative framework for the development of social skills. *Psychological Bulletin, 136,* 39–64.

Centers for Disease Control and Prevention (CDCP). (2017, May 09). *Autism spectrum disorder.* Retrieved August 9, 2017, from www.cdc.gov/ncbddd/autism/index.html

Cohen, D. J., Volkmar, F. R., & Paul, R. (1986). Issues in the classification of pervasive developmental disorders and associated conditions: History and current status of nosology. *Journal of the American Academy of Child Psychiatry, 25,* 158–161.

Constantino, J. N., & Todd, R. D. (2003). Autistic traits in the general population: A twin study. *Archives of General Psychiatry, 60,* 524–530.

Eliz. 2. (1959). *Mental Health Act, 1959.* Retrieved August 9, 2017, from www.legislation.gov.uk/ukpga/1959/72/pdfs/ukpga_19590072_en.pdf

Emerson, R. W., Adams, C., Nishino, T., Hazlett, H. C., Wolff, J. J., Zwaigenbaum, L., . . . Kandala, S. (2017). Functional neuroimaging of high-risk 6-month-old infants predicts a diagnosis of autism at 24 months of age. *Science Translational Medicine, 9*(393), eaag2882. Retrieved from http://stm.sciencemag.org/content/9/393/eaag2882

Evans, B. (2013). How autism became autism. *History of the Human Sciences, 26*, 3–31.

Folstein, S., & Rutter, M. (1977). Infantile autism: A genetic study of 21 twin pairs. *Journal of Child Psychology and Psychiatry, 18*, 297–321.

Gilliam, J. E. (2014). *Gilliam Autism Rating Scale* (3rd ed.). Orlando, FL: Houghton Mifflin Harcourt.

Howe, Y. J., O'Rourke, J. A., Yatchmink, Y., Viscidi, E. W., Jones, R. N., & Morrow, E. M. (2015). Female autism phenotypes investigated at different levels of language and developmental abilities. *Journal of Autism and Developmental Disorders, 45*(11), 3537–3549.

Hus, V., & Lord, C. (2014). The autism diagnostic observation schedule, module 4: Revised algorithm and standardized severity scores. *Journal of Autism and Developmental Disorders, 44*, 1996–2012.

Itard, J. M. G. (1802). *An historical account of the discovery and education of a savage man, or of the first developments, physical and moral, of the young savage caught in the woods near Aveyron, in the year 1798.* London: Printed for Richard Phillips.

Kanner, L. (1943). Autistic disturbances of affective contact. *The Nervous Child, 2*, 217–250.

Kuhn, R. (2004). Eugen Bleuler's concepts of psychopathology. *History of Psychiatry, 15*, 361–366.

Lai, M. C., Lombardo, M. V., Pasco, G., Ruigrok, A. N., Wheelwright, S. J., Sadek, S. A., . . . MRC AIMS Consortium. (2011). A behavioral comparison of male and female adults with high functioning autism spectrum conditions. *PLoS One, 6*(6), e20835.

Lord, C., Rutter, M., DiLavore, P. C., Risi, S., Gotham, K., & Bishop, S. (2012). *Autism diagnostic observation schedule* (2nd ed.). Torrance, CA: Western Psychological Services.

Lord, C., Rutter, M., & Le Couteur, A. (1994). Autism diagnostic interview—revised: A revised version of a diagnostic interview for caregivers of individuals with possible pervasive developmental disorders. *Journal of Autism and Developmental Disorders, 24*(5), 659–685.

Lotter, V. (1966). Epidemiology of autistic conditions in young children. *Social Psychiatry*, 124–137.

Mahone, E. M., Crocetti, D., Tochen, L., Kine, T., Mostofsky, S. J., & Singer, H. S. (2016). Anomalous putamen volume in children with complex motor stereotypies. *Pediatric Neurology, 65*, 59–63.

The National Archives. (1959). *Ministry of health: Mental Health Act 1959 general policy, registered files (95,200 Series).* Retrieved September 17, 2017, from http://discovery.nationalarchives.gov.uk/details/r/C10978

National Institute of Mental Health (NIMH). (2016) *Behavioral assessment methods for RDoC constructs.* Retrieved September 17, 2017, from www.nimh.nih.gov/about/advisory-boards and-groups/namhc/reports/rdoc_council_workgroup_report_153440.pdf

National Institute of Mental Health (NIMH). (2017a). *Behavioral assessment methods for RDoC constructs.* Retrieved August 9, 2017, from www.nimh.nih.gov/about/advisory-boards-and-groups/namhc/reports/rdoc_council_workgroup_report_153440.pdf

National Institute of Mental Health (NIMH). (2017b). *Research domain criteria (RDoC).* Retrieved August 9, 2017, from www.nimh.nih.gov/research-priorities/rdoc/index.shtml

Odom, S. L., Boyd, B., Hall, L., & Hume, K. (2010). Evaluation of comprehensive treatment models for individuals with autism spectrum disorders. *Journal of Autism and Developmental Disorders, 40,* 425–436.

Olshansky, S. (1962). Chronic sorrow: A response to having a mentally defective child. *Social Casework, 43,* 190–193.

Pathological Demand Avoidance (PDA). (2017). Retrieved August 9, 2017, from www.pdasociety.org.uk

Robins, D., Fein, D., Barton, M., & Green, J. (2001) The modified checklist for autism in toddlers (M-CHAT): An initial investigation in the early detection of autism and pervasive developmental disorders. *Journal of Autism and Developmental Disorders, 31*(2), 131–144.

Rutter, M., Bailey, A., Berument, S. K., Lord, C., & Pickles, A. (2003). *Social communication questionnaire.* Los Angeles, CA: Western Psychological Services.

Schopler, E., & Van Bourgondien, M. E. (2010). *Childhood Autism Rating Scale* (2nd ed.). Torrance, CA: Western Psychological Services.

Truffaut, F. (1970). *L'enfant sauvage, [Motion picture].* France: Les Artistes Associés.

Wetherby, A. M., & Prizant, B. M. (2002). *Communication and symbolic behavior scales developmental profile.* Baltimore, MD: Paul Brooks Publishing Co.

Wing, L. (1997). The autistic spectrum. *The Lancet,* 1761–1766.

Wing, L., & Gould, J. (1979). Severe impairments of social interaction and associated abnormalities in children: Epidemiology and classification. *Journal of Autism and Developmental Disorders, 9,* 11–29.

Wong, C., Odom, S. L., Hume, K., Cox, A. W., Fettig, A., Kucharczyk, S., . . . Schultz, T. R. (2014). *Evidence-based practices for children, youth, and young adults with autism.* Chapel Hill: The University of North Carolina, Frank Porter Graham Child Development Institute, Autism Evidence-Based Practice Review Group.

World Health Organization (WHO). (1992). *The ICD-10 classification of mental and behavioural disorders: Diagnostic criteria for research* (10th ed.). Switzerland: World Health Organization.

8 Disorders of Academic Learning

Historical Considerations

There has been an interest in atypical learning patterns throughout the study of human development. Toward the end of the 1700s, Franz Joseph Gall began to assert that specific cognitive functions were associated with different areas of the brain (Franz Joseph Gall, n.d.). This was the beginning of the concept of "localization" of brain function, which received further support in the 1800s through the work of individuals studying language disorders, such as Pierre Paul Broca (n.d.), who localized speech functions to the inferior left frontal lobe, and Carl Wernicke (n.d.), who described "sensory aphasia" in which individuals had fluent and yet non-sensical speech associated with lesions more posterior in the left temporal lobe of the brain. Continued study of the neuroanatomy of language progressed from this point, to the current state where we have a fairly good understanding of how the brain processes language (Bauer, 2014) and the nature of language-based information processing and learning disorders.

At the turn of the twentieth century, there were growing mandates for compulsory education for all children in the United States. This movement led teachers to join with brain researchers in attempting to tease apart all the various areas of the brain that are involved in academic learning. Samuel Orton, who later partnered with Anna Gillingham, was one early pioneer in studying what caused some children to have trouble learning to read. Orton and Gillingham developed an approach to the remediation of reading problems that stressed the need for explicit instruction in phonics and sound blending, using a multisensory approach. The lessons from their approach, as laid out in the 1936 book *Remedial Work for Reading, Spelling, and Penmanship* (Gillingham & Stillman, 1936), continue to shape current-day strategies for helping children learn to read.

The scientific study of academic learning challenges therefore existed long before the public even became familiar with the idea that some children had learning disabilities. Widespread recognition of learning disorders was driven by parent movements in the 1940s for intellectual disabilities and in the 1960s for specific learning disorders. These parent organizations called upon state and federal legislatures to acknowledge the needs of children with learning and developmental disorders, despite the fact that there was little in the way of concerted efforts toward programmatic development other than vague medical terminology being applied to such children, including terms such as "brain injured" and the "perceptually handicapped" (Hallahan & Cruickshank, 1973). Beginning in the 1960s, however, parents began to call for scientific conferences regarding the non-intellectually disabled, struggling student. It was at the First Annual Meeting of the Conference on Exploration into the Problems of the Perceptually Handicapped, held in Chicago, that a presentation by Dr. Samuel A. Kirk began to draw smaller groups of parents and fledgling organizations together. Kirk's comments included the statement: "Recently, I have used the term 'learning disabilities' to describe a group of children who have disorders in development in language, speech, reading, and associated communication skills needed for social interaction" (Kirk, 1963). Following this meeting, professionals and parents attending the conference met and decided to form the Association for Children with Learning Disabilities (ACLD) (Learning Disabilities Association of America, 2017a). This organization ultimately changed its name to the Learning Disabilities Association, which continues to advocate for children and adults with learning disabilities, and their families. Individuals interested in more information about the history of the field of learning disabilities are encouraged to read the work of Daniel Hallahan and colleagues (Hallahan & Cruickshank, 2013).

Categorical Diagnosis

Stemming from the above initial movements, various legislation was passed at the national level, perhaps most significantly in 1975 with the passage of Public Law 94–142, the Education for All Handicapped Children's Act. This law codified what has become a familiar definition of learning disabilities:

> The term 'children with specific learning disabilities' means those children who have a disorder in one or more of the basic psychological processes involved in understanding or in using language, spoken or written, which disorder may manifest itself in imperfect ability to listen, think, speak, read write, spell or do mathematical calculations. Such disorders include such conditions as perceptual handicaps, brain injury, minimal brain dysfunction, dyslexia, and developmental aphasia. Such term does not include children who have learning problems which are primarily the result of visual, hearing, or motor handicaps, of mental retardation, of emotional disturbance, or environmental, cultural or economic disadvantage.
>
> (20 USC 1401(4) A)

What was not clear in PL 94–142 was how such children should be identified, other than that each state should establish procedures by which they would be "located and evaluated" (20 USC 1412 Sec 612(2)(C). One of Kirk's former students, Barbara Bateman, had earlier introduced the concept of examining the "discrepancy" between an individual's measured intellectual abilities and academic achievement, as a means of quantifying a learning disability. Bateman stated:

> Children who have learning disorders are those who manifest an educationally significant discrepancy between their estimated potential and actual level of performance related to basic disorders in the learning process, which may or may not be accompanied by demonstrable central nervous system dysfunction.
>
> (Bateman, 1965)

Efforts to include this operational definition in the implementation of PL 94–142 were unsuccessful at the federal level; however, state departments of education grasped the idea of an IQ-Achievement discrepancy as an objective method by which children with learning disabilities could be identified, and extensive effort was expended to define the methodology, severity levels, "acceptable" tests, etc. that could be used to bring local educational districts into compliance with the law. Unfortunately, different school districts often used different formulae and had different requirements, leading to lawsuits being filed by parents over the decisions made by school districts as to whether their child had a "severe discrepancy" and therefore qualified for services (Herr & Bateman, 2013). The process indeed became somewhat ludicrous, with some districts deciding, for example, that a child with a 16-point discrepancy qualified for services whereas a child with a 15-point discrepancy did not qualify!

Since these early days of special education, a great deal of research has been performed looking at both the IQ-Achievement discrepancy strategy as well as the core underlying characteristics of learning disabilities. Over time, the reliability and validity of the discrepancy strategy has come under significant fire, to the extent that the current iteration of special education law, the Individuals with Disabilities Education Act (IDEA), as amended in 2004, indicates that states may no longer require districts to use a severe discrepancy model when identifying specific learning disabilities (34 C.F.R. § 300.307(a)). In part, this shift came about because research into learning disabilities began to recognize that children with various forms of learning disorders, for example, dyslexia, had similar cognitive profiles regardless of whether they had significant IQ-Achievement test discrepancy scores, and studies of children who did versus did not have a significant discrepancy were not shown to differ in longitudinal studies of how well they ultimately learned to read (Fletcher, Stuebing, Morris, & Lyon, 2013).

Rather than requiring a discrepancy, IDEA suggests that determination of the existence of a specific learning disability (SLD) may rest upon findings that:

(1) The child does not achieve adequately for the child's age or to meet State-approved grade-level standards in one or more [of eight academic areas]

when provided with learning experiences and instruction appropriate for the child's age or State-approved grade-level standards. . . .

(2) (i) The child does not make sufficient progress . . . when using a process based on the child's response to scientific, research-based intervention; or (ii) The child exhibits a pattern of strengths and weaknesses in performance, achievement, or both, relative to age, State-approved grade-level standards, or intellectual development, that is determined by the group to be relevant to the identification of a specific learning disability.

(IDEA, 2004)

Dimensional Diagnosis

Contained within the above sections of federal law lies the essence of a debate that has waged over recent decades, regarding exactly how we should identify specific learning disabilities. There are two primary "camps" or schools of thought: 1) we should focus upon a child's progress and response to intervention, and 2) we should focus upon a child's pattern of strengths and weaknesses as they are relevant to the identification of SLD.

Jack Fletcher, of the University of Houston, has repeatedly asserted, "Comprehensive cognitive assessments are not necessary for the identification and treatment of learning disabilities" (Fletcher & Miciak, 2017). Similar to Barkley's argument that cognitive measures don't correlate well with behavioral indicators of ADHD (Barkley, 2014), Fletcher argues that measures of academic achievement are correlated with measures of cognitive abilities and that the process of determining formulae for the identification of SLD is fraught with statistical and conceptual problems, such as how one should determine the point of "cutoff" beyond which a student is found eligible for services. Fletcher suggests that the addition of neuropsychological testing to documentation of poor achievement may not improve identification and treatment, over a more intensive focus upon whether a child who is identified early on as having academic difficulties actually responds to quality, research-based academic instruction. Fletcher thus emphasizes that poor achievement is all that is required for the identification of children in need of intervention services, regardless of the cause. Fletcher cites guidance from the regulations accompanying the IDEA (2004):

The Department does not believe that an assessment of psychological or cognitive processing should be required in determining whether a child has an SLD. There is no current evidence that such assessments are necessary or sufficient for identifying SLD. Further, in many cases, these assessments have not been used to make appropriate intervention decisions.

(IDEA, 2004, p. 46651)

Alternatively, what has come to be known as "response to intervention" (RTI) (RTInetwork, 2017) has, in many parts of America, replaced the concept of an individually administered battery of assessment techniques in the identification of SLD. RTI is based upon the concept that a student who has been referred for a traditional eligibility evaluation often must wait for an extended period to receive an evaluation, following which a student is determined eligible or not eligible for special education services, only following which is the student referred for intervention that may or may not be helpful. RTI, alternatively, is based upon screening of all children to identify those who may be at-risk for learning challenges and the immediate provision of evidence-based interventions. Progress is monitored to determine whether the student "responds to intervention," with non-responders then subjected to eligibility testing for more individualized instruction (Fletcher, Stuebing, Morris, & Lyon, 2013).

RTI models thus suggest that, because SLD can be considered one component of low overall academic achievement, it is more appropriate to consider whether a student would benefit from intervention based upon evaluating the outcome of such intervention, rather than attempting to search for the cause of the student's challenges. This seems to be sensible—we should help those who struggle to learn and see if our efforts are successful. RTI is not without its critics, however. In 2010, the Learning Disabilities Association of America performed a survey of 58 "doctoral-level scholars in special education, psychology, medicine and the law with expertise in and public recognition for their work in SLD identification and intervention" (Hale et al., 2010). The survey concluded that *both* response to intervention and a comprehensive assessment of a student's psychological processes related to ability and achievement are needed to optimize service delivery for children both with and without SLD, but that neither was sufficient. The expert panel concluded that "a 'third method' approach that identifies a pattern of psychological processing strengths and weaknesses, and achievement deficits consistent with this pattern of processing weaknesses, makes the most empirical and clinical sense" (Hale et al., 2010. p. 223). This position thus emphasizes that interventions for SLD should rely upon individualized assessment and treatment planning, not just more intensive intervention for all students.

The "processing strengths and weaknesses" (PSW) models to explain learning disorders seems to fit the other implication of IDEA, emphasizing the importance of the identification of profiles of abilities as they are relevant to the identification of SLD. Approaches attempting to characterize the cognitive profiles of different types of learning disabilities posit that one can identify academic achievement impairment based upon a cognitive "footprint." Examples of strategies based upon this approach include the "concordance-discordance method" (Hale & Fiorello, 2004); the "discrepancy/consistency method" (Naglieri, 2010); and the "cross-battery assessment" method (Flanagan, Ortiz, & Alfonso, 2007). The core concept underlying these models is that SLD reflects truly different brain organization and function, not just low achievement or delays in the development of academic skills. Brad Hale has cogently argued that genetic and neuroimaging studies of children with SLD identify specific types of brain-based information processing dysfunction, which require focused remediation rather than compensation (Hale et al., 2016). Clearly, each child is unique and the product of variations within a multitude of genetic, perinatal, developmental, familial, and educational experiences. This perspective led me to have previously suggested that, with regard to the causes of SLD, "Much as a log jam alters the flow of the river and causes collateral pathways and pools, each brain's unique development forces us to respect that there will never be a singular cause or treatment for dyslexia" (Nicholls, 2010).

The debate regarding the merits of RTI versus PSW approaches in identifying learning disabilities is likely to continue; however, Hale raises a provocative consideration regarding how our brains grow and develop, relative to how and when SLD should be identified, and when intervention should be initiated. Citing Donald Hebb's classic phrase that "neurons that fire together wire together" (Hebb, 1949), Hale reminds us that our brains enjoy a period of relative "plasticity" when we are young. Should our assessments, perhaps initiated secondary to either early warning signals or strong genetic pedigrees, identify the footprint for a specific cognitive pattern very early in a child's life, it seems that we would be more likely to be able to promote the development of the skills found to be weak or missing or to recruit other brain regions to take over for the brain's identified weaknesses in circuitry, as compared with waiting until the child is older.

As an example, recent studies of the brain suggest that, after initial perceptual processing, visual input to the brain splits into two pathways: a more top of the brain or "dorsal" pathway that analyzes the "how" and "where" aspects of the image versus a more bottom of the brain or "ventral" pathway that analyzes the "what" aspects of the image. Phonological dyslexia has been found to be associated with weak "dorsal" stream processing connecting occipital and parietal regions in the brain, which is involved in developing an understanding of *how* the sound building blocks (phonemes) are combined within words. The identification of poor phonological awareness is a red flag for future reading disorders, intervention for which has proven effective in remediating and preventing further challenges in reading skills development (Shaywitz, 2004). If such neural plasticity is ignored, however, and the child is taught "compensatory" strategies that emphasize, for example, using a "ventral" ("what") stream process of memorizing sight words rather than learning to decode the phonics, further troubles will appear as the child grows older and reading comprehension requires rapid decoding of an increasing number of unfamiliar words. Simply memorizing the most frequent words in a language is therefore insufficient. Understanding the meaning of words and gaining an appreciation of higher-order language functions such as syntax and grammar must combine with competence in sounding out unfamiliar words, so that we focus about the meaning of what we read rather than decoding itself.

Our brains are built around the concept of automaticity. The more automatic a behavior becomes, the less we need to use conscious thought and cognitive resources to function. Consider, for example, the experience of a new driver as they get behind the wheel of a car. There is so much to pay attention to—pedals on the floor, mirrors reflecting different angles of vision, dials on the dashboard, and the relative position of your car within a stream of traffic. New drivers are bombarded by demands upon their information processing systems and must learn to differentiate important from unimportant information and integrate sensory input with decisions regarding actions such as turning the steering wheel and adjusting pressure on the accelerator, etc. There is good sense to the argument that new drivers should not have peers in the car and that the radio be turned off. As experience is gained, however, many of the processes of driving become automatic and relegated to "subcortical" brain mechanisms—they become habitual. Indeed, by the time a driver has accumulated thousands of hours behind the wheel, their attention is often distracted by conversations and thoughts unrelated to the process of moving some 4,000 pounds of metal and plastic through space at a speed almost beyond comprehension as little as two generations ago.

Appreciation of this concept of habituation and automaticity quickly leads to the idea that, the earlier we can identify variations in brain development and function that are known to result in later dysfunction, the more likely we will be to help modify or correct the identified problems. "Early identification" has become a rallying cry among child developmental specialists, and a focus upon the preschool and toddler years is now reaching downward to infancy and the very first signs of potential impairment, with subsequent intervention being provided. It may therefore not make sense to wait to screen kindergarten students to identify those who need early intervention and the support of research-based interventions. The identification of SLD seemingly must occur much earlier than the earliest screenings within a RTI model.

One positive aspect of a focus upon processing strengths and weaknesses, and the science of developmental/cognitive/neuropsychology in general, has been the development of a growing body of research that seeks to describe and characterize the pattern of brain functions that are associated with identified disorders. As opposed to a categorical diagnostic strategy of focusing upon whether a student does or does not meet the criteria for diagnosis as defined by DSM-5 (American Psychiatric Association, 2013); ICD-10 (World Health Organization, 1992); or the special education laws of various locations across the world, a dimensional approach emphasizes description rather than membership. If an individual has a family history of a certain learning disorder, shows early signs of the cognitive profile of that disorder, and will likely respond to interventions that have been proven to remediate that disorder, service eligibility should not be tied to whether one meets all the diagnostic criteria that have been codified, at a level that is necessary over a prescribed duration of time. A young child who clearly shows evidence of a developmental language disorder should not "wait to fail" before receiving intervention.

The dimensional approach to understanding specific learning disabilities must therefore take the perspective that we have a growing understanding of how cognitive functions emerge and support the development of the end products of reading, writing, math, and receptive-expressive language. Such cognitively based research is increasingly backed up by neuroimaging data and more finely discriminatory genetic analyses.

As a case in point, Emily Ross, Joel Schneider, and I presented a poster in 2016 that compared the cognitive profiles of 7-year-old twins reared together, one of whom had been diagnosed with Sotos syndrome (Nicholls, Ross, & Schneider, 2016). This genetic syndrome has been found to be characterized by neuroimaging anomalies including enlarged ventricles, increased extracerebral fluid, and midline abnormalities (Schaefer, Bodensteiner, Buehler, Lin, & Cole, 1997), along with implications of hypoperfusion of frontal brain regions (Horikoshi et al., 2006). Our comparison of the twins emphasized the need for analysis of individuals with learning disorders at the neuropsychological level, as simple comparison of global intellectual and achievement test performance was inadequate in describing their abilities. A specific profile of impairment was identified in the twin diagnosed with Sotos, primarily involving impaired spatial reasoning, working memory, novel learning skills, and mathematics, along with significant executive function weaknesses. This cognitive and academic profile is reminiscent of early discussions of non-linguistic learning problems by Johnson and Myklebust (1967) and the subsequent development of a model of brain functioning by Byron Rourke (1989). Rourke described multiple syndromes and clinical conditions (including Sotos syndrome) as demonstrating a suggested profile of strengths and weaknesses that he called the "Nonverbal Learning Disability (NLD) Syndrome." Rourke argued that this profile of information processing strengths and weaknesses was found among children with many types of brain insults, including certain genetic disorders, adverse neurological events associated with prematurity, endocrine anomalies, and others. Rourke felt that the profile was associated with problems in the "white matter" or the long circuits that connect various areas of the brain.

For those who align with a categorical model of understanding neurodevelopmental disorders, however, NLD causes a problem. NLD has not been recognized within DSM-5 or ICD-11, and those who have examined the validity of a categorical syndrome involving this concept have dismissed its utility. For example, Otfried Spreen, in a critical review of the concept, concluded:

> After a brief historical introduction, the article focuses on the apparent rarity of NLD; the hypothesis of the frequent co-occurrence of emotional disorder, depression and suicide in NLD; the white matter hypothesis as an explanation of the origin of NLD; and the question of NLD as part of a variety of other disorders. It is argued that NLD presents a broad hypothesis, but that there is little evidence to support its use in clinical practice.
> (Spreen, 2011)

As opposed to the professional rejection of the concept of NLD by some, clinical experience suggests that many families are astounded that Rourke's model of information processing in NLD captured their child in a way that is not only extremely accurate and helpful but is a conceptualization that they had never heard of before. Providing such families with references to the many works describing educational and emotional strategies for helping their children has been, for many, a tremendous relief from the burden of repeatedly being told by professionals that their child's problems were secondary to low intelligence, poor parenting, psychiatric illness, or a host of other inaccurate causative factors. Continuing work with NLD is finding that this umbrella category likely has multiple subcomponents, which if evaluated from a dimensional perspective make sense, not only biologically, but also in terms of educational planning. It seems critical that those of us who work with childhood developmental disorders continue to keep an open mind and resist the temptation to reject ideas simply because they don't fit mainstream thinking.

Another example of the habit of some professionals to "throw the baby out with the bathwater" is found in the analysis of some children who have reading disorders. Since the time of Orton's original work, it has become quite clear that phonological dyslexia is associated with inadequate functioning of the area of the brain that translates individual letters and letter sequences into sounds ("phonemes"). Evidence for this conclusion has derived from autopsy evaluations of adults who had a history of dyslexia (Galaburda, 2005), as well as from functional magnetic resonance imaging of the brains of children who could versus could not read competently (Shaywitz, 2004). These findings resulted in the extensive commercial development of reading intervention programs that, for some, have resulted in fairly rapid remediation of the core cognitive weaknesses and subsequent improvement in reading competence. It seemed to some that the problem was solved! We now know what causes dyslexia, and we know what we must do to fix it! Many clinicians have joined this bandwagon and confidently assert that reading disorders are definitively caused by poor phonological awareness and that any other explanations simply does not reflect current scientific knowledge. Unfortunately, it seems that they may be wrong.

Bruce Pennington has performed very careful genetic analyses of reading disorders and has concluded that the case for weak phonological awareness as a cause of reading problems is not airtight (Pennington, 2011). Pennington suggests that, while phonological awareness can be important in learning to read, reading also influences phonological awareness in a bidirectional manner. Children with chance-level phonological awareness can also use letter names to learn rather than sounds, and some children who have speech-sound (articulation) disorders with persisting phonological awareness deficits do not become reading disabled. Pennington suggests that reading disorders are genetically heterogeneous, with at least six candidate genes having been identified at four of nine well-confirmed loci. The appealing hypothesis that

dyslexia is purely a phonological awareness problem therefore may not be completely true.

It is also the case that reading disorders overlap and are comorbid with multiple other neurodevelopmental disorders, including speech-sound disorders, other language impairment, ADHD, etc. In fact, reading disability and ADHD have been found to co-occur (ranging from 25% to 40% in both disorders) much more frequently than would be expected by chance (Willcutt & Pennington, 2000). Analysis of a multiple deficit model of reading disorder and ADHD symptom dimensions has in fact found that they shared a common predictor—information processing speed.

Virginia Berninger (2008) further warns against treating each child with reading disorders as being the same, as if there are no individual differences between the children. Berninger suggests that there are multiple components to successful reading, including phonological awareness, orthographic awareness, knowledge of language morphology, intact phonological and orthographic working memory, attention variables, and executive functions. Understanding reading disorders requires an appreciation that different variations emerge at different stages of development and that interventions must be tied to the specific needs of the individual child. Dimensional thinking dictates that we not take on a "cookbook"-driven mentality.

Emerging research indeed questions the centrality of phonological awareness as tied to the specific brain region implicated and is identifying other areas of the brain that can reliably differentiate good versus poor readers. Eckert and colleagues, for example, found that carefully matched children with dyslexia and controls with good reading skills were reliably differentiated on the basis of an area on the right side of the cerebellum, correctly classifying 72% of dyslexics and 88% of controls (Eckert et al., 2003). Others have suggested that, while impaired cerebellar function is probably not the primary cause of dyslexia, it may be involved in more fundamental neurodevelopmental abnormalities that lead to differences throughout the brain's reading network (Stoodley & Stein, 2011). This line of thinking is consistent with other conceptualizations of how clinicians working with neurodevelopmental disorders should think about the evaluation of children. An emphasis upon large-scale brain systems and neural "networks" is likely to be the future of understanding learning disabilities.

So what is the clinician to do? Although it is "easy" to accept categorical models of disorders and to apply the cookbook strategies we are taught for their identification and diagnosis, a nagging question of whether such methods, which admittedly may be necessary in today's world, are sufficient. If one works within an environment where categorical eligibility decisions are based upon models such as achievement-potential discrepancies, meeting DSM-5 diagnostic criteria, or some other list of required data to compile in one's evaluation, then it does not serve the children and adolescents we work with to ignore such requirements in favor of our own personal conception of learning disabilities. The clinician in such situations is in some ways obligated to gather data that "makes sense" to the individuals who will make the categorical eligibility decisions, whether or not additional evaluation procedures can expand an understanding of why this particular student is struggling. It does not take too long to look up the eligibility or documentation requirements of various schools, government agencies, or programs on the internet or to place a quick call to the office that will end up making the decisions. At least on some level, our job as advocates for our patients requires that we provide information that will help them to obtain services that they need. A dimensional assessment may enhance the patient and family's understanding of their condition; however, it has reduced value if the patient is denied services because we didn't check all the boxes the eligibility coordinator looks at for their program.

As with all neurodevelopmental disorders, our evaluations should begin with detailed gathering of information. Particularly with learning disabilities, a wealth of information can be gathered from review of provided records, report cards, and a comprehensive developmental history. When evaluating learning challenges, however, it is invaluable to simply ask the child or adolescent in front of us about how they experience their own learning. Our own testing and assessment methodologies can help provide quantitative indicators of the presence/absence or severity of various information processing disorders; however, it is from the perspective of the child/adolescent that we can often gain a unique understanding of their daily struggles. Clinicians should ask the student about both their areas of strength and capabilities, as well as their areas of difficulty in learning. Whether the difficulties are limited to certain subject areas or are present across the schooling experience is important, as is asking about what the student feels is the most helpful support that they have been provided thus far. It is not uncommon for students to praise some teachers because "they know how to teach me," while expressing frustration in other classrooms where they feel lost and confused. It is useful to ask students what they feel is their preferred modality of learning. Do they like to listen to lectures or audio presentations of material, or do they prefer to read books and articles on the subject matter? Do they prefer to watch YouTube videos or other multimedia presentations in order to learn, or do they learn better with hands-on experience with new concepts and information? Do they take notes in class, and if so, are those notes helpful? Do they even look at the notes once they leave the class? Does it help them to have preorganized summaries of the main points to be taught, or do they utilize study guides or book synopses to grasp the main ideas? How do they approach the tasks of expressing their ideas either in writing or orally? Have they learned to use an outline or graphical organizer prior to initiating their expression? When assessing troubles with math, does the student feel they have more difficulties with the concepts involved or the calculations themselves? These questions can be covered in a fairly brief period of time and give the clinician insight as to where the student's difficulties may lie. Such reports can be compared with findings from formal testing, but it is important to remember that *how* a student obtains a specific score on a given test is more important than what the score is.

Clinicians need to learn to engage in the process of qualitatively evaluating our test results. If a student scores below expectations on a measure of passage length reading comprehension, what is the source of their low score? Asking the student to read out loud, as is required on some tests, allows for the clinician to track the accuracy of the student's reading decoding. Although letter reversals and sequencing errors may not be tied to the core components of a reading disorder, recognition that the child has not yet inhibited this natural tendency to perceive visual information irrespective of directionality is important. In reading, does the student painstakingly sound out words in a phoneme-by-phoneme manner, or have they achieved a level of automaticity that allows them to "see and say." Some students make errors in looking at the first few letters of the word and guessing at the rest and subsequently may or may not recognize their errors. Is their oral reading fluid with appropriate intonation and emphasis, or is it halting, monotonic, or characterized by emphasis upon the wrong sound patterns within the sentence? Does the student seem to recognize words and understand their meaning, or is it clear that they have a reduced level of vocabulary knowledge, which may in fact derive from their poor reading skills? Does the student skip lines when they are reading, need to use their finger to keep their place, or otherwise seem confused about where to start reading on a page? When errors are made, does the student recognize that they have made an error and attempt to correct it, or did they continue reading without an appreciation that what they have said makes no sense?

Asking these questions of how a student reads helps the clinician to select the types of tests or instruments that will be used in the assessment process. While larger batteries of academic achievement are useful in evaluating a student's profile of academic strengths and weaknesses, different test instruments assess similar concepts through different methodologies. As an example, the assessment of reading comprehension is performed differently on the Wechsler Individual Achievement Test (Psychological Corporation, 2009); the Woodcock-Johnson Tests of Achievement (Schrank, McGrew, & Mather, 2014); and the Academic Achievement Battery (Messer, 2014). The Wechsler test asks the student to read a passage and then answer questions about what they have read. The Woodcock asks the student to read a passage and supply a missing word within the passage. The Academic Achievement Battery asks the student to punctuate reading passages. Each of these approaches makes some degree of theoretical sense; however, comparison of a score from one test with another test is complicated by the fact that the processes involved are different. There is also a difference between asking the student to read a passage and answer questions while the passage is still visible, as opposed to asking questions after the reading passage has been removed. The former allows the child to scan back over the passage to find the answers to the question, whereas the latter requires conceptual integration of and memory for the passage, possibly tapping a higher level of understanding and "comprehension."

In the evaluation of mathematics, there tends to be more consistency across the various test batteries, most of which measure straightforward mechanical calculation skills, on the one hand, and more conceptual or quantitative reasoning skills based on word problems, on the other. Once again, a process analysis can be revealing in terms of identifying the nature of where the student's deficits may lie, in contrast to what aspects of mathematics remain intact. Our understanding of the underlying brain processes involved in mathematics is unfortunately much less complete than our understanding of language disorders; however, the study of "normal" acquisition of mathematical knowledge has suggested that there are core building blocks which must be mastered, as well as essential processes of information management that are necessary.

A full understanding of mathematical learning disabilities is not yet possible; however, the clinician can ask multiple questions that can assist in understanding how a particular student may fare. Does the student recognize numbers, and can they correctly draw the shapes associated with numbers? Do they reverse numbers either in their production or in sequencing multi-digit numbers? When performing calculation, does the student seem to understand the process of the various operations involving addition, subtraction, multiplication, division, etc.? Can they follow the steps necessary to reach a correct solution, or do they make procedural errors? When performing rows of calculation problems, does the student pay close attention to the operational signs, for example, continuing to perform addition after the problems become more varied and involve subtraction and multiplication? Does the student demonstrate spatial errors, as evidenced in their capacity to line up columns of numbers, and their understanding and completion of the processes of borrowing and carrying? Do they have automatic math fact knowledge, or do they need to count on their fingers and toes? Do they seem to understand the language involved in word problems and understand the terminology used in mathematics, such as percentages, fractions, etc.?

When it comes to oral language, does the student show any evidence of auditory processing or language perception difficulties? Conversely, is their speech clear and without articulatory errors? Does the student seem to have a good understanding of vocabulary, both through receptive and expressive measurements? Is their language interesting and varied in its use of vocabulary, and how well does the student use adjectives, adverbs, and other aspects of language morphology? What is the student's attention span like, and how well does the student hold orally presented information in their short-term and working memory? Can they process multiple-step instructions or complex lines of reasoning, or are they more focused upon concrete details while losing "the big picture?" Does the student seem to understand the concepts of grammar and syntax? Is the student able to process non-literal language such as the use of metaphors or idioms? What is the student's command of the social pragmatics of communication?

In written language, clinicians should evaluate the quality of the student's handwriting. Can they consistently create letters and words of uniform size and spacing, or is their written product difficult to decipher? Is the student able to spell most words, or can you at least decipher the words to grasp the meaning the student is producing? How creative is the use of vocabulary, and does the written product "sparkle" or engage the reader through the use of narrative and theme development? Does the student seem to appreciate the perspective of the reader and use appropriate structural conventions such as organization, transitions, paragraphs, etc.? Is it easy for the reader to grasp a mental image of what the student is trying to convey through their writing, or is their written product continually distracting? Does the passage represent a stream of consciousness that is difficult to follow? How well does the student use punctuation? Is there a "flow" to the writing that helps the reader with understanding the messages to be conveyed?

In summary, the evaluation of academic and learning disabilities should not be a robotic and formula-driven process. Simple achievement/potential discrepancy analysis is clearly inadequate, and the proponents of an RTI approach to addressing learning disorders are correct in asserting that the response of a student to particular styles of intervention may be more telling than simply identifying whether a student exceeds a cutoff score designed to make categorical eligibility decisions. Nevertheless, the processing strengths and weakness school of thought is correct in asserting that our goal is not necessarily to diagnose learning disabilities but, rather, to describe how someone learns. The greater we can learn to identify the associations between biological aspects of genetics and brain development, and their subsequent learning profiles, the earlier we can identify profiles that place a student at risk and provide intervention even before the student reaches the age of starting school. The future of learning disabilities assessment will likely focus upon the precursors to academic skills development, and interventions will likely occur increasingly at a preschool level. It also it is also important, however, to remain vigilant to the fact that children and adolescents are highly complex organisms influenced by multiple factors beyond simple information processing strengths and weaknesses.

Brain development is dimensional, with various brain functions coming "online" at different stages of development. How effectively a student develops executive functions may determine at what age or stage of schooling a problem may be evident or arise. Maintenance of a developmental perspective is therefore essential, as is the recognition of the science of evaluation and assessment including key concepts such as the Flynn effect (Flynn, 1984) and the Matthew effect (Stanovich, 1986). The Flynn effect refers to the fact that new versions of published tests often present/produce scores that are different from previous versions of the same test, while the Matthew effect states that "the rich get richer and the poor get poorer." Students who have language-based learning disabilities often demonstrate a profile of falling farther behind their peers on language-based measures, as they get older. We must remember that most of content learning occurs through exposure to language-based instruction, both in reading and lectures, and that any impediments in learning through this process means that non-disabled peers will begin to distance themselves over time. We should also be cognizant that as the world changes and is entering yet another phase of the information revolution, a growing emphasis will be placed upon science, technology, engineering, and mathematics (STEM) education and that students with "non-verbal" learning disorders may increasingly become disadvantaged.

Ideas Regarding Intervention

From an intervention perspective, it is clear that a one-size-fits-all model will not work. Interventions must be targeted, developmentally appropriate, and operate from a building block model. Clinicians regularly encounter students who cannot manage more advanced instruction because they do not have core skills that they somehow missed or failed to learn at an earlier age. While it may not be appropriate to expect that educational institutions will work at the pace of the slowest students, it seems that the requirement that students pass high-stakes tests in order to be promoted to the next level misses the concept that students with learning disabilities learn differently, not that they can't learn.

Interventions for specific learning disabilities typically involve three broad concepts. The first line of effort may be to try to teach the skills that are missing, based upon our assessment and formal testing, as well as the needs identified by the student and their teachers/caregivers. Focused intervention should follow a "bottom-up" approach of reducing the needed skills down to their core components, building the missing skills to automaticity, and gradually incorporating higher levels of integration of the skills into learning strategies. It might seem obvious, but this should initially always consider sensory acuity and motor competence. There are applications for smart phones and tablets that allow clinicians to screen for visual acuity, color blindness, hearing impairments, etc., and initial observations of the child's competence in holding and manipulating a pencil are important. Should concerns arise from these screenings, it is important to make sure that the student is referred for a more comprehensive eye or hearing examination, and possibly to occupational or physical therapies.

Interventions for SLD should also work in a scaffolded manner. Should one have phonological dyslexia, for example, with poor awareness of phonemes and how they are identified, manipulated, and sequenced, initial efforts should be to teach these skills prior to moving on to memorizing the most common words in the language. Building phonological awareness is therefore a substrate to effective reading development. But what if the student has significant distractibility, an elevated activity level, and poor working memory? Investing heavily in what can become quite expensive private tutoring programs may be minimally effective if the core skills of sitting down, paying attention, and remembering presented material aren't addressed first. Although many caregivers are wary regarding the use of medications with young children, clinicians can share research as to the safety and effectiveness of medication use when monitored closely by appropriate medical professionals. Some caregivers will ask, "But my child is not hyperactive—why do they need medicine?" Clinicians are advised to be aware of and refer to research such as Shaywitz et al.'s (2017), studies that proved that the use of atomoxetine (Strattera) improved reading scores in patients with ADHD and comorbid dyslexia, as well as in children with dyslexia *without* ADHD. This finding suggests that medicines for ADHD may help a child with reading even if they don't have ADHD. Our interventions need to consider the totality of the child's needs, rather than focusing upon one specific or commercial strategy.

The effectiveness of SLD interventions also needs to be closely monitored for effectiveness and intensity. A greater frequency and/or intensity of core skills training may facilitate the process of making the skill use automatic, which then frees up cognitive reserves for the next level of intervention. Some intervention programs even recommend taking a child with SLD out of school so that they can attend day-long interventions, every day for several weeks, to ensure that the skill base is established. Naturally a family's financial resources and the level of the child's education need to be considered in this regard; however, it may be that greater intensity for shorter periods of time will work better than lower-intensity skills training, spread out over a longer period of time.

All interventions for SLD should be recommended based on published evidence of effectiveness, and clinicians are encouraged to research all programs they recommend and to understand such evidence. Information in this regard can be found on several websites, including the Florida Center for Reading Research (Florida Center for Reading Research, 2017) and InfoAboutKids (InfoAboutKids, 2017). Such websites perform careful reviews of the evidence supporting various programs and/or resources, with an eye to their research base, their freedom from commercial influence, and other factors that might affect the credibility of their recommendations.

Once the clinician has recommended a specific skill-based approach to building core competencies, the next step is ensure that the environment is supportive of the intervention programming and provides accommodations for the student's core learning impairments. As an example, students who are distractible benefit from preferential seating within learning environments and higher levels of structure in their education. Some children need repetition/clarification of instructions, a reduced quantity of work (scored proportionately), or the opportunity to have examination of their knowledge performed in alternative ways (e.g. the ability to use a keyboard/laptop rather than handwriting to show one's knowledge). It is important to question the basis and effectiveness of accommodations, however, as new research suggests that many of the most commonly used accommodations in academic testing (e.g. extended time, reduced distraction environments, use of a calculator, etc.) may not actually result in better reading or math performance (Pritchard et al., 2016). The Learning Disabilities Association of America offers many ideas about the use of accommodations for students with SLD (Learning Disabilities Association of America, 2017b). The focus of intervention should be on building a student's capabilities, rather than continually confronting them with their impairments. Keeping children in during recess or restricting them from "the fun classes" of art and music should be avoided.

Any evaluation and treatment plan for SLD should focus upon a child's strengths as well as their weaknesses, and clinicians should emphasize to caregivers the importance of investing as much time and energy into building on what the child can do well, as opposed to just focusing upon their weakness. Many students with SLD have areas of substantial talent that should be nurtured, whether involving art, music, athletics, leadership, or any other area in which the child can learn to be proud of themselves, rather than feeling inadequate secondary to their learning struggles. Clinicians should be alert to any indication that the child or adolescent is experiencing a low level of self-esteem, anxiety, depression, or somatic distress, as a sign that psychological interventions may be indicated to accompany academic interventions. As with other neurodevelopmental disorders, the message needs to be that this is a child with a specific learning disorder but that most of the child's abilities are strong and the disorder is only one small part of who the child is. We need to celebrate successes and be our children's cheerleaders and biggest fans.

Conclusions

It seems that the pace of learning and acquired knowledge is growing at a logarithmic rate. Our ancestors learned to communicate through pictures, hieroglyphs, and eventually written materials that required formal education to understand. Mathematics evolved from a method of exchanging goods to advanced calculus. Education moved from hands-on experience to structured teaching to the new information world of the internet. Anything that gets in the way of acquiring academic knowledge therefore becomes a stumbling block in human development, and rather than focusing upon waiting for a child to fail, clinicians today must recognize the earliest manifestations of learning disorders. This requires asking questions as to what core skills are required to advance, what they look like at different ages, and how we can remediate difficulty in their acquisition. Wouldn't it be great to intervene at a level before the child experiences failure?

Bibliography

American Psychiatric Association (APA). (2013). *Diagnostic and statistical manual of mental disorders* (5th ed.). Arlington, VA: American Psychiatric Association.

Barkley, R. A. (2014). *Attention-deficit/hyperactivity disorder* (4th ed.). New York: Guilford.

Bateman, B. (1965). *Learning disorders: An educational view of a diagnostic approach to learning disorders*. Seattle: Special Child Publications.

Bauer, R. M. (2014). *Functional neuroanatomy and essential neuropharmacology* (p. 34). New York: Oxford.

Berninger, V. (2008). Defining and differentiating dysgraphia, dyslexia, and language learning disability within a working memory model. In M. Moody & E. Silliman (Eds.), *Brain, behavior and learning in language and reading disorders*. New York: Guilford Press.

Broca, P. (n.d.). *In Wikipedia*. Retrieved August 9, 2017, from https://en.wikipedia.org/wiki/Paul_Broca

Eckert, M. A., Leonard, C. M., Richards, T. L., Aylward, E. H., Thomson, J., & Berninger, V. W. (2003). Anatomical correlates of dyslexia: Frontal and cerebellar findings. *Brain, 126*, 482–494.

Flanagan, D. P., Ortiz, S. O., & Alfonso, V. C. (2007). *Essentials of cross-battery assessment* (2nd ed.). Hoboken, NJ: Wiley.

Fletcher, J. M., & Miciak, J. (2017). Comprehensive cognitive assessments are not necessary for the identification and treatment of learning disabilities. *Archives of Clinical Neuropsychology, 32*, 2–7.

Fletcher, J. M., Stuebing, K. K., Morris, R. D., & Lyon, G. R. (2013). Classification and definition of learning disabilities: A hybrid model. In H. L. Swanson, K. R. Harris, & S. Graham (Eds.), *Handbook of learning disabilities*. (pp. 33–50). New York: Guilford.

Florida Center for Reading Research (FCRR). (2017). *Resources*. Retrieved August 9, 2017, from www.fcrr.org/resources/

Flynn, J. R. (1984). The mean IQ of Americans: Massive gains from 1932 to 1978. *Psychological Bulletin, 95*, 29–51.

Gall, F. J. (2017). *In encyclopaedia britannica*. Retrieved August 9, 2017, from www.britannica.com/biography/Franz-Joseph-Gall

Galaburda, A. M. (2005). Dyslexia—a molecular disorder of neuronal migration. *Annals of Dyslexia, 55*, 151–165.

Gillingham, A., & Stillman, B. W. (1936). *Remedial work for reading, spelling and penmanship*. New York: Sackett & Wilhelms Lithographing Corporation.

Hale, J., Alfonso, V., Berninger, V., Backen, B., Christo, C., Clark, E., . . . Yalof, J. (2010). Critical issues in response-to-intervention, comprehensive evaluation, and specific learning disabilities identification and intervention: An expert White paper consensus. *Learning Disability Quarterly, 33*, 223–236.

Hale, J. B., Chen, S. H. A., Tan, S. C., Poon, K., Fitzer, K., & Boyd, L. A. (2016). Reconciling individual differences with collective needs: The juxtaposition of sociopolitical and neuroscience perspectives on remediation and compensation of student skill deficits. *Trends in Neuroscience and Education, 5*, 41–51.

Hale, J. B., & Fiorello, C. A. (2004). *School neuropsychology: A practitioner's handbook*. New York: Guilford.

Hallahan, D. P., & Cruickshank, W. M. (1973). *Psychoeducational foundations of learning disabilities*. Englewood Cliffs, NJ: Prentice-Hall.

Hallahan, D. P., Pullen, P. C., & Ward, D. (2013). A brief history of the field of learning disabilities. In H. L. Swanson, K. R. Harris, & S. Graham (Eds.), *Handbook of learning disabilities* (pp. 15–32). New York: Guilford.

Hebb, D. O. (1949). *The organization of behavior: A neuropsychological approach*. New York: John Wiley & Sons.

Herr, C. M., & Bateman, B. D. (2013). Learning disabilities and the law. In H. L. Swanson, K. R. Harris, & S. Graham (Eds.), *Handbook of learning disabilities*. (pp. 51–68). New York: Guilford.

Horikoshi, H., Kato, Z., Masuno, M., Asano, T., Nagase, T., Yamgisihi, Y., . . . Kondo, N. (2006). Neuroradiologic findings in Sotos Syndrome. *Journal of Child Neurology, 21*, 614.

IDEA. (2004). *Sec. 300–309-Determining the existence of a specific learning disability.* Retrieved September 17, 2017, from https://sites.ed.gov/idea/regs/b/d/300.309

InfoAboutKids.org. (2017). Retrieved August 10, 2017, from infoaboutkids.org

Johnson, D. J., & Myklebust, H. R. (1967). *Learning disabilities: Educational principles and practices.* New York: Grune & Stratton.

Kirk, S. A. (1963). *Behavioral diagnosis and remediation of learning disabilities.* Proceedings of the Conference on Exploration into the Problems of Perceptually Handicapped Child: First Annual Meeting, Chicago.

Learning Disabilities Association of America (LDAA). (2017a). *Accommodations.* Retrieved September 17, 2017, from https://ldaamerica.org/?s=accommodations

Learning Disabilities Association of America (LDAA). (2017b). *History.* Retrieved August 10, 2017, from https://ldaamerica.org/about-us/history/

Messer, M. A. (2014). *Academic achievement test.* Lutz, FL: Psychological Assessment Resources.

Naglieri, J. A. (2010). *Essentials of specific learning disability identification* (pp. 145–172). New York: Wiley.

Nicholls, C. J. (2010). [Review of the book: *Brain, behavior and learning in language and reading disorders* by M. Mody & E. R. Silliman]. *Archives of Clinical Neuropsychology, 25*, 78–79.

Nicholls, C. J., Ross, E. K., & Schneider, W. J. (2016). The neuropsychological profiles of twins discordant for Sotos Syndrome: A case study. *Journal of Pediatric Neuropsychology, 2*, 131–148.

Pennington, B. (2011). *Multiple deficit models of reading disability and comorbid disorders.* National Academy of Neuropsychology Annual Convention, FL.

Pritchard, A. E., Koriakin, T., Carey, L., Bellows, A., Jacobsen, L., & Mahone, E. M. (2016). Academic testing accommodations for ADHD: Do they help? *Learning Disabilities: A Multidisciplinary Journal, 21*.

Psychological Corporation. (2009). *Wechsler Individual Achievement Test* (3rd ed.). San Antonio: Psychological Corporation.

Rourke, B. P. (1989). *Nonverbal learning disabilities: The syndrome and the model.* New York: Guilford Press.

RTInetwork.org. (2017). *What is RTI.* Retrieved August 10, 2017, from www.rtinetwork. org/learn/what/whatisrti

Schaefer, G. B., Bodensteiner, J. B., Buehler, B. A., Lin, A., & Cole, T. R. P. (1997). The neuroimaging findings in Sotos syndrome. *American Journal of Medical Genetics, 68*, 462–465.

Schrank, F. A., McGrew, K. S., & Mather, N. (2014). *Woodcock-Johnson IV.* Rolling Meadows, IL: Riverside.

Shaywitz, S. (2004). *Overcoming dyslexia.* New York: Alfred A. Knopf.

Shaywitz, S., Shaywitz, B., Wietecha, L., Wigal, S., McBurnett, K., Williams, D., . . . Hooper, S. R. (2017). Effect of atomoxetine treatment on reading and phonological skills in children with dyslexia or Attention-Deficit/Hyperactivity Disorder and comorbid dyslexia in a randomized, placebo-controlled trial. *Journal of Child and Adolescent Psychopharmacology, 27*, 19–28.

Spreen, O. (2011). Nonverbal learning disabilities: A critical review. *Child Neuropsychology, 17*, 418–443.

Stanovich, K. E. (1986). Matthew effects in reading: Some consequences of individual differences in the acquisition of literacy. *Reading Research Quarterly, 21*(4), 360–407.

Stoodley, C., & Stein, J. (2011). The cerebellum and dyslexia. *Cortex, 47*, 101–116.

Wernicke, C. (n.d.). *In Wikipedia*. Retrieved August 9, 2017, from https://en.wikipedia. org/wiki/Carl_Wernicke

Willcutt, E. G., & Pennington, B. F. (2000). Psychiatric comorbidity in children and adolescents with reading disability. *The Journal of Child Psychology and Psychiatry and Allied Disciplines, 41*(8), 1039–1048.

World Health Organization (WHO). (1992). *The ICD-10 classification of mental and behavioural disorders: Clinical descriptions and diagnostic guidelines*. Geneva: World Health Organization.

Section III

The Role of the Clinician

The first two sections of this book focused upon the dimensions of being different and the most common clusters of impairment that result in children and adolescents coming to the attention of developmental clinicians. We have reviewed some of the important considerations and questions the clinician needs to ask him- or herself and have seen that dimensional thinking can help to organize the volumes of data that we can gather.

Section III attempts to integrate the foregoing into strategies that the clinician can use to perform an evaluation of childhood developmental disorders, including issues of consent, diagnostic interviewing, the formulation of questions to be asked, the use of questionnaires and standardized testing, and concerns regarding process and performance validity. Next, we review considerations relevant to writing a report of our findings and touch on questions of expediency, writing for one's audience, common pitfalls in report writing, and the process of giving feedback to our patients and their families. We discuss variables to consider in formulating and implementing interventions for the challenges we identify, including questions of the scope of intervention; compliance with patient wishes; the setting for the interventions; and the need to remember the dimensions of development, familial resources, and comorbid conditions.

We end Section III by turning attention onto ourselves. How much education do you need to engage in being a clinician who works with neurodevelopmental disorders? Why did you choose this field of study and for whom are your services really designed? We end with a call for clinicians to strive for excellence while remembering to take care of ourselves. The career of a developmental specialist is challenging, rewarding, and ultimately satisfying.

9 Considerations for Assessment

Consent

Clinicians who work with neurodevelopmental disorders are, by definition, often working with individuals who lack the legal capacity to give consent for their participation in an evaluation and/or treatment. It is therefore essential that clinicians have clear intake paperwork that clarifies who is the legal guardian of the child/adolescent beforehand and spells out your policies regarding needed consent from relevant parties. In today's age of the internet, many of your forms can be posted online, on your website, or sent via an email address that you obtain at the time of the initial telephone contact. Having background questionnaires that clarify family members and background information can help you to not ignore potentially critical information, while gathering such information in a straightforward manner. Readers who would like to see the forms used in my office may do so at www.thenichollsgroup.com.

It is also important to clarify exactly who is your client. Although this seems simple, many referrals for evaluations come from parties who are not, themselves, the legal guardians of the child. Take for example, a call from a step-mother who has not discussed the fact that she is seeking an evaluation with the child's biological mother, who has joint legal custody. What about a referral from a private school that will be paying for an evaluation of a child to guide their educational programming—is the school your client or is the caretaker of the child? What about a request for you to provide an "independent evaluation" of a child who is engaged in some form of civil or criminal court proceeding? Is your client the child, their caregivers, the attorneys involved, or the court? Clinicians are advised to very carefully review the laws governing the jurisdiction within which one works and to discuss these issues with the relevant parties prior to providing services, to follow best practices, avoid confusion, and prevent a licensing board complaint. I recommend having written policies, procedures, and intake forms. Consider asking a colleague to review these forms to make sure they are consistent with the laws of your region and cover all the important information.

If the biological parents are not currently married, and depending upon the laws of the country, state, territory or province in which the child lives, some jurisdictions require both legal parents to give permission for various services, including developmental evaluations, to be performed. It may be prudent to request a copy of a divorce decree, or other documentation of legal guardianship, to clarify roles and responsibilities. Unfortunately, parents sometimes use the opportunity of consulting with a behavioral health specialist to undermine another caregiver, criticize them, or sometimes even plant the seeds of suspicion regarding a non-involved caregiver's suitability, such as implicating child abuse or neglect. How much weight does the clinician give information one parent provides about the other, in the absence of external corroboration? Whose wishes should predominate in serving the best interests of the child? If the family involves other than a two-biological parent family and an evaluation is to be performed, to whom will feedback be given? Should feedback sessions be held jointly or separately? Should non-biological caregivers be invited (e.g. step-fathers)? My recommendation is that a clinician's default position should be that input is requested from and feedback given to all relevant caregivers, unless there is a clear prohibition or risk to the child. Sometimes this may require separate appointments; however, it is critical for clinicians involved in this line of work to have well thought-out policies and procedures for dealing with postdivorce families. The clinician's role is not that of the courts.

The Initial Interview

Most families who come to see a developmental specialist have a story to tell. Clinicians often form hypotheses about the purpose and scope of an evaluation based on referral information or what has been learned in an intake telephone call; however, it is important to allow caregivers to have enough time to tell their story. Perhaps the simplest opening line for the clinician is something to the extent of "How may I help you?" Such open questions provide an opportunity for the caregiver (and if present the patient) to tell the clinician all about their concerns, in an unstructured and free-form manner. The clinician at this stage of the process should use good reflective listening techniques to encourage discussion of the concerns, without interjecting too many questions or imposing too much structure. Some caregivers have carefully prepared notes and a mental outline of what they wish to share, while others may need encouragement to tell the clinician what they hope to get out of the consultation. Taking notes regarding (or even recording) this opening discussion allows the clinician to circle back, later, and rephrase the concerns to make sure that the caregiver feels listened to and that the purpose of the assessment is clear.

Allowing the caregiver to share their story also allows the clinician to get a sense of who has the concerns and something about the dynamics of the child's family system. Is the primary spokesperson one caregiver versus another, or is there shared discussion of the concerns? Not infrequently I have experienced one caregiver to arrive with a clear agenda, while another caregiver arrives late to the appointment and isn't sure who I am or why they are coming to visit. Often, one of the caregivers has experienced their own struggles that are like those of the child, or an assertive caregiver offers thinly veiled comparisons of the child to the other caregiver, even in their presence. How does the caregiver who has their own neurodevelopmental disorder cope with our evaluation processes? If they have their own reading challenges, how might they cope with our provision of stacks of questionnaires and forms for them to complete? One can gain initial understanding of a child's challenges if the clinician senses difficulties in the caregiver's ability to organize and express their thoughts.

Parents sometimes will tell you that their child is simply lazy, apathetic, unmotivated, and any number of other adjectives and that they don't "believe" in all this junk about neurodevelopmental disorders. Many a caregiver has come to my office and, within the first 5 minutes, pointedly told me that their child will never, ever, take medicine to manage what they got past themselves with grit and determination. Sensitive clinicians must help such parents through gently structuring the intake interviews, providing support to those who have trouble reading or expressing their ideas, and not embarrassing or shaming caregivers who may secretly be terrified that their child's problems are "all my fault." In general, it is counterproductive to begin arguing with a caregiver about the utility of specific interventions, before the clinician even knows if that intervention is indicated. Simple acknowledgment and validation of caregiver concerns and beliefs may be more productive in securing their alliance and in obtaining a clear understanding of the child's struggles.

Indeed, it may be worth considering the fact that the *family* is the patient, not just the individual whose name is at the top of your referral sheet. Most parents are at some level anxious and possibly defensive about the fact that their child has a problem, and it is important to remember that, when a caregiver enters your office in an angry or hostile manner, such emotions are less likely to be about you and are more likely to reflect their own pain and history. We must strive to join with the family and to some degree share their pain, if we don't want to come off as an arrogant and uncaring ivory tower professional. When you encounter resistance to your incredibly reasonable plan of action, consider the nature of your relationship with the individual and carefully examine your own assumptions and attitudes.

Background Questionnaires

The goal of the initial interview is to find out who has concerns, what those concerns are, why your services are being sought currently, and what the caregiver or referring source views as the best outcome of meeting with you. To answer these questions, it is helpful to have a method for efficient gathering of background historical information. Few parents can recall the details associated with early medical, developmental, and academic progression, and providing a questionnaire or format for them to report this information allows for the individual to find their baby books, dig out report cards, obtain other professionals' records, and share this information with you in an organized manner. I have found that having a background history questionnaire on my website allows parents to provide the information I want to know in a manner that I can review systematically and store in the child's file. Background questionnaires also allow the clinician to specify the kinds of information desired, by offering checklists or prompting recall of information the caregiver may not have at their fingertips.

As an example, we often want to know about the patient's family history of neurological, developmental, and psychological/psychiatric disorders. Simply asking, "Is there a family history of any problems?" typically results in caregivers stating, "No, not really." On the other hand, asking, "Has any family member has experienced any of the following:" under which is a list of common conditions (migraines, depression, sleep disorders, etc.) allows caregivers to perhaps recognize that "You know, my uncle had. . . ." Similar facilitation of recall can be effected in asking about mother's pregnancy and delivery; the perinatal period and early development; the child's temperament, preschool experiences, transition to schooling; etc. Instead of asking whether the child gets along well with others, questions can be posed about numbers of friends, activities engaged in, the presence of bullying, etc.

Questionnaires that are completed before an intake appointment also allow for caregivers to acknowledge and share sensitive information that may be hard to talk about when first meeting a stranger. We now know that adverse childhood experiences are strongly associated with physical and mental health/illness, with higher numbers of experiences associated with greater severity of impairment. Asking questions on a background form can allow caregivers (and children/adolescents capable of responding) to report incidents of abuse (emotional, physical, sexual); household challenges (domestic violence, substance abuse, criminality, mental illness and parental separation/divorce); and childhood neglect (emotional or physical). Sensitive follow-up by the clinician can explore these issues, which may become easier to talk about if they are recognized as common and not a topic shrouded by secrecy (Centers for Disease Control and Prevention [CDC], 2017). As an example, I recently evaluated a severely emotionally dysregulated 4-year-old girl who objectively demonstrated no areas of developmental impairment but became aggressively defiant, hitting our psychometrist repeatedly, throwing office materials on the floor and engaging in times of screaming and crying secondary to simple requests. The little girl was clearly not on the autism spectrum, was quite bright, and when not asked to do something she didn't want to do, was quite pleasant and engaging. In the feedback session, however, when I suggested that mother consider a second opinion consultation with a child psychiatrist, the mother exploded in much the same way as the child, screaming that she had been the victim of unrelenting abuse as a child, had been psychiatrically hospitalized herself, and wanted no part of medicating her child.

A quick review of textbooks that discuss important historical information to be gathered identifies that there are multiple broad areas to cover. These include family history and genetics, pregnancy, the perinatal period, early development and temperament, separation from the nuclear family and the transition to schooling, academic progression, medical history, social relationships, extracurricular activities, and the transition to adulthood/emancipation from caregiver control. Once again, while interviewing a caregiver to obtain this information is a standard strategy, having a background questionnaire can complement review of records that can be obtained from other sources. Clinicians should ask whether the child has been previously evaluated and ask to see any reports of such evaluations. One should ask to review report cards, reports of school standardized testing, and any evaluations by allied school professionals such as occupational and speech/language therapists. Request copies of Individual Educational Programs, Student Accommodation Plans, and Functional Behavioral Assessments/Positive Behavioral Intervention Plans. I recommend paying close attention to the comments written by teachers on the child's report card, and therapists in their notes, as they are often more revealing than grades or progress ratings. Clinicians might consider developing their own teacher questionnaires that cover desired information and asking caregivers to make sure that the child's teachers provide input to the evaluation. It is sometimes easier and more comfortable for a teacher to share concerns on a questionnaire that is sent directly to the clinician, rather than handed back to the caregiver who may question or take exception to the teacher's impressions. It can also be helpful to invite teachers and other school personnel to telephone the clinician should they be reluctant to put their thoughts into writing.

Formulating the Key Questions That Need to Be Answered

The review of caregiver concerns, input from teachers and other professionals, and background history should lead clinicians to formulate key questions that will be addressed through the evaluation process. It can be helpful at this stage to clearly state what those questions are and to obtain agreement with the caregiver requesting the evaluation. Confirmation that the questions are an accurate summary of the concerns can next point to the specific strategies the clinician will use to try to answer the questions. Some questions can be answered by direct interview as to the what, when, how, and where of the behaviors of concern. Other questions will need more objective data gathering through the use of a standardized assessment process. This process will sometimes also require observation, such as through a Functional Behavioral Assessment that looks at and records data regarding the behaviors of concern, their antecedents, and consequences, which serve to identify the function of the behavior.

Commonly, clinicians will turn to the use of standardized questionnaires and rating scales. Such instruments allow respondents to rate the presence/

absence and/or severity of carefully defined behaviors, and the comparison of the respondent's ratings with a sample of similar respondents' responses about the child (sometimes with age- and gender-specific norms). These forms of data gathering are important in that the individuals who complete these questionnaires generally observe the child daily and across multiple settings. The results from these screening tools therefore have "ecological validity," meaning that they reflect the child's performance in the usual settings in which they live. To legitimately evaluate the information obtained, however, clinicians need to assess the similarity of the child being rated with the standardization sample used to develop the questionnaire. The use of a questionnaire that was developed primarily for acculturated, suburban, middle-class students may suggest misleading information when utilized with an individual from a different cultural background. Likewise, some questionnaires are developed and normed on a specific type of respondent, for example caregivers, and using the questionnaire with a different type of respondent, for example teachers or other non-caregivers, may not be appropriate. One of the strongest mandates in assessment is therefore that the clinician must learn about their tools and technologies before using them. In three summary words: READ THE MANUAL(!)

Additional considerations in the choice of questionnaires to use include an appraisal of whether one wants a broad overview of the child/adolescent's adjustment and psychosocial functioning, or whether one wants a more focused assessment of an area of specific functioning, such as social skills, study skills, or levels of anxiety, depression, etc. It may be best to use a combination of both approaches to obtain a broad overview of the child while narrowing down to specific features of the areas of specific concern. This strategy helps by ensuring that the clinician is considering the child's overall adaptation and doesn't ignore an area of need. As an example, ADHD as a diagnostic entity is rarely found in isolation. Indeed, in most developmental disorders, comorbidity is the rule rather than the exception. ADHD often co-occurs with oppositional and defiant behavior, anxiety or depression, social skills impairment, or other symptoms depending upon the unique experiences of the patient. While one could use only a focused questionnaire that teases apart the components of ADHD, there is a risk that this strategy might overlook other causes of the child's current levels of impairment. Think of your assessment as needing to cover a variety of systems and try not to overlook areas that may reveal critically important information.

It is also important to try to obtain questionnaire data from several sources or respondents. It is not uncommon, for example, that behavioral ratings provided by teachers are very different from those provided by parents. Rather than assume that one is in denial while the other is exaggerating, the clinician should consider whether the different environments in which the child is observed impacts the level of severity of reported concerns and even the nature of the concerns. Consider, for example, a seasoned second grade teacher's observations of a child's behavior within their structured and organized classroom versus a young parent's first encounter with the challenges of child rearing and each emerging developmental stage. Conversely, consider the new teacher's frantic efforts to manage the overwhelming demands of corralling thirty-plus energetic children while struggling to develop each day's curriculum, as opposed to a parent who has had three other children go through this developmental stage and has acquired a repertoire of effective parenting techniques. Sometimes caregivers will state that it seems that the child "keeps it together" during the hours of the school day but then "unloads" upon the parent the minute they get home.

Asking children and adolescents to complete questionnaires about themselves is also important, if they have the needed levels of reading skills and can understand the questions. A caregiver who is dealing with their own depressive disorder may see symptoms of depression in their child which, when asked directly, the child indicates is not their experience. Alternatively, some parents gloss over a child's experience and state, "He's fine," when direct questioning of the child reveals a tremendous sense of inadequacy as compared with peers, difficulties falling asleep secondary to worries about the next school day, or fears of once again being bullied or teased by other students at school, to the point that they are having stomach aches or other stress-related symptoms.

On the basis of the intake interview, review of historical data and the information gathered through questionnaire completion, the clinician can next decide upon the key questions to be addressed and answered by the evaluation. In some instances, formulation of these questions leads to a conclusion that the clinician already has sufficient information to answer the questions and move on to intervention. As an example, if the clinician observes a pattern of coercive family interaction and defiance on the part of the child/adolescent, and there are no reported concerns regarding the academic skills or school performance of the patient, the clinician may decide that there is little to be gained by putting the patient through an extensive battery of direct testing, the information gathered from which would probably not make a big difference in what the clinician chooses to do. There is no necessary need to rule a categorical diagnosis in or out, if it will not make much difference in the choice of an intervention strategy. Patients don't care so much about diagnoses—they want solutions.

The Use of Standardized Testing

While intervention may not require additional testing, it is often the case that many clinicians will want to directly evaluate a child's performance on a structured set of objective tasks, against which comparisons can be made with appropriate normative data. Some systems, such as schools or disability determination organizations, in fact require that the clinician provide objective test scores to facilitate decision-making as to whether the child meets criteria for eligibility or diagnosis. In some circumstances, there is a "fixed battery" of tests that is requested, such as an intelligence test and a broad battery of academic achievement to determine the presence or absence of a specific learning disability. This approach, like categorical diagnosis, is comforting, familiar, and well recognized by the schools or agencies used to making eligibility decisions. This approach may also not always be either necessary nor sufficient. Simply documenting a student's levels of ability on such tests does not tell the clinician *why* the child obtained the scores or point to the specific form of intervention that may be best for remediation of the underlying deficits. The choice of tests used must therefore balance competing purposes for the overall assessment. If one intends to utilize standardized tests of various developmental factors, the clinician must be prepared to justify which tests were chosen, for what purposes, and how the test scores answer the questions formulated during the initial interview and data-gathering phase. Was the test developed and standardized on a sample of children like your patient? How well does the test accurately measure the construct underlying the behaviors in question? Sometimes the "fixed battery" requested may not be appropriate for a given child, such as asking a hearing impaired child to engage in a testing process that involves only direct questioning and reliance upon auditory presentation of test materials, rather than allowing the child to demonstrate their knowledge in other ways. In sum, most clinicians use a more flexible approach to developing their test batteries, with the goal of answering referral questions but in a manner that is individualized to the specific child and the specific questions being asked.

Behavioral Observations and Consideration of Validity

Testing that occurs in the clinician's office presents an unfamiliar experience for most children, who may find the process to be quite stressful. The child who must disrupt their regular routine to get bundled up to travel to the clinician's office, undoubtedly knows that their trip is atypical. Traveling to a clinic or provider's office can also be stressful for the caregiver, who may need to arrange for transportation or must follow directions to a sometimes hard to find place. The process can be nerve wracking and expensive, and the stress experienced by the caregiver is not lost on the child.

Next, the child is ushered into the setting in which the evaluation is to occur and is typically asked to wait in some entrance area until they are checked in and the provider is available, during which time they may be exposed to other children and families. Most staff members who work in such settings are kind and sensitive individuals, but they are still strangers to the child. Children check each other out, wondering why the other is here. If another child has a visible difference or disability, the child may question whether their own challenges might be equally obvious to others. Depending upon the child's level of social competence and anxiety, such encounters can either be interesting or frightening but inevitably involve stress, as defined by the *Oxford Dictionary* as "A state of mental or emotional strain or tension resulting from adverse or demanding circumstances" (Oxford Living Dictionaries, 2017). All of us who evaluate developmental disorders have experienced the stress of examination of our knowledge within our training programs, and we know that while a little stress can enhance performance of well-learned competencies, it can also negatively influence performance on tasks for which we are less competent or prepared.

I suggest that first thing clinicians do is to recognize and normalize the experience of the child. Often we are too quick to "get started" and don't spend sufficient time to allow the children and adolescents who come to visit us become acclimated to the situation. It is important to ask them what they know about why they came to see you and what their understanding is as to what will happen to them in the next minutes and hours. I think it is important to stress that we will not be doing anything to hurt them, such as giving shots, which is what many, many children fear when they go to the doctor. I like to tell the child that they should speak up if they need to use a restroom, take a break, or if they want to check in with their caregiver(s). Asking the child their perspective offers respect for their dignity and is a source of tremendous information, such as a child who shakes your hand, smiles, looks you in the eye, and says, "You know, I may not have autism!"

It has also recently become clear that we are particularly incompetent at determining whether a child is giving good effort in our testing if we rely only upon our impressions and observations. The work of Paul Green (Green & Flaro, 2003), Mike Kirkwood (2015), and others has clearly shown that sometimes the "little darlings" who come to us for assessment produce performances that are non-credible and resemble that of individuals with severe neurological impairment, even though they are sweet and cooperative and look like they are trying their best! While the clinician should be very resistant to stating that such children are "malingering," the formal assessment of effort and performance validity is crucial to our interpretation of other data and the formulation of our conclusions. While performance validity testing has become the standard of care in forensic practice, I recommend always using some objective strategy for evaluating effort in every case. Suggestions for how this should be done are provided in Kirkwood (2015); however, the process of determining whether a child is giving reliable and valid performance on our assessment tools can be addressed through both dedicated or "standalone" measures or tests, as well as through analysis of "embedded" indicators of the level of effort extended by our patients.

Standalone tests typically involve the presentation of tasks that seem to be legitimate measures of some cognitive skill but which have been found to be sufficiently easy that almost all persons who perform the task will have very little if any difficulty. Common measures involve skills such as recognition memory, for example asking the child to choose between two images or words, one of which they have seen before. Accumulated research has found that even young children can perform these tests competently and that, if a child's performance drops below certain standards as have been identified by the test's developers, it is likely that the child is not giving optimal effort.

Embedded measures use a similar strategy of looking at how a child performs on a test to assess how reliable and valid the obtained scores on that test might be. If a child makes errors on many easy items on the test, and yet gets quite difficult problems correct, it may be that they were disengaged in the early portions of the task but became more interested as the item difficulty level increases. Their overall score, nevertheless, is artificially lowered by the early item failures and may misrepresent the ability level of the child on the construct measured by the task.

It is important for the clinician to ask themselves how long of a testing session should be utilized, to maximize the individual's capacity for full engagement with testing. Although it may be convenient for us to perform an entire assessment battery across the course of a full, 8-hour day, such extended testing sessions may overtax the patient's resources and produce unreliable/invalid findings, as compared with a process of breaking the assessment up into several shorter segments of time, which might result in more accurate measurement. Many other conditions must be addressed in determining the appropriateness of an evaluation and include environmental factors such as ambient noise, lighting, temperature of the room, and size of the table and chair utilized. Asking a small child to sit in an adult chair, where their feet do not hit the ground, adds complications to an assessment of their fine motor control, since many of their postural muscles must be utilized simply to keep them upright in the chair. Asking an individual to pay attention in an environment where there is significant background noise may also compromise the accuracy of the findings obtained. It is generally better to find some small and quiet room in which to perform testing, as opposed to testing in a school cafeteria or other noisy and active environment. Sometimes clinicians can use simple environmental modification, such as the use of a white noise machine to mask background noise, or more substantial strategies, such as putting up sound-absorbing panels in rooms within which testing frequently occurs. Maximizing the comfort of the child while reducing distractions and competing stimuli will help the clinician obtain the most reliable and valid findings.

Minimizing Error in the Assessment Process

Categorical thinking is based upon convenience and our assumptions. As science moves forward and we test our assumptions, we learn that there are multiple sources of error in evaluations, which can be broadly reduced into a 2 × 2 table. If our methodology of evaluation is useful, we will identify true cases as having the condition and true non-cases as not having the condition. Unfortunately, our diagnostic accuracy is often not that good, and we are prone to making errors. One kind of error occurs when we assert that something is present when in fact it is not present. This is termed a Type I error and is demonstrated in diagnosing a child with ADHD when it is subsequently learned that they have obstructive sleep apnea and their attention problems disappeared following surgery to remove their tonsils and adenoids. The other type of error is when we assert that something is not present when it truly is: a Type II error. An example here is when schools make the assumption that, just because a student with ADHD doesn't get poor grades, they don't need supportive or special education services (Lhamon, 2016). Teachers sometime assume that a student understands what they have read because the student says so; however, subsequent questioning of their understanding reveals misunderstanding. Many other errors are also possible, and as we grow in our sophistication as diagnosticians, we consider variables with names such as "positive predictive power," "base rates," and "areas under the curve." All individuals who perform clinical diagnostic evaluations should develop some degree of understanding of these statistical concepts, as they ultimately affect how accurate we are in reaching our conclusions.

Take, for example, the issue of base rates. This is the statistical phenomenon that, as we administer more and more measures or tests, we increase the likelihood that we will get one or two scores that seem to be suggestive of a specific area of strength or weakness. A low subtest score on a large battery of cognitive abilities therefore entices us to conclude that the individual has a specific weakness in the skill set that score reflects. While that that may in fact be the case, it may also be the case that the individual scored poorly on that specific subtest for reasons that are independent of whether or not they have the ability. Often a youngster's performance on the first few tests they are administered is affected by a natural tendency to be somewhat nervous going into an evaluation. A child who is worried about why they must go through this testing and what might be wrong with them, and the unfamiliarity with the evaluation environment, may be prone to guessing impulsively, giving up too easily, or in some other manner not demonstrating their true knowledge base. The child who needs to go to the bathroom but is reluctant to speak up may be distracted and again less likely to show their true ability levels. It is therefore essential for clinicians to ask themselves not only what the score is that an individual may have obtained on a certain measure, but perhaps equally importantly, how did they get that score, and how reliable/valid is the score? A child who fails an item on a test involving arrangement of colored blocks to resemble a pictured design may obtain an item score of 0 if they take one second over the time limit for the item, if they rotate one of the blocks so that it is different from the model design, if they lose the 2×2 or 3×3 configuration of the blocks, or if they eat one of the blocks! Clinicians should observe and document behavioral observations throughout an evaluation, as they are ultimately very revealing when it comes time to write a report.

Scoring developmental testing is not always easy. Most standardized measures offer rules for determining if a response provided by the patient is correct and sometimes whether they should receive scores of 0, 1, or more based upon the quality of the response. Most standardized tests, for example, give sample responses indicating whether an answer is a 1-point or a 2-point response, or whether the item should be considered failed. What is often not appreciated, however, is that not all possible correct responses are given and that sometimes a patient will give an answer to a question which represents a superior response that is much better than the examples provided in the manual. It is common for younger clinicians to fail to give points for such an answer, which nevertheless indicates that the child has a clear understanding of the concept being measured, even though the answer is not one listed in the manual. Clinicians must, again, read the manual to determine the spirit of how tests should be scored and recognize the implications for a student if scoring is either too strict or, alternatively, too lenient. It is dangerous to consistently penalize a child who is "close but inaccurate" in their responses, just as it is not helpful to always give a child's responses credit even though they are not precise. The clinician should always consult with colleagues about ambiguous scoring questions or, if not possible, use an alternating strategy of giving credit for the first ambiguous response while not giving credit for the next. Should a testing protocol be full of such scoring questions, the clinician could score the test twice—once giving credit and the other not giving credit, to see if the outcome is significantly different and might alter conclusions reached.

Were the Questions Posed Actually Answered?

Once the clinician has formulated an assessment battery, administered the procedures, and performed the scoring, it is helpful to circle back to review the original formulation of questions to be answered by the assessment. We may be proud of our brilliant battery of tests and extensive tables of scores; however, they are of little use if the questions which prompted the referral remain unanswered. It is also easy to become sidetracked and to focus upon areas of intellectual interest to us, the clinician, and to lose track of what is important to the individual, their caregiver, or the referral source who sent you the patient. Clear definition of referral questions ensures that we will utilize methodologies that will answer the questions and concerns brought to us, and if we cannot clearly answer those questions, we may need to ask what else needs to be done before we finish our assessment. Clinicians should also recognize that some children do in fact have developmental delays in certain areas, even if our evaluations and assessment don't end up telling us exactly what the problem or cause is or was. Our job in these circumstances is to carefully document the child's level of performance in as reliable and valid a manner as we can, to speak about the strengths and limitations of our assessment processes, and to occasionally say something to the effect of "I don't know" in response to the questions that are posed. Younger clinicians often are reluctant to express such uncertainty, out of fear that the caregivers or others will deem them incompetent. More seasoned clinicians are comfortable with the concept that we do our best to figure things out but that we don't know everything.

Conclusions

The evaluation of child and adolescent neurodevelopmental disorders is a process. There are multiple steps and stages within the process, and the gathering of information needed requires a combination of open-ended interviewing, the review of clusters of typical systems involved in the genesis or maintenance of a disorder, and direct data gathering through both subjective and objective methodologies. Clinicians can approach the task systematically but should regularly question the assumptions being made in our choice of procedures or our interpretation of the findings. There are multiple sources of error in assessment, which can be reduced but likely not eliminated. Recognition of this fact requires that clinicians remain humble, report the limitations within our procedures and findings, and consider alternative explanations for the results we obtain. An initial process of clearly formulating the questions we wish to have answered should end up with our review of whether, in fact, we actually answered those questions.

Bibliography

Centers for Disease Control and Prevention (CDCP). (2017). *Adverse childhood experiences (ACEs)*. Retrieved August 10, 2017, from www.cdc.gov/violenceprevention/acestudy/index.html

Green, P., & Flaro, L. (2003). Word memory test performance in children. *Child Neuropsychology*, 9(3), 189–207.

Kirkwood, M. W. (Ed.). (2015). *Validity testing in child and adolescent assessment*. New York: Guilford.

Lhamon, C. E. (2016). *United States Department of Education: Office for Civil Rights*. Retrieved August 10, 2017, from https://www2.ed.gov/about/offices/list/ocr/letters/colleague-201607-504-adhd.pdf

Oxford Living Dictionaries. (2017). *Stress*. Retrieved September 18, 2017, from https://en.oxforddictionaries.com/definition/stress

10 Putting It All Together and Writing a Report

The Importance of Expedience

When a caregiver has finally mustered up the courage to take their child in for an evaluation, they are often dismayed at how long the process will take. Usually a visit to a healthcare provider, such as a physician or a dentist, results in immediate feedback and a plan of action. This period is agonizing for the families of the children seeking an evaluation, and they are often waiting on the edge of their chairs for the news. Families who visit developmental specialists must wait even longer. They must often wait a long time to get an appointment, a period of time after the intake appointment before the formal assessment, and then must again wait for the feedback session before they learn what has been concluded and what needs to be done about it. For some practitioners, getting the written report to the family may then take even longer. The time between completion of the evaluation and providing the feedback is therefore critical. Some of our colleagues take weeks or even months to mail the report to the family, claiming that they are too busy to produce a report in a timelier fashion.

Clinicians should realize, however, that it takes the same amount of time to complete a report in a timely fashion as it does to complete it 3 months later. Indeed, it is even more efficient to perform your report immediately after evaluating a child, while the particulars of the history and your impression of the child are still fresh in your mind. If you wait too long to write the report, you have to relearn all the information contained in the child history form, review your notes, and conjure up an image of who the child was. Alternatively, writing the report as soon as you have completed the evaluation is comparatively easier because you have a fresh memory and sense of the child. This is also more professional and kinder toward the parents who are figuratively baring their soul to the examiner. I recommend building report-writing time into your schedule so that it is immediately performed just as soon as the evaluation data is available. Preorganizing your thoughts into a report template can allow you to drop information into the relevant sections as you become aware of the information, and rather than having to write the report start to finish once all data is gathered, clinicians need to learn to be flexible and to create portions of the report independently of each other, tying together the findings at the end.

As an example, if one performs an intake interview one day and has the child come back for testing on a later date, build time into your schedule to write up the intake interview and review of the background information and summarization of provided reports and other professionals/school evaluations, on the day of the first interview. Again, it will probably take less time in the long run because the information is fresh in your mind. Summarizing your review of intake information also helps to remind you why you are evaluating the child, if there is a longer period of time or if you see several other new patients between the intake appointment and subsequent testing or further evaluation. Typically, younger clinicians remember everything about the first few patients they see and wonder why you might not remember all the details; however, as your schedule fills up and you see more and more patients, often multiple patients each day, it gets harder and harder to separate out any individual patient from the others and remember their unique story. So, as a rule, it is most efficient and effective to perform documentation as soon as possible—even before the family has left the building if possible. Adding a few minutes at the end of the intake (or stopping the intake a few minutes earlier) can build in time to do this. Don't strive for perfectionism: just get it done, and do it today!

Integrating the Data

By the time we reach the stage of putting it all together, we have typically amassed a large volume of data and findings. Now is the time for the clinician to flexibly shift between grasping the big picture while organizing the details. One strategy that may be helpful is to enter all data into tables that allow for simultaneous analysis of the findings. Some clinicians list test findings in columns as shown in Table 10.1.

This approach tends to focus the attention of the clinician upon the numbers, however, and potentially leads to an over-interpretation of the

Table 10.1 Test Name

Cluster/Subtest Name	Raw Score	Scaled Score	Percentile	Description
Full Scale Score	xx	yy	zz	abc
Cluster 1	xx	yy	zz	abc
Subtest A	xx	yy	zz	abc
Subtest B	xx	yy	zz	abc
Subtest C	xx	yy	zz	abc
Cluster 2	xx	yy	zz	abc
Subtest A	xx	yy	zz	abc
Etc.	xx	yy	zz	abc

discrepancies between them. If someone gets a score at the 35th percentile on one test and the 59th percentile on another, that "looks like" a fairly big difference, and the clinician may tend to try to interpret the meaning of such a discrepancy. On the other hand, data could be presented in a different format, as shown in Table 10.2.

The format of Table 10.2 allows the clinician to "see" the relationships between scores more readily and to draw certain conclusions fairly quickly. Thus, the child whose performance is depicted in Table 10.2 clearly is very bright on a conceptual level but has significant difficulties with the skills measured in aspects of the abilities measured in Cluster 4. Based on this overview, the clinician could next look at data from other tests that may examine component functions at a finer level, to see if a similar pattern of relative weaknesses emerges. Interpretation of findings to families and patients is also easier when scores are presented in a visual format and performance is anchored— i.e. showing where the Average range is and pointing out that the patient has both strengths and weaknesses. If a child is highly competent and intelligent, relative to peers, this fact stands out quickly, while the same is true if the child has a significant intellectual disorder.

Keeping in mind the fact that the more tests we administer, the greater the likelihood we will obtain scores that are "outliers" or different from the remaining scores, the clinician should next formulate hypotheses about how the data relates to the key questions that were posed at the outset of the evaluation. If one of the questions had something to do with the patient's comprehension of spoken language, for example, the clinician can look at the various test scores to determine whether there is objective evidence that the

Table 10.2 Test Name

Scale/Subtest	Scaled Score SS/T	1	2	3	4	5	6	7	8	9	10	11	12	13	14	15	16	17	18	19
Full Scale	120														x					
Cluster 1	136																	x		
Subtest A	16																x			
Subtest B	17																	x		
Cluster 2	109												x							
Block Design	12												x							
Visual Puzzles	11											x								
Cluster 3	121														x					
Subtest A	11											x								
Subtest B	16																x			
Cluster 4	82						x													
Subtest A	8								x											
Subtest B	7							x												
Subtest C	6						x													

child has a receptive language processing disorder, as opposed to difficulties with attention, memory, speed of language processing, or expressive language skills. Through this process, the clinician can start to examine the evidence supporting or refuting the concept that the patient has one of the usual suspects of neurodevelopmental disorders or possibly something else causing their difficulty.

When considering one's findings, it is sometimes useful to keep in mind the differentiation between whether a patient can't perform the specific skills; whether they can under the structure of the evaluation process but doesn't show the skills on a day to day basis; or finally whether the patient can perform the skills, does sometimes, but won't perform on a consistent basis. This is where the value of the behavioral questionnaires and rating scales can be integrated with one's behavioral observations and the history. Why does a child perform poorly on a given task? Is it because of a "Swiss cheese" performance of passing or failing items within a given task, or does the child correctly answer problems until they become too difficult and they reach a "ceiling?" Is the poor performance secondary to anxiety and a lack of confidence on the part of the child, or is it secondary to scattered attention and/or high levels of impulsive responding? Analysis of one's data must integrate the obtained scores with all other information, prior to reaching a conclusion about the child's native abilities. Is it competence? Or is it performance?

The next task facing the clinician is the differentiation of important versus unimportant findings in the evaluation. Sometimes we identify a finding that, while interesting, may not be that important to our overall conclusion. Color blindness is one example. During testing, the clinician might identify that a child has trouble differentiating red and green, which may have affected performance on a couple of subtests where such color discrimination is important. This might lead to a recommendation for a referral to a vision specialist for confirmation of our hypothesis; however, it may be unlikely that being color-blind is a significant contribution to some of the key questions we are trying to answer, such as whether the child has a developmental social disorder. Some data that we gather is interesting in its own right but may not pass the "So what?" question.

Once our findings have been looked at from the big picture level, the clinician should next ask him- or herself whether the pattern of findings is consistent with what is known about the hypothesized underlying condition. If a child has trouble with reading, for example, do the findings match the science that suggests challenges with phonological awareness, rapid naming, etc.? Or, alternatively, does the child show intact core language skills and phonological awareness but struggles with reading secondary to a lack of automaticity of decoding skills? This is the point at which it is essential to have reference texts that describe current findings for given conditions, such as the *Handbook of Pediatric Neuropsychology* (Davis, 2011) or the *Handbook of Neurodevelopmental and Genetic Disorders in Children* (Goldstein & Reynolds, 2010). Clinicians are also advised to secure some form of electronic library search access and to perform literature reviews on clinical conditions presented by our patients, if one is not familiar with the most recent findings regarding the condition. Working with neurodevelopmental disorders requires a lifelong commitment to continuing education. Science is moving so rapidly that it is impossible for any clinician to remain current in their knowledge, and therefore optimally helpful to their patients, without the use of resources.

One final point in the analysis of one's data is the necessity of considering whether the data are explained by one specific kind of disorder or, more likely, the interactive contributions of multiple, comorbid conditions. Clinicians should ask whether the data is consistent with the history we have obtained. For example, one doesn't usually "catch" a neurodevelopmental disorder later in childhood without some earlier signs having been present. Next, one should question the relationship between the child's findings and normal developmental milestones, or how an early-onset or acquired disorder might have altered the normal developmental course the child has gone through. The impact of a significant neurological insult at age 2 is different from the same insult at age 10, and the clinician should ask him- or herself how this child's brain may have been altered by their early experience, need for adaptation and coping with acquired impairments, etc. Even if there is a clear developmental progression of symptoms without intervening factors affecting brain growth and maturation, what is the environment in which the child has grown, and what have been the impacts of opportunity, poverty, or marginalization secondary to ethnic and cultural difference? It is easy to become nearsighted, professionally, and fail to consider the total life experience of our patients and the role their disorder may have played.

Consider Your Audience

The end product of our work typically takes the form of either an evaluation report or letter to a referring party. This document, which may be all some people ever know about you, should represent a summary of your findings, recommendations as to interventions, and a "roadmap" for the patient and/or family to utilize in moving forward. Your report will become a living document that will follow the patient, often for many years. If you're done a good job, the patient may return for a re-evaluation or update of their status, several years later, and your report may be all that you have to help you to remember the specific situation of the patient, your impressions and findings, and a summarization of your thinking. Evaluation reports are therefore helpful for the clinician and serve to document the work we have done.

But who reads our reports? Many reports from clinicians are so long and so full of needless details that the average recipient of the report simply jumps to the impressions and recommendations section, without considering what you have written. Caregivers who take a greater interest in our evaluation reports may attempt to wade through long reports but are often driven to distraction by what has been appropriately termed "psychobabble." Indeed, Karen Postal et al. (2017) found that, in a survey of several hundred neuropsychologists and referral sources, only 15% of neuropsychologists believe that referral sources read their entire reports, while slightly more than half of the referral sources reported that they actually do read the entire report. Nevertheless, referral sources felt that a slow turnaround of neuropsychologists' reports negatively affected patient care, and the most frequent complaints were that reports were "difficult to understand, vague, long [and] inaccurate" (Postal et al., 2017, p. 15).

Jacobus Donders has published an article entitled "Pediatric Neuropsychological Reports: Do They Really Have to Be So Long?" (Donders, 1999). In this article, Donders laments the fact that developmental evaluation reports are often quite lengthy, with large portions devoted to recitation of test scores, confidence intervals, and other information that is often meaningless to the recipients of the report. It is important that the clinician be well grounded in assessment theory and consider important concepts such as sensitivity, specificity, and the kinds of errors that can be made in performing evaluations. It is not necessary that the clinician bore the recipient of the report with such information, however, and it often appears that an overemphasis upon detail-level information, about how the child or adolescent performed on this or that test, leads to the reader becoming lost in the trees while missing the forest. Indeed, there may be an inverse relationship between the length of a report of findings and the clinician's true understanding of the nature of the child or adolescent's difficulties. Many clinicians continue to write as if they are being evaluated by their instructor in their first assessment class and seem to feel that they must justify every conclusion drawn through reference to statistics, standardization samples, etc.

Alternatively, clinicians should try to take the perspective of the audience of their reports. Most often, the audience is the patient and/or their caregivers. These individuals have little interest in or understanding of the psychometric science involved in our assessments and alternatively are asking more basic questions such as "What is wrong?" and "What can I do about it?" To this end, effective report writing should tend to focus upon being shorter, using plain language, and striving to answer the primary questions presented by the family. As noted in the previous chapter, these questions include "Who is this patient?" "What are the concerns?" and "Who has the concerns?" It is important to clearly define what the referral questions are and to then evaluate one's report by determining whether those questions were answered. In plain language, the effective communicator can say what they found, what that means, and what can be done about it.

Common Pitfalls in Report Writing

There are multiple common pitfalls in report writing, most of which are easy to avoid when recognized. As above, one of the biggest pitfalls in report writing is inclusion of information that ultimately doesn't matter. As opposed to writing pages and pages of text regarding the individual's background history and developmental milestones, if there is no useful or meaningful information contained in the history, simply say that their history is unremarkable. Conversely, some evaluation reports neglect information that is important. As an example, an adolescent who presents to your clinic with concerns about emerging difficulties with critical thinking and executive functions may seem far removed from a detailed examination of their birth history. Most clinicians ask about perinatal events when dealing with a younger child with developmental delays but often neglect to do so with older individuals. Nevertheless, the conclusion the clinician might reach will likely differ if one is aware that the patient was the product of a late-term premature birth complicated by significant jaundice and feeding difficulties, rather than if an assumption is made that the perinatal period was unremarkable. The necessity of writing concise reports, therefore, does not mean that all relevant data should be ignored, only that data that is within normal limits may not need to be detailed exhaustively.

Another common perform report writing is a tendency for the clinician to talk about the tests that were administered, rather than talking about the child or adolescent who is their patient. Some clinicians extensively detail the scores that were obtained, often in a minimally organized list or table of scores, score ranges (e.g. "low average"), and stock phrases about what each test measures. I am regularly amazed to see 30- or 40-page reports that are clearly a template into which the clinician has cut and pasted specific numbers from specific tests. Not only does this style of writing lead to extremely long, boring reports, it likely reflects a poor understanding on the part of the clinician as to what the evaluation scores truly mean or measure. Many tests and subtests have names that are inconsistent with what the test measures. Likewise, two tests with similar names (e.g. working memory) from two different scales, may measure very different components of the purported skill being measured. If one is testing memory span by presenting sequences of digits to be recalled, one would likely find different results if the digits are presented at a rate of one per second as opposed to two per second. If reading comprehension is measured with the reading passage still in front of the patient as they are asked questions, is that the same skill as if the questions are asked after the passage has been removed?

Clinicians should strive to describe the patient they have evaluated, instead of talking about scores on tests they administered. When test scores are reported in language that is inaccessible to the general public, the patient, and their caregivers, the reaction is often one of confusion, anxiety, and even anger on the part of the family. It doesn't matter how eloquent you are in explaining statistical analyses if the point you are making seems unrelated to the concerns for which the child is brought to the evaluation.

A third area of common pitfalls in report writing is found in clinicians who are overconfident in their findings and draw conclusions which may not be supported by the data. As we have discussed, when looking over tables of test scores, there is a natural tendency to identify a low score and decide that it represents an area of significant impairment for the patient. In reality, the more tests one administers, the more likely you are to obtain a few low scores. What is the base rate of the discrepancy between that score and other obtained scores? Although a low score may be statistically below the mean of other scores, if 25% of people who took that test had a similar low score, is it meaningful? Kyle Boone (2013) cautions that many clinicians "over test" and obtain large numbers of test scores, with no consideration of the statistical characteristics of comparing such a volume of information. Boone cautions that we should not assume that a low score means brain impairment; that our patients had average premorbid abilities; or that, even if a patient suffered a documented significant brain injury, that they can't recover and ultimately even have completely normal cognitive functions. Clinicians should therefore always question the logic of their reasoning when presenting the findings of our assessment, and not make logical errors including jumping to a conclusion, ignoring data that is inconsistent with our conclusion, failing to consider alternative possibilities, or failing to investigate the truth of information suggested to us when we are performing our initial intake interviews.

It is natural for clinicians to want to try to be "correct" in their formulation and diagnosis; however, in some cases, it is simply not possible to draw firm conclusions, and brazen statements of conclusions which are clearly not supported undermine our credibility. Our evaluations always have limitations. The failure to consider the limitations in one's findings, or other factors that were not evaluated, suggests the level of professional arrogance that tends to lead patients to seek services from other sources. Our evaluations represent a brief photograph at a single point in time. Life is a movie, and sometimes our best efforts to take an accurate photograph are inadequate in describing the life script of our patients. Returning to the referral questions can often be a helpful process at this stage, in trying to tie evaluation findings to the specific questions that were asked at the outset. If one's evaluation cannot answer the questions, perhaps the strategy utilized should be questioned or consultation with a trusted colleague sought. Asking for help when one is not sure of one's findings is a sign of maturity and competence. Failing to ask for help, or failing to answer the referral questions in favor of simply reporting what you are sure about, serves no one.

An easily avoidable pitfall in performing evaluations is the failure to consider all of the facts of a case and the research evidence supporting any conclusions that are drawn. For example, child development professionals are increasingly called in to offer testimony within a myriad of "bad baby" lawsuits and legal actions, and the conscientious practitioner needs to devote sufficient time and energy into evaluating the scientific literature relevant to the case at hand, rather than just assuming that a child's later developmental problems are secondary to the birth trauma. Recently, I was asked to review another clinician's evaluation of a child who had experienced shoulder dystocia (dystocia means slow or difficult labor or birth). In this condition, the infant's head was delivered. but the baby's shoulder became "stuck" behind the mother's pubic bone. The result was an injury to the nerves of the shoulder, arm, and hand. The professional who performed the original evaluation of the child in this case concluded that the child was at risk for the development of learning difficulties "consistent with hypoxia associated with delivery complications." The professional's opinions were, in their mind, confirmed when follow-up evaluation of the child demonstrated early signs of reading problems. My review of the birth records nevertheless revealed that the infant had no medical record indications of having suffered a significant hypoxic injury (including acidemia, prolonged Apgar scores of 5 or less for longer than 5 minutes, multiple organ involvement, etc.), based upon parameters defined by the American Academy of Pediatrics and the American College of Obstetrics and Gynecologists (Task Force on Neonatal Encephalopathy, 2014). Furthermore, a computer search of the professional literature found no evidence to support a specific link between hypoxia and reading disorders, whereas in this case there seemed to be a strong family history of poor academics. The point is that just because a child's history contains events which, to the untrained eye, look like they would cause later problems, such an outcome is not necessarily the case. Professionals in child development must move beyond assumptions and hunches to examine the evidence. Careful review of a child's early history is essential in the competent evaluation of developmental difficulties; however, professionals must not jump to conclusions. Our review of the history adds data to our ultimate conclusions, but we must remain objective and impartial. If you don't know whether something is important, ask someone or *look it up*.

Giving Feedback That Makes Sense

One final pitfall that should be emphasized is the level of vocabulary used by the clinician when writing their report. Most clinicians have an advanced level of education and training. We are fortunate to have well-developed vocabularies, strong writing skills, and an appreciation of higher-order conceptual reasoning. When discussing cases among ourselves, there is an assumption that we can use technical terminology and multisyllable words with complete understanding on the part of the colleague with whom we are speaking. Such an assumption is not always valid when giving feedback to our patients and their families.

My experience has been that the process of giving feedback works best when one starts with a brief review of the history that is provided to you, the questions that were posed at the outset of the evaluation, and acknowledgment from the family that everyone is on the same page. I then provide information in terms of the characteristics or description of the child, without necessarily referring to numbers or diagnostic categories. I try to discuss both the patient's strengths and weaknesses, with an emphasis upon the strengths. Any areas of difficulty should be discussed in terms of daily examples in the child's behavior and an integrative explanation of what the findings likely mean. My goal is to see the individuals in the feedback session nodding their heads and agreeing with my descriptions. By using plain language and talking about the child, clinicians allow caregivers and patients alike to give you feedback about the accuracy of your findings. As we have discussed throughout this book, diagnostic labels and categorical descriptions are often less important than a clear understanding of the child and the nature of any challenges that they may face.

Ending With Recommendations, Not Diagnoses

Some evaluation reports seem to end at the diagnostic impressions. It appears that the clinician has focused only upon the assessment process, has gathered and integrated the provided data, and has reached a conclusion but has also stopped at that point before providing information that can be functionally helpful to the patient. This is analogous to a beam of light coming through a window and illuminating a spot on the floor. Our evaluations, conversely, should be more of a lighthouse, in which gathered information leads to an understanding of what we are seeing and in turn leads to the generation of recommendations that patients and caregivers can take and use, as a roadmap for effective intervention for their concerns.

Some reports seem to cut and paste pages and pages of generic recommendations, including some recommendations that may not even apply to the patient at hand. This is not to say that having a bank of recommendations from which one can pick and choose is unhelpful, as many developmental disorders will have a need for similar interventions and it can be more efficient for the clinician to insert previously well thought-out strategies for dealing with various problems. Some caregivers will tell you that they only used two or three of the forty recommendations they were provided, however, and it is always embarrassing to receive a phone call back from a caregiver, asking why some other child's name is included throughout the recommendations you provided, rather than the name of their own child. As a general strategy, I recommend avoiding the "cut and paste" strategy in report writing. We should recognize that our evaluation reports will often follow our patients for years and years and, in some cases, cause significant changes in their lifestyle or services provided. Remember to first do no harm.

It is also important to think about how we provide feedback regarding our findings. While we may have benefitted from university-level and graduate school education in statistical concepts and the psychometric basis of our findings, describing a child's functioning by referencing standard scores and confidence intervals typically results in caregivers glazing over and not understanding what we are saying, even though they appear to be attentive and may even nod in agreement with what we say. It was important to prove to your professors that you comprehend concepts such as regression to the mean and split-half reliability, but the use of such language with caregivers does not impress anyone and does disservice to those who seek our advice. The wisest of mentors demonstrate how to speak in plain language, using concepts that are readily understandable, and talk about the child rather than the tests and their results for that child. I strongly recommend the book *Feedback That Sticks: The Art of Effectively Communicating Neuropsychological Assessment Results*, by Karen Postal and Kira Armstrong (2013), for all clinicians who perform evaluations of children, not just for neuropsychologists.

Conclusions

Clinicians are encouraged to recognize that their evaluation reports are similar to a self-portrait. Other professionals, patients, caregivers, and referral sources will draw conclusions about your competence as a clinician, your thoughtfulness, sensitivity, and your humility, all on the basis of your several pages of text. Considering the old saying that one never gets a second chance to make a first impression, clinicians should take a second to look over their reports with a critical eye. Does the report "look" presentable, with appropriate margins, justification, headers, and use of white space? Did you proofread the report for typographical errors and/or grammatical gaffes? Would it be helpful to ask someone else to review your report before you sign it, to be sure that you have communicated effectively and at a level that is accessible by the patient and/or caregivers? In some ways, your report is similar to your business card. It is what people will remember you by and on some level determine whether they choose to refer other patients to you. If your treatment recommendations reflect a lack of understanding of the nature of the concern the patient has, or has a "one-size-fits-all" style, future referrals are likely to go to other clinicians (often without your awareness). Individuals involved in the evaluation and treatment of children and adolescents with developmental disorders must recognize that we are in a customer service business. It may be helpful to remember that, if one goes to a restaurant where one does not like the food or receives poor service, there are plenty of other restaurants.

Bibliography

Boone, K. B. (2013). *Clinical practice of forensic neuropsychology* (pp. 208–226). New York: Guilford Press.

Davis, A. S. (Ed.). (2011). *Handbook of pediatric neuropsychology*. New York: Springer Publishing Company.

Donders, J. (1999). Pediatric neuropsychological reports: Do they really have to be so long? *Child Neuropsychology, 5*, 70–78.

Goldstein, S., & Reynolds, C. R. (2010). *Handbook of neurodevelopmental and genetic disorders in children*. New York: Guilford Press.

Postal, K., & Armstrong, K. (2013). *Feedback that sticks: The art of effectively communicating neuropsychological assessment results*. New York: Oxford Press.

Postal, K., Chow, C., Jung, S., Erickson-Moreo, K., Geier, F., & Lanca, M. (2017) The stakeholders' project in neuropsychological report writing: A survey of neuropsychologists' and referral sources' views of neuropsychological reports. *The Clinical Neuropsychologist*. Published online: 17 Sep 2017. doi: U10.1080/113854046.2017.1373859

Task Force on Neonatal Encephalopathy. (2014). Neonatal encephalopathy and neurologic outcome, second edition. *Obstetrics & Gynecology, 123*(4), 896–901.

11 Considerations for Intervention

We have discussed certain forms of intervention for specific clinical conditions, within the four chapters of Section II. This chapter focuses upon some more general considerations that cut across specific dimensions or areas of impairment. There are overriding considerations that should guide the clinician in their recommendations and principles that should be followed regardless of the focus of the intervention.

Interventions Should Be Based Upon Evidence of Need

The beginning of the twenty-first century has been characterized by many clinicians identifying with a given theory, school of thought, or intervention strategy that is applied to multiple conditions and presenting complaints. One hears of certain cognitive training or psychotherapeutic techniques being practiced by clinicians as if that specific technique is a "one-size-fits-all" miracle. It is common for clinicians to advertise that they are practitioners of this or that technique, which they can effectively use with all kinds of disorders. This movement is found among professionals from multiple healthcare disciplines, and local, national, and international organizations are formed around various specific interventions or theoretical models. And yet it seems unlikely that the same technique could be effective with the myriad of disorders that present to clinicians, suggesting that a healthy degree of skepticism should arise when a psychotherapeutic technique is offered as treatment for a cognitive disorder, or when an occupational or physical therapy approach is offered as treatment for an emotional symptom profile. I do not challenge the validity of the techniques themselves, which can be very helpful to those whose needs are aligned with the therapeutic effect of the treatment, but it makes sense for the clinician to ask what kinds of needs are specific to our patients and how can we address those needs, rather than whether we can apply a favored therapeutic strategy to a need for which there is no indication.

A question sometimes arises as to whether one should intervene to remediate a deficit or simply provide accommodations to bypass the deficit. Should children with math challenges be allowed to use a calculator? Should children who can't read well have all instruction orally? It is important to keep in mind that simply bypassing areas of weakness may actually reinforce an individual's disability, instead of helping the child to overcome their impairment (Hale et al., 2010). Bypass strategies may be necessary for children with severe disabilities, and alternative teaching techniques may help students with disabilities, but it is important to help our patients learn to overcome their challenges and not just avoid them.

Interventions Should Follow Patient Wishes

I view the clinician's task as one of taking a patient or caregiver's concerns and performing an evaluation of the underlying dimensions of need. Clinicians should then offer recommendations based upon what strategies might best address the needs identified in the assessment. The determination of which interventions are applied, however, is not the purview of the clinician and alternatively lies primarily with the patient and their family. Returning to the example of medication usage, clinicians may understand that certain kinds of medicines may reduce symptom severity in a certain condition and enhance the application of other intervention teachings and strategies. It is up to the patient, however, as to whether they agree to take the medication, and clinicians should support the patient's wishes rather than argue with them or give a message that the patient will not get better unless they follow our specific instructions.

Among neurodevelopmental disorders, for example, it is common for teenage youngsters who have ADHD to assert that they do not wish to take a stimulant medicine because they feel that it changes their personality or because they don't want to have a stigma attached to them because of their taking medicine. Rather than argue with the teenager, I recommend supporting their assertion of responsibility for performing the behavioral strategies that are necessary for success in school, family life, etc. Often supporting a teenager's assertions while building in a monitoring strategy for compliance with expectations, and the suggestion "Let's follow up in three months to see how you are doing" not only builds an awareness on the patient's part that *they* are responsible for their behaviors but also allows for feedback about whether they are able to perform the steps necessary without the support of medicine. Caregivers may be reassured that the adolescent's level of responsibility can and will be monitored, typically through the preparation of a written behavioral contract with specific criteria identified, by which compliance can be monitored. Often, this will require some flexibility on the part of the caregiver and an understanding that the goal should be progress rather than perfection. I suggest tying specific privileges and freedoms desired by the adolescent to explicit evidence that the adolescent is meeting their responsibilities ("Yes I trust you, but show me evidence that you have completed the task"). Help adolescents to recognize that good intentions are admirable but insufficient.

Interventions Should Be Focused, and Not Generic

Clinicians sometimes learn that their patient's school has performed an evaluation that identified a need for academic support, found the child eligible for services, and has provided that child with one of the school's intervention programs for students with similar needs. Unfortunately, after 6 months, a year, or sometimes even longer, the student has not responded to the offered interventions. The clinician should then question whether the failure of the student to respond to intervention may be secondary to generic programming for such students, rather than an individualized, needs-based strategy. As an example, a school district may contract with a company to provide Brand X reading intervention services. Such services have been found helpful for many students struggling to read, it is argued, and the school is unable to purchase every reading program available secondary to budgetary restrictions. This argument makes sense in that school administrators have a set amount of money to spend on cafeteria tables, athletic field maintenance, crossing guards, etc. It is nevertheless not helpful for the student whose areas of impairment are not effectively treated with Brand X. Parents, in frustration, suggest that the school doesn't seem to care about their child, while teachers, also frustrated, sometimes suggest that the student just isn't trying hard enough. What should a parent do?

Interventions Should Be Evidence Based

Clinicians should become advocates of scientifically validated recommendations for improving the welfare of those who consult with us and advise against practices that could have from minimally helpful to devastating consequences if followed. An example here would be the topic of what we should do if a parent tells us that they will not vaccinate their children because of the potential for the vaccines to cause autism and other problems. It is difficult to argue against a parent's wanting to make intelligent choices for their children's health and wellbeing, and when faced with familial preferences for a vegetarian diet or the avoidance of medications in favor of behavioral strategies for symptom management in certain disorders, we should avoid professional arrogance in favor of providing an understandable explanation of the science, in language that parents can understand. I learned early in my career that there is little value in telling a mother that she is wrong in her beliefs about what is best for her children. Society, in the guise of the legal system, takes responsibility for interfering in parenting practices when the practice involves potential abuse or neglect of the child; however, our job is to compassionately inform and correct misconceptions held with conviction based upon partial information. Often this is best accomplished by providing summaries of research in digestible forms or reference to the positions of the Centers for Disease Control (CDC, 2017) or the World Health Organization (WHO, 2017). We must be kind and deferential to the ultimate authority of the choices made by those who seek our services. We can do great harm if we make an insensitive remark or dismiss a parent's concerns as not relevant.

Similarly, when informed that an agency or school declines to provide services we recommend, one approach a parent and/or clinician can take is to share with school administrators the research evidence for or against various intervention programs, relative to the specific impairments that our patient has. Research showing that a whole word memorization approach to reading is ineffective for a child with phonological dyslexia, for example, may enlighten administrators that they may be wasting their resources rather than saving money. Likewise, we need to help teachers learn that it isn't productive to hold a hyperactive child in from recess, for them to complete work they were too distracted to finish in class. Most clinicians are not teachers, and we should offer input without telling teachers what to do. At the same time, offering information about which focused intervention has been found to work well with what specific impairments may allow the well-meaning teacher to be more effective in their classroom and even to consider applying that strategy with other students.

Interventions Can Be at Least Partly School Based

The quest for academic excellence has led some schools to reduce the opportunities for "specials" such as music, art, and other creative outlets. What is sometimes lost in the process is the fact that these activities are equally important in the development of executive functions as are more formal exercises in academic training and homework. Learning to play a role in a theatrical play, cooperating with other students in a team sport, or coordinating one's music with the rest of an orchestra are all methods of improving both cognitive and behavioral self-regulation. Play and exercise are essential in the development of strong bodies and strong minds, and even though most students will never become elite athletes, it is the process of exploring one's capabilities and testing one's limits that leads to confidence and a differentiated self-concept. Some children are great leaders but may not be very artistic. Some children may have athletic prowess but be socially shy. Even good-natured "pickup games" on the playground are being replaced by highly organized athletic teams where children are required to have matching uniforms and equipment (at sometimes great expense to families who can't spare the money). Alternatively, unstructured games, the process of choosing players for your team, and arguing over whether the pitch was a ball or a strike is a part of building resilience. Left to their own devices, children are remarkably strong and able to weather the minor frustrations involved in growing up but cannot do so if their every move is micromanaged.

And who are we paying to teach these life lessons? Teacher pay is among the lowest of individuals who are so qualified and who have such responsibility placed upon them. Many school systems are handicapped by the failure to pass referenda or bonds to fund education and are required to make do with minimal funding. The average teacher also has only an introductory level of education in the special techniques and strategies that are often necessary for educating children who have developmental disabilities. In some states, the number of hours of training in special education, which is required to get a teaching certificate, is in the single figures (meaning class hours). Many teachers will explain that, although they wished they could help children with special needs, they don't know how to do so and don't get support in the process. Child development specialists who can offer teachers specific, concrete recommendations of what to do in the classroom are often appreciated; however, it must be kept in mind that a teacher who is trying to meet the needs of thirty or more children may not have the energy to provide the level of care many parents hope for.

This also means that special education is not the only, or even primary, answer to developmental difficulties, simply because of the burden placed upon teachers. IDEA calls for students to be placed in a "least restrictive environment" (U.S. Department of Education, 2017), and there is ample evidence that teaching children who have developmental needs alongside more typically developing children benefits both. Children who have special needs should not be viewed as "handicapped" or defined by their condition. Many of the accommodations necessary to optimize children's learning can be managed within the mainstream classroom and are recognized by the student's peers as justifiable. It is the job of the diagnosing professional to suggest evidence-based treatment guidelines at the level which can be utilized by the average teacher or at least offer accommodations for all students with learning differences, such as those promulgated by the International Dyslexia Association (2017) or the organization Children and Adults with Attention Deficit Disorders (CHADD, 2017). Encouraging parents to work collaboratively with school personnel typically works better than suggesting that parents demand optimal services that may not be possible in the given situation.

Interventions Need to Be Developmentally Appropriate

Certain forms of developmental interventions have been designed to be implemented at specific ages or developmental levels. Our brains have "windows of opportunity" for maximal effectiveness of different forms of intervention, and it is important to try to match recommended strategies with specific developmental stages. A preschool child who shows signs of a developmental social disorder would benefit from training to increase eye contact and respond verbally to communication from others. This makes sense and can serve as a building block for later skills training in reciprocal social interaction. Focusing upon this skill set in an adolescent may also be helpful; however, the teenager may benefit more from learning about the "dance" of social interaction at a process level, how they might interpret non-verbal cues as expressed in body language and tone of voice, or how they might politely ask for explanation when they are confused by the use of non-literal language or metaphors.

First- and second-grade children with reading decoding problems will likely have a better response to focused training in decoding strategies, while the junior high school–aged poor reader who is developing anxiety and avoidance of all things reading may better be taught how to use audiobooks and the humorous approaches to studying offered by Sparklife (n.d.).

Thankfully, school systems are gradually learning to accept electronic tools in the classroom, which can be of tremendous assistance to those students who learn differently. Voice recognition software that can translate oral lectures into printed text, or the use of audio devices that record teacher lectures as the student takes notes, can be very helpful to the student who has dysgraphia, short-term memory problems, or other forms of difficulty with notetaking. Multimodal instruction often bypasses specific learning disabilities and can enhance learning through the use of videos, internet-based learning supports, etc. Children who have difficulties organizing their thoughts and expressing them may use graphic organizer software or mind mapping techniques. Recommendations should be geared toward the developmental level of the child and modified as the child grows older. Older students can learn to use advanced technologies to bypass their developmental challenges (e.g. cell phones, iPads), while younger students may still be developing an understanding of how best to access these tools. Young adults who grew up with developmental difficulties continue to need help and support but likely in a different manner and delivery system than that used with younger children.

Recommended Interventions Must Be Accessible

The very best program for a given patient's needs is not helpful if it is only provided in a location that is geographically inaccessible—whether in another town or even in the same area the patient lives if they lack transportation to get to the program. Clinicians can begin to develop a list of resources/referrals for various types of providers and interventions that are cross-referenced by location and provide that list to families when giving feedback about certain recommended interventions. There are likely multiple occupational therapists within an accessible geographical range, for example, and giving families a list of phone numbers and/or websites allows the family to investigate the providers, determine the specific nature of their services, and other logistical factors in deciding to obtain services.

Clinicians should also consider how much time our recommended interventions will require and how practical they are for the family as a whole. If our patient has siblings, each of the children will likely have extracurricular activities in which they are involved, and caregivers often find that they are the family taxi, shuttling children here and there according to each one's schedule. Parenting young children is exhausting and involves juggling the schedules of all involved. As such, clinicians should consider the time commitment required by various recommended interventions and whether it is practical for the family to pursue. If we tell our patients that the only intervention that

makes sense is one that requires 5 hours per week within a geographically distant provider's office, we must recognize that there will be a minimal half-hour
drive time added to each end of that daily commitment and that the caregiver
will need to sit and wait for the child to complete their training—representing
time that could be spent helping siblings with homework, grocery shopping or
meal preparation, and any of the hundred other things that need to be done.
Such recommendations add a sense of guilt to the caregiver whether they
follow your recommendation and neglect something else, or if they choose to
not follow your recommendation and then worry that they are not giving the
patient every opportunity to overcome their developmental difficulties.

Whenever possible, I like to provide caregivers with intervention strategies
that can be performed within the home or suggest professional-based interventions that can be extended by home practice. Some interventions can be
woven into the daily routine of the family and might benefit siblings or the
cycle of family interaction. Educating caregivers around principles of social
learning theory, for example, can enhance their ability to put a structured
behavioral system into place within the home setting. Having family meetings in which all members of the family are assigned tasks and "jobs" for which
they can earn privileges and rewards helps to avoid some of the impairments
in activities of daily living that often plague youngsters with developmental
difficulties. Toilet training can be achieved by virtually everyone, including
individuals with severe intellectual disorders, and there is no need for parents
to have to cope with such issues among youngsters who are increasingly physically large and mature. All children should receive developmentally appropriate education in sexuality and be taught how to manage the manifestations of
puberty in a responsible manner. Pretending that one's child just won't engage
in masturbation is less helpful than discussing issues of privacy.

If one recommends interventions for developmental disorders, how much
of the patient's life is involved in pursuing these interventions? Children are
increasingly over-scheduled, with little time programmed to play, relax, or
simply "veg out." Societal over-concern about ensuring that our children have
the best opportunities in every arena has taken away time that the child can
use to experiment with the world and develop their own understanding and
feelings of competence. Take social interactions as an example. Many youngsters with more significant disabilities tell me that they are ok with just one
or two activities or friends. Younger children with autism spectrum disorders
can be quite content with parallel play. The development of virtual gam-
ing has allowed many to develop online communities of "friends" that they
may never have met and yet with whom they feel a close bond. For others,
however, it may be necessary to encourage involvement in structured activities and groups. Spiritual groups associated with religious organizations often
provide supervised group activities within which children can test out their
social skills without fear of rejection or bullying. Engaging children in musical
groups such as school bands and orchestras can promote identity development
equal to that of the athlete who joins the school team. Student government,

theater, and even group-format individual sports such as swimming and karate all foster the sense in the child that "I can!" Above all, however, children need to be loved, and perhaps one of the best sources of such love can come from a pet—a dog, a cat, a horse—something that loves unconditionally regardless of your appearance, your intelligence, or your social skills.

Financial Considerations

Interventions need to be financially realistic. Some children are fortunate to live in advantaged families who can afford to send the child to expensive tutors, therapists, and programs. Such children seem to all have their own cell phone, computer, and/or iPad. Some families can even afford for therapists to come to their homes to provide service or hire helpers to transport their children across town. It is more likely, however, that the interventions we recommend for our patients are received by the caregivers, at least on some level, as a financial burden. Do caregivers pay for some expensive intervention or pay down their credit card each month? Does the family have to take out a loan to pay for the services we recommend, or do they ask extended family members for help? Many parents will tell clinicians "whatever it takes" in response to expressed concerns about their resources; however, clinicians should seriously consider the impact of their recommendations upon the total family finances and resources. Clinicians need to guard against a position of "out of sight, out of mind" in recommending services.

Self-Esteem and Comorbid Conditions

Everyone is good at something, and it is essential that a student's strengths be emphasized with as much time and energy as their areas of difficulty. Building self-esteem and a sense of confidence that one is good at something can help to overcome the shame and anxiety that accompanies the realization that one cannot perform some skills at the same level as others one's age. Resilience and persistence should be trained, and all students should be taught that they should never, never, never, never give up.

As I have hinted earlier, some caregivers also "don't believe in" various developmental difficulties or assert that it is their contention that the child or adolescent willfully chooses not to perform the skill in question because they are "lazy" or "unmotivated." Many family systems will engage in shaming of the individual with a developmental disorder and refuse to seek out necessary services for the individual either out of a sense of the caregiver's own guilt, embarrassment, or the blaming of another caregiver such as a divorced parent. Children and adolescents, themselves, also often engage in behaviors suggesting that they are denying the existence of their difficulty. Similar to the youngster who is non-compliant with the management of a chronic medical condition, such as diabetes, some individuals with developmental disorders seem to have belief systems that interfere with managing the symptoms of their impairments and performing the activities that will ultimately help the disorder to be less impactful. In part, this may result from an inadequate understanding on the individual's part of the true specifics of their disorder or disability. Putting one's head in the proverbial sand to not listen to the specifics of their challenges may result from a student who "doesn't want to hear it." As such, it is critical to involve the child and or adolescent in the feedback sessions following our evaluations, so that the clinician can assess the individual's level of understanding and knowledge of the news that is being provided. Placing the news in perspective and emphasizing that the individual has many strengths in addition to some areas of difficulty sometimes can achieve buy-in that was not there previously. Our goal is to have the individual accept responsibility for their own challenges and to recognize that there is always hope and potential for improvement, which often requires a one-step-at-a-time strategy of working to make things better.

Conclusions

The identification of the dimensions along which our patients struggle helps to focus our intervention efforts. These efforts should in fact be tied to the patient's needs and not just the application of a favorite therapy that may not have been proven to help our patient's specific challenges. We should also be sure that our recommendations are consistent with our patients' wishes and probably keep the number of interventions recommended to a reasonable number. Some caregivers have expressed feeling overwhelmed when they receive several pages of recommendations and ask what they should do first. It is important that our recommendations be developmentally appropriate, geographically available, and something that the family can afford. Asking the child or adolescent to buy-into the intervention can assist with compliance, and the focus of interventions should focus upon what the child thinks is important, as well as the wishes of the caregivers.

Bibliography

Centers for Disease Control and Prevention (CDC). (2017). Retrieved August 7, 2017, from www.cdc.gov

Children and Adults with Attention Deficit Disorders (CHADD). (2017). Retrieved August 8, 2017, from www.chadd.org

Hale, J., Alfonso, V., Berninger, V., Bracken, B., Christo, C., Clark, E., . . . Dumont, R. (2010). Critical issues in response-to-intervention, comprehensive evaluation, and specific learning disabilities identification and intervention: An expert white paper consensus. *Learning Disability Quarterly*, 33(3), 223–236.

International Dyslexia Association (IDA). (2017). Retrieved August 7, 2017, from https://dyslexiaida.org

Sparklife. (n.d.). Retrieved August 21, 2017, from http://community.sparknotes.com/2017/08/21/vintage-auntie-sparknotes-new-kid nerves

U.S. Department of Education. (2017, June 6). *Individuals with Disabilities Education Act*. Retrieved August 7, 2017, from https://www2.ed.gov/about/offices/list/osers/osep/osep-idea.html

World Health Organization (WHO). (2017). *Disabilities*. Retrieved August 7, 2017, from www.who.int/topics/disabilities/en/

12 Questions to Ask Oneself

How Much Education Do You Need?

Becoming a clinician who works with neurodevelopmental disorders typically requires an advanced level of education. Depending upon the profession one chooses, clinicians typically start with a college degree and then pursue advanced training that can lead to a Master's or Doctoral degree. There is some degree of prestige associated with having advanced levels of education and degrees. According to the most recent United States Census, 88.4% of individuals aged 25 or older had achieved a high school degree or more, 58.9% had attended some college coursework, 42.3% had earned an Associate's degree or better, 32.5% had achieved a Bachelor's degree or higher, but only 12% had earned a Master's degree or higher, and less than 2% had achieved a doctorate. Obtaining an advanced degree therefore places an individual within a fairly small group of individuals (Census, 2017).

The process is highly competitive, however, and from the perspective of an individual just starting down the path, it seems very long. Does one become a generalist or a specialist? Some trainees define themselves early in their career by choosing a very narrow field to pursue. Others have a broader perspective that they wish to obtain as wide a knowledge base as possible, recognizing that they can specialize later. The advantage of the specialty focus is that one can ensure that they take the right courses, get focused clinical training and experience, and possibly take a faster path to their eventual goal. The disadvantage of such an approach is that one may gradually recognize that one doesn't really like the direction they have chosen to pursue but feel it is too late to change. The advantage of the generalist strategy is that one can be exposed to a wide array of clinical settings and processes and find that one has a fascination with an area that hadn't previously been considered. Generalists also tend to develop a bigger toolbox of available strategies to apply in their work and learn multiple theoretical viewpoints of the world. The disadvantage of the generalist approach is that one may not be chosen for specialty training programs because they are "beaten out" by colleagues with very narrow and yet extensive training in the specialty. Generalists may also be denied a fast-track route to prestigious job opportunities and may recognize that they know a little about a lot, but not a lot about anything.

For many, the road to a specialty is found after one's initial training. Most professions that involve licensure require continuing education, and for some, it is the process of regular attendance at conferences on a specific topic that begins to shape the focus of our practice. If this is the case, clinicians can hone their skills in certain areas, obtain supervision from experts more competent than oneself in the area, and gradually devote oneself to learning all that one can about a narrow field. This book, for example, is designed to prompt your developing an interest in the complexities and yet fascination of working with neurodevelopmental disorders. Such a focus nevertheless requires an ongoing commitment to lifelong learning. It is easy to become complacent and to cite our growing years of experience as an excuse for avoiding the work of staying up to date, of reading and attending conferences, of seeking advanced certification, and of limiting our work to the areas in which we truly have competence. We have also all known individuals who lose sight of these goals. These are professionals who seem more focused upon disorders than the people who are impacted, professionals who can "do it all" and whom you never see at continuing education conferences. I wish to emphasize the importance of challenging dogma, of constantly questioning how and why we do things, and of collaborating with colleagues both within our own discipline as well as those with different training.

Why Are You Doing This?

How did you come to want to be a clinician? For some, there is a desire to learn more about one's own developmental struggles. Perhaps you personally struggled with math; perhaps you have always been somewhat impulsive and distractible. Some clinicians openly discuss their own challenges while others are less likely to share their histories and their own challenges. If one returns to the first chapter of this book, we remember that Gregor Mendel scored poorly on some of his early academic work. Other figures both currently and in history are famous for their battles with neurodevelopment, including King Charles II of Spain who had an intellectual disability (Charles II of Spain, n.d.); Temple Grandin who has an autism spectrum disorder (Templegrandin.com, 2012); and Charles Schwab who has dyslexia (Aboutschwab.com, 2017). One can find lists of individuals who dealt with developmental disabilities on the internet and on the web pages of multiple major organizations, which is sometimes helpful when giving feedback to a child or adolescent ("You are like this really famous actor/athlete/politician/writer. . . .").

Others among us entered our chosen field because we have a family member who has struggled with some form of disability or health impairment. Growing up as the sibling of such a family member is a source of both joys and sorrows, as is watching the impact upon the family system over time. Some family members quietly care for their adult siblings or another relative who has more significant impairments and cannot manage life's demands on their own. I recently evaluated a gentleman with a lifelong intellectual disability who spent his educational career in special education but was able to obtain steady employment as a groundskeeper on a local golf course. This individual lived independently and was self-sufficient for some 40 years, until he suffered a stroke. His siblings were immediately there for him, arranged for his evaluation with me so that he could obtain social security benefits, but told me their story of gentle support and supervision throughout their brother's life.

Most of us will probably identify a desire to be of some help for others. We have goals of understanding and perhaps in some way easing the burden of those with whom we work. At their core, most health and developmental specialists are caring individuals who have empathy for those who struggle and wish to do what we can to lighten their load. Still, for most of us there is a secondary drive that is founded in intellectual and scientific curiosity. We want to learn about the conditions we work with; we think about their origins, manifestations, and treatment. We may become involved in the study of some specific component of a disorder, such as how the brain processes visuospatial information or how memory traces are formed and fade. Most clinicians pursue advanced educational degrees in a specific area of interest and invest time and money in becoming a knowledgeable specialist in a certain area. This requires delay of gratification and for some a substantial financial investment. Some current professional school students graduate with jaw-dropping student loan debt that may take half of their career to repay. Why on earth would we do this when our friends and peers from college may have found well-paying jobs and seem much more financially stable than we are?

Healthcare and education are nevertheless bastions of power differentials, of "white coat fever," and of multiple relationships whether we choose to acknowledge them or not. We are, after all, pursuing our professions at least in part to achieve some level of financial success, recognition by our peers, and admiration for our brilliance. Some of our colleagues unfortunately seem focused upon self-importance and may lose sight of the true value of our contributions, although hopefully the numbers are small. What is more admirable, is the desire most professionals have to make a real difference in the world. Increasingly, society, government, and legal bodies look to our guidance and scientific understanding of the human condition, and it is important that we remember that our contributions have great value for many.

One of the choices early career clinicians must face is the determination of which arena they will choose for their professional home. Some will choose to work in schools, local agencies, or for government services, where the workload will be heavy, the remuneration limited, and the needs of our patients great. Such a commitment early in one's career is often defensible since one's need for financial security may be less and one has a longer career ahead of oneself. Acquiring credentials from working "in the trenches" often serves to validate one's breadth of experience, as the patients who are seen are often complex, underserved, and very grateful for our commitment. The choice of this path nevertheless often means less financial reward during the early years but may involve added benefits in terms of insurance coverage, perhaps a retirement plan, and clearly defined vacations and other time off. Such experience often leads to more lucrative careers within the private sector after a period of time and serve to establish one's name in the community, referral sources for a private practice, and a database of clinical experiences upon which one can evaluate new theories, findings, and science. Ours is an honorable profession which is held in high regard by others around us.

Some clinicians will shoot for more competitive employment in medical centers or more outwardly prestigious institutions. The colleagues with whom one will compete to land such placements are often hard working, high achieving, and test one's drive to excel and exceed expectations. There is excitement in pursuing a career that mixes research, clinical work and teaching, and having one's name affiliated with a major regional institution can feel gratifying and partial payment for all of the hard work one has put in. Such career paths often have their own price, however, as the hours are often very long and time with new families or for oneself seems to be constantly in short supply. Stress levels can also be quite high, as one often feels that one's performance is constantly being evaluated and judged against standards of organizational politics over which one may have little control. Clinicians are not immune to the impact of chronic stress, and several of my colleagues over the years have suffered health and emotional consequences from constantly pushing hard and demanding more on themselves. Often these are the individuals who seem more focused upon the excellence of their work, than they are in taking care of themselves.

Yet another option is to form one's own private practice or to join an already established group of similar clinicians. Solo practice provides complete autonomy in decision-making and no need to worry about the desires or issues of others. If one has established connections in the community, a solo practice can gradually grow into a strong brand of one's name and removal of the fear that you may be let go from someone else's company. Solo practice entails significant costs, however, as one must buy phones, copiers, assessment tools, etc., all at a time when one doesn't have a rolling cash flow. Much as is the case in law or medicine, many early career clinicians choose to benefit from the established businesses of more senior clinicians, in terms of a "ready-made" practice that provides referrals, administrative staff, an office and furniture, etc. The practice's overhead costs are shared across several providers, and as one becomes established within the group, opportunities may be provided for the junior staff to purchase stock in the company and potentially make it their own. These decisions are individual and often depend upon whether one has a partner who already has a job, one's phase of family life and decisions about having children, and one's long-term goals.

Whose Needs Are Important?

I remember the pride I felt on the first occasion that someone called me "Doctor." Although I was young and many patients seemed to wonder if I actually knew what I was doing, I had completed a training program and had become licensed, and as far as it appeared on paper, I was someone to be consulted and whose opinions might be important. Individuals in other professions seemed to think that I knew more about something than they did, and I gradually realized that I had a role on a team of healthcare providers—I fit in! But how should I introduce myself? It seemed arrogant to introduce myself as "Dr. Nicholls," and I became aware of the power differential between clinicians and patients. Although some families seemed unimpressed, most seemed to act in a deferential manner and to hang on the words that I offered in my consultation with them. What a responsibility!

I began to observe other clinicians around me and came to some important realizations. The clinicians I admired and respected the most tended to be humble and to use small words when they spoke with their patients. They would sit down, occasionally hold the hand of, and in general, connect with their patients on a personal, equal level. They tended to introduce themselves using their first and last names and made sure to ask their patients about their own names and identities. This was true collaboration, with the clinician and patient working together toward a goal, rather than there being a power differential in which the clinician was more important than their patient. My point here is that clinicians play a very small role in the lives of our patients. We offer suggestions for how they may address certain concerns; however, we hold little power over whether or not our recommendations are followed. It may well be that the opinions of an extended family member have a greater impact on whether our patients pursue or receive various treatment options and that our suggestions or recommendations written in a report may not actually be read.

How Good Is Good Enough?

Some clinicians fall into an easy routine of performing their work and manage the stress of their profession by not thinking too deeply about the implications of their work. Convenience and expedience easily replace critical thinking and consideration of ethical principles and remaining current on licensing laws and professional standards. A simple example is the clinician who fails to maintain adequate records of their involvement with a patient or one who charges an insurance company for more hours of service than they actually provided. Who will know? Who will check? Most professions have licensing boards that are designed to evaluate complaints filed by consumers regarding a professional's behavior, and a periodic visit to such a board meeting can be a reminder that we don't have an unregulated right to do whatever we please.

One strategy of avoiding a slide into mediocrity and substandard practice is to subject oneself to peer review. This can take the form of a peer mentoring group that meets periodically to discuss cases or professional issues, or it can be a simple lunch meeting with a trusted colleague to anonymously discuss a perplexing situation. Joining one's local, state, or national professional organization can allow one to periodically attend conferences or continuing education classes that help us to keep up with what is new and with evolving standards of care. In medicine, it is expected that most physicians will pursue advanced levels of board certification as an indication of the physician's need for periodic assessment of competency and maintenance of certification. Unfortunately, such a process is still emerging in other healthcare fields and is followed by relatively few individuals within those fields where a process has been established. It is my strong recommendation that all clinicians seek advanced certification in their field of specialty. The additional study and examination process may seem daunting at first but is achievable by all with dedication and persistence.

One can also open oneself up to the thoughts of others through giving presentations on certain topics, through writing a newsletter article or even a peer-reviewed journal article. Forcing oneself to sit down and prepare a presentation of one's thoughts can help clinicians to critically self-evaluate and to step outside of one's daily routine to question what one is doing. This process also allows one to contribute to one's profession either through teaching younger colleagues, through participation in some professional organization's governing board, or by serving in a public service fashion by joining the board of directors for an advocacy group. Clinicians should write letters to government officials and offer opinions about current events in a manner that serves society through our often unique perspectives. Performing some kind of public service is a good way to maintain self-awareness and motivation toward excellence.

Perhaps most importantly, however, is the necessity of clinicians taking care of themselves. We can be of little service to others if we are battling our own demons, if we are over-tired or over-committed. Clinicians must take time to smell the proverbial roses, take time for oneself, and engage in some activities that have nothing to do with our profession. It is essential to balance time and commitment, so that you have the energy to give to others who are in need. This requires that we be honest with ourselves and recognize when we, too, may have needs for professional services. Many clinical training programs require their graduates to have at least some form of experience as a patient themselves, and clinicians are not invulnerable to our own medical and mental health challenges. I encourage all to have a personal physician with whom one has yearly checkups, and it is a convenient reminder to schedule such appointments as one approaches their birthday, each year. Taking care of oneself is important in all aspects of life, including exercise, stress management, relationships with friends and families, and the avoidance of succumbing to unhealthful habits and practices. Clinicians cannot be as helpful as they might, when there are demons in their own closets.

Conclusions

Clinicians who work with neurodevelopmental disorders are tasked with trying to understand highly complex systems of medical, sociocultural, developmental, and psychological knowledge. The pace of growth in such fields, as in others, seems to be growing faster and faster. The goal of maximizing factual knowledge must change to one of managing dimensional thinking and asking good questions. Our information-based world is rapidly moving toward artificial intelligence and machine learning, which will soon perform many of the tasks that clinicians previously were assigned. As such, clinicians must learn to integrate data, consider both the details but also the big picture, and become more efficient members of the healthcare marketplace. Fortunately, child-oriented clinicians have fairly good job security, as new generations of patients steadily emerge. Our job is capitalize upon what we know, while continuing to challenge old patterns of thinking, and to ask the hard questions that will keep us up with the pace of progress.

Bibliography

Aboutschwab.com. (2017). *Charles Schwab*. Retrieved August 21, 2017, from www.aboutschwab.com/leadership/charles-schwab

Census. (2017). *Educational attainment in the United States, 2016*. Retrieved August 7, 2017, from www.census.gov/data/tables/2016/demo/education-attainment/cps-detailed-tables.html

Charles II of Spain. (n.d.). *In Wikipedia*. Retrieved August 21, 2017, from https://en.wikipedia.org/wiki/Charles_II_of_Spain

Templegrandin.com. (2012). *Temple Grandin*, PhD. Retrieved August 21, 2017, from www.templegrandin.com/templehome.html

Index

Page numbers in bold indicate tables on the corresponding pages.

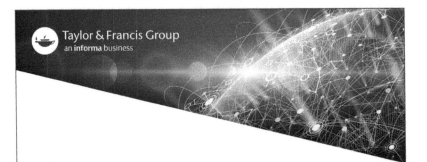